Words of Conscience

Religious Statements on Conscientious Objection

WORDS OF CONSCIENCE

Religious Statements
on
Conscientious Objection

TENTH EDITION
©Copyright 1983

edited by
Beth Ellen Boyle

published by the
**NATIONAL INTERRELIGIOUS SERVICE BOARD
FOR
CONSCIENTIOUS OBJECTORS**

NISBCO

550 Washington Building
15th & New York Avenue, N.W.
Washington, D.C. 20005
Telephone: (202) 393-4868

Warren W. Hoover, Executive Director

First Edition	December, 1951
Edited By	A. Stauffer Curry
Second Edition	August, 1953
Edited By	A. Stauffer Curry
Third Edition	April, 1957
Edited By	C. LeRoy Doty, Jr.
Fourth Edition	March, 1963
Edited By	Michael L. Yoder
Fifth Edition	October, 1966
Edited By	Robert C. Heath
Second Printing	December, 1967
Sixth Edition	November, 1968
Edited By	P. Wayne Wisler and J. Harold Sherk
Seventh Edition	February, 1970
Edited By	Gerald E. Shenk
Second Printing	November, 1970
Eighth Edition	February, 1973
Edited By	Richard Malishchak
Ninth Edition	March, 1980
Edited By	Shawn Perry
Tenth Edition	June, 1983
Edited By	Beth Ellen Boyle

Table of Contents

Introduction 9
War and Hope, an essay 11
THE WITNESS OF CONSCIENCE—Past, Present and Future
   American Objectors' Heritage: Conscience Since
      Colonial Times 15
   Conscience in the Current Age: The Birth Of
      Nuclear Pacifism 31
         Pope John Paul II 32
         Billy Graham 35
         Rabbi Isidor B. Hoffman 38
WHERE DOES MY CONSCIENCE LEAD ME?
   Am I a Conscientious Objector? 41
   Where Do I Go From Here? 47
   Resources 51
   Worksheet on War 54
WORDS OF CONSCIENCE
   Words of Conscience: Official Statements by Religious
      Bodies 61
      American Ethical Union 62
      American Humanist Association 63
      Assembly of Covenant Churches 64
      Assemblies of God — General Council 64
      Association of Bible Students 65
      Baha'i 65
      Baptist
         American Baptist Churches—USA 66
         Seventh Day Baptist General Conference 67
         Southern Baptist Convention 68
      Brethren
         Church of the Brethren 69
         Dunkard Brethren 73
         Old German Baptist Brethren 74
      Brethren in Christ Church 76
      Buddhist 78
      Catholic (see Roman Catholic) 153
      Christadelphians 79
      Christian Church (Disciples of Christ) 80
      Christian Reformed Church 82
      Christ's Sanctified Holy Church 85
      Church of Christ 87
      Church of Christ, Scientist 88
      Church of God (Anderson) 89
      Church of God (Oklahoma) 90

Church of God (Seventh Day) 91
Church of God (7th Day, Salem, W.V.) 93
Church of God of the Abrahamic Faith 93
Church of God, General Conference 94
Church of the Gospel 96
Church of the Lord Jesus Christ of the Apostolic Faith 97
Church of the Nazarene 99
Doukhobours 99
Episcopal
    Episcopal Church 100
    Episcopal Peace Fellowship 102
Evangelical Covenant Church of America 103
Fellowship of Reconciliation, The 104
Friends
    Friends, The Religious Society of (Quakers) 105
    American Friends Service Committee, The 107
Greek Orthodox 109
Hutterian Brethren, Church of Christ (Hutterites) 109
Hutterian Society of Brothers 111
International Society for Krishna Consciousness 112
Israelite House of David 113
Jehovah's Witnesses 115
Jewish
    Synagogue Council of America 117
    Central Conference of American Rabbis 119
    Jewish Peace Fellowship 120
    Rabbinical Assembly 120
Lutheran
    American Lutheran Church, The 121
    Association of Evangelical Lutheran Churches 123
    Lutheran Church in America 123
    Lutheran Church—Missouri Synod 125
Megiddo Mission Church 128
Mennonite
    Beachy Amish Mennonite 130
    Mennonite Churches 131
Methodist
    Free Methodist Church 136
    United Methodist Church 136
    Wesleyan Church, The 139
Missionary Church, The 139
Moravian Church (Northern Province) 140
National Council of Churches of Christ in the USA 141
Presbyterian
    Presbyterian Church in the U.S. 145
    Reformed Presbyterian Church, Evangelical Synod 146
    United Presbyterian Church in the U.S.A., The 147
The Reformed Church in America 150

Reorganized Church of Jesus Christ of Latter Day Saints... 152
Roman Catholic
   Pope John Paul II on Violence and Law 153
   United States Catholic Conference 154
   Catholic Peace Fellowship 157
   National Federation of Priests' Councils 158
   Pax Christi—USA 159
   Pax Christi—USA Center on Conscience and War 160
Salvation Army, The 160
Seventh-Day Adventists 161
Sojourners Fellowship 162
Unitarian Universalist Association 165
United Church of Christ 167
United Molokan Christian Association.................... 169
United Pentecostal Church, International 171
Worldwide Church of God
  (formerly Radio Church of God)...................... 172
World Council of Churches 172

Words of Conscience: "Unofficial" Statements of Religious Groups 177
American Indian 178
Black Muslim... 182
Hindu.. 184
Islam 186

Words of Conscience: Individuals Speak 189
Albert Camus... 190
Dorothy Day.. 193
Mahatma Gandhi 195
Martin Luther King, Jr. 196
Peter Maurin 199
Thomas Merton....................................... 201
A. J. Muste 204
Henry David Thoreau.................................. 208
Leo Tolstoy 210
Mark Twain 214

Acknowledgements 217

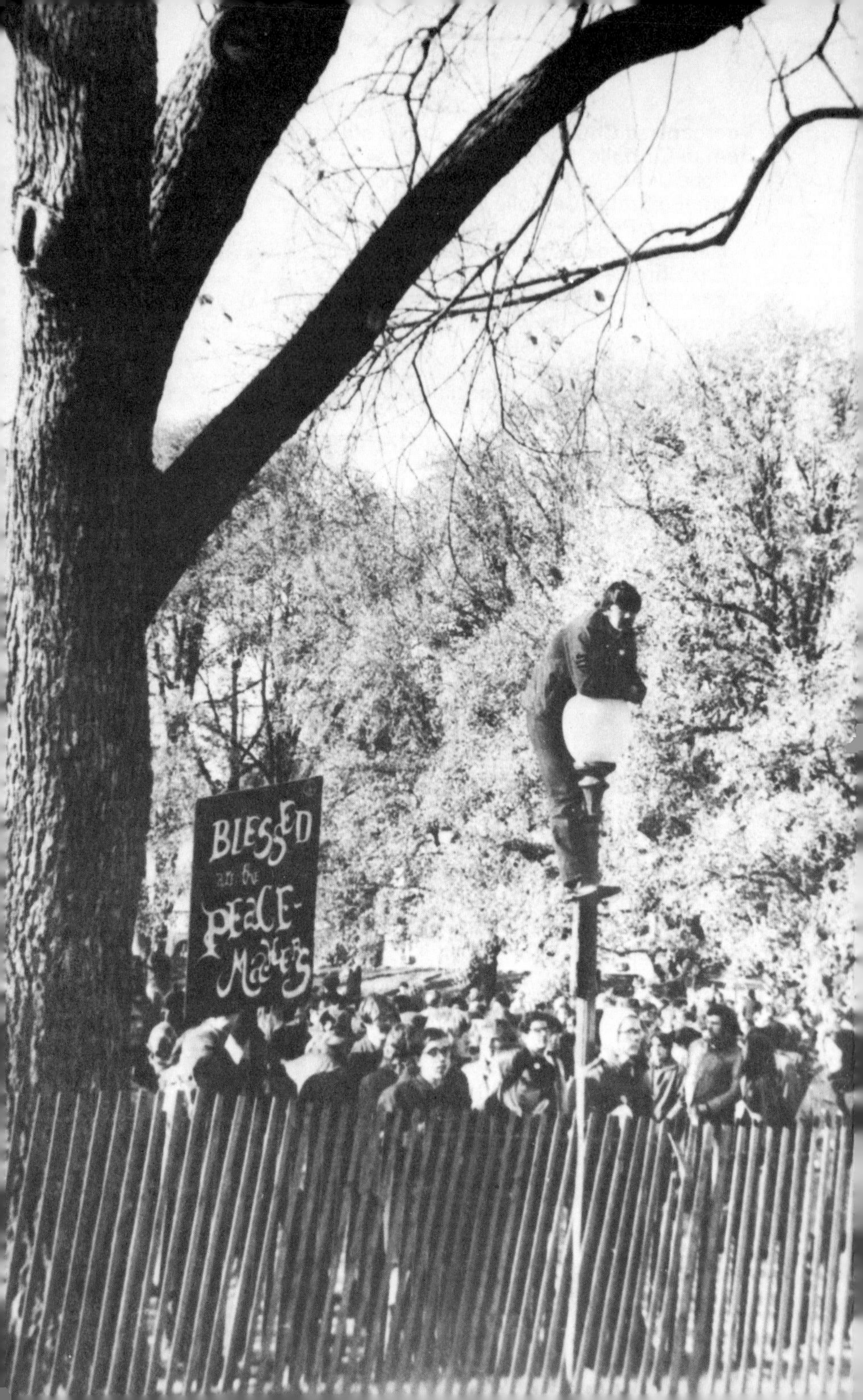
BLESSED
are the
PEACE-
MAKERS

Introduction

For over thirty years, NISBCO has published a collection of statements by religious bodies on conscientious objection. The compilation —the only one of its kind—has served as a useful reference for anyone wishing to know the official stand of the particular churches. These statements stand, collected, a common religious witness against the evil of war. That witness has not only survived, but strengthened during the last three decades of international conflict.

This tenth edition of **WORDS OF CONSCIENCE** offers not only an expanded section of official religious statements but also a collection of writings by noted individuals which exemplify the basis of conscientious beliefs.

This edition is also expanded to become more useful as a peace education tool. For young people asking the question "But what do I believe about war?" the book offers articles, questions, and a worksheet to help each person in determining their own position on participation in war. It explains various types of conscientious objection and the process under current SSS regulations for recognition as a conscientious objector. It offers guidelines for documenting one's beliefs and provides a reading and resource list.

This edition places the simple witness of conscience in historical perspective with a chapter on conscientious objection in the United States from colonial times until now, and in the current perspective with essays and articles on the meaning and implications of war and pacifism in the nuclear age.

It is our hope this new book will serve you well in your witness and work for peace.

—Beth Ellen Boyle

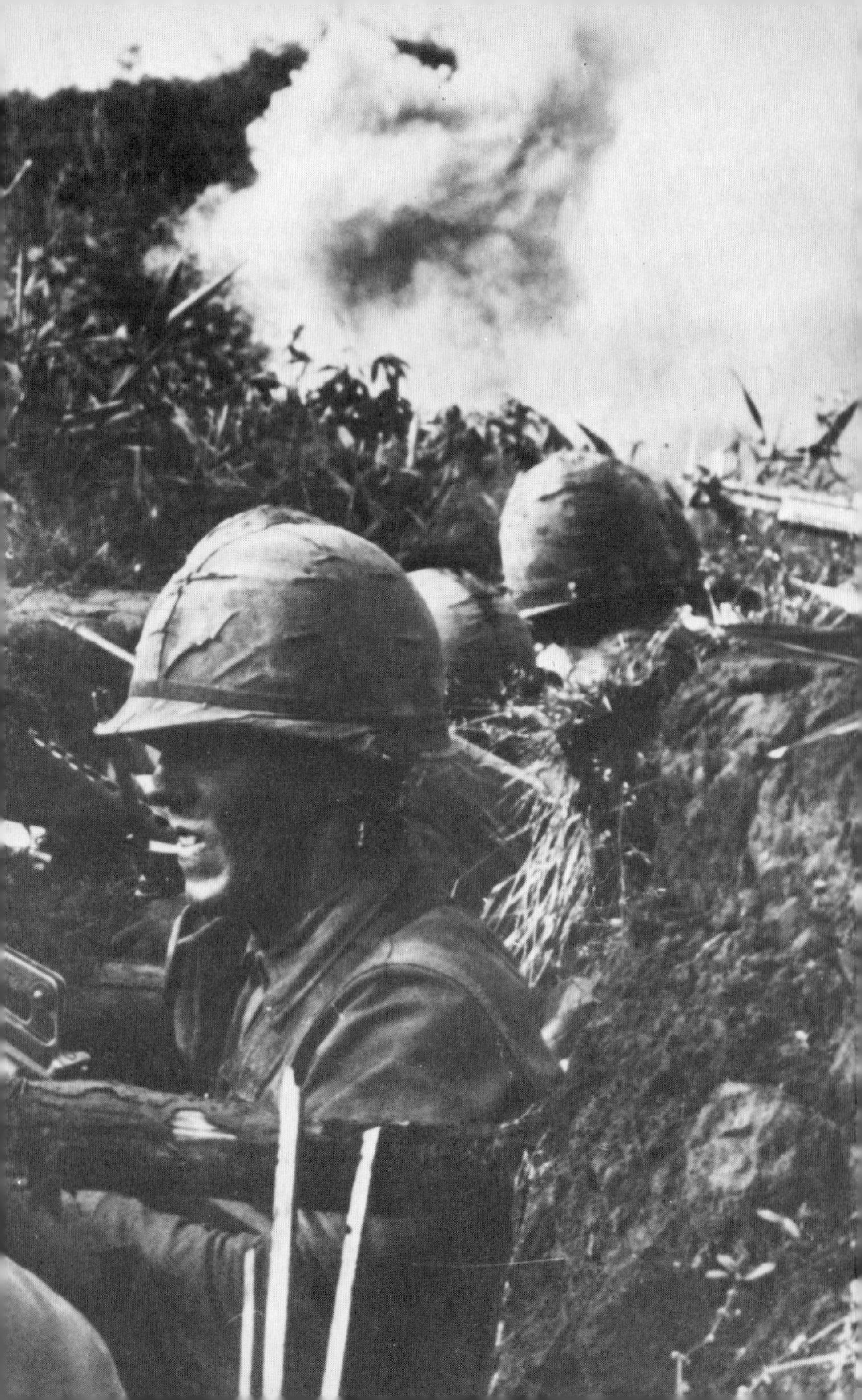

War . . . and Hope
an essay

Have you ever wondered what historians will write when they begin to assess the twentieth century?

Will they write about the unprecedented developments in automation; humankind's ability to invent and produce new things?

Will they write about the tremendous growth of different forms of transportation, such as automotive and air travel?

Will they write about new forms of communication; radio, telephone, television, and satellite?

All of these are twentieth century developments that have had a profound impact on the world. Unfortunately, however, these developments may pale in comparison to other aspects of the twentieth century.

Historians of the twentieth century will write about one hundred years of cold and hot war. They will review a century that began with World War I (the "war to end all wars"), which led inevitably to World War II, which led to the Korean War, and the Vietnam War, and many smaller conflicts in between.

They'll find that at the dawn of the 1980's America was spending more of its national budget preparing for war than for anything else.

Indeed, despite all of our incredible technological advancement, we have not been able to do away with humankind's oldest plague—war. Instead, and ironically, that same technology has been used to improve the destructive capabilities of nations.

While bringing much good, technology has also brought us the ultimate weapon in nuclear arms which can stamp out life as we know it. We stand within the shadow of a nuclear threat that could plunge us into a holocaust in which the losers would be the survivors.

If war ultimately leads to this, then what use is it anyway? What glory could there be in conquering a radioactive wasteland?

There are those who contend that every war need not lead to nuclear confrontation. Even if this were true, we've seen that, in this century, one war has simply led to another, with no end to killing and preparations for killing in sight.

There are signs of hope, however. The nuclear threat has forced many more to consider what they believe about war more urgently than those who came before them. The incredible consequences of a war in our time have amplified the horror of the killing that has taken place on previous battlefields.

This realization has led many to act. Many young people who register for the draft have started files declaring their conscientious objection to war. Others have conscientiously refused to register and have accepted the legal consequences of their action. Still others, who are not required to register, are doing what they can to support conscientious objectors. Sometimes that support, even for the legal CO, is given at some risk.

Millions of people of faith have stepped forward to protest the continued blind production of nuclear weapons. Many of them call themselves nuclear pacifists. This movement has been supported and encouraged by official church bodies.

People are also beginning to realize that it is impossible to fashion genuine peace in the world if they can not bring peace to their own homes and communities.

In short, people from every walk of life are not leaving it up to government to find peace. They are taking personal responsibility. Because of this the peace movement has begun to transcend "liberal" and other political labels and started to become a truly "popular" concern. We see more men and women saying "no" to the never-ending battle.

Those who say "no" to war do not make an empty gesture. The decision of a human heart is more important than a political agreement. History has shown us that it is more difficult to break the individual and collective human spirit than it is to break a treaty. A universal spiritual resolve could put an end to all war. But, that can only happen after a long series of heartfelt decisions made one at a time around the world.

Many American grade-school children learned a simple song during the 1960's that began "Let there be peace on earth, and let it begin with me. . ." The childlike simplicity of such a sentiment may embarrass those accustomed to dealing with harsher political realities. Yet, in what other way will genuine peace be achieved? Any peace that does not start with a profound conviction of the heart is doomed to failure. Those convictions affect the actions we take in shaping our world. So what we believe does make a difference.

We may often find ourselves discouraged. The task ahead seems so large. Our own efforts appear so small. Yet what we fail to see is that in each small effort there is a great deal of power.

Several years ago I read an account of a meeting between U.S. Senator Mark Hatfield and Mother Teresa of Calcutta. Upon seeing the incredible environment of poverty and death in which she works, Hatfield asked the Nobel laureate how she kept from becoming discouraged. Mother Teresa replied that she was not called to be successful—only faithful.

If we set our sights on the goal of faithfulness, we can never "lose." If we are faithful to the vision of peace, that, in itself, becomes its own reward. When one person has the courage to act faithfully in the face of overwhelming odds, that action gives courage to others. There is tremendous power in one small faithful act.

It appears that greater threats to world peace will emerge in the final years of this century. Men and women will have to make important decisions about how they will respond to the call to arms.

What decision will you make?

The answer you give to this question will have a profound effect on the rest of your life. If you choose not to answer, that too will have a profound effect on the rest of your life. The decision should be yours—don't let anyone make it for you.

The conclusions you come to will influence what historians write about the final decades of the twentieth century.

—Shawn Perry

Discussion Questions

1. What are some of the reasons nations go to war?
2. What are some of the reasons individuals go to war?
3. Is war the same today as it was centuries ago? How has war changed?
4. Is there any way a nation can defend itself without war?
5. How will future historians write the history of the twentieth century—particularly the remaining years of the century?

They shall beat their swords into plowshares . . .

Conscientious objectors in the Civilian Public Service (WW II alternative service program)-planting trees in Coshocton, Ohio, May 1942

American Objectors Heritage:

Conscience Since Colonial Times

> All our history gives confirmation to the view that liberty of conscience has a moral and social value which makes it worthy of preservation at the hands of the state. So deep in its significance and vital, indeed, is it to the integrity of man's moral and spiritual nature that nothing short of the self-preservation of the state should warrant its violation; and it may well be questioned whether the state which preserves its life by a settled policy of violation of the conscience of the individual will not in fact ultimately lose it by the process.
>
> Chief Justice Harlan F. Stone, "The Conscientious Objector," *Columbia University Quarterly,* vol. 21, October 1919.

Conscientious objection is as ancient as the book of Psalms and as current as the young man turning 18 today who will not register for the draft. The history of conscientious objection in America represents one chapter of the larger history of opposition to war which stretches back to man's first days as a free thinker. American conscientious objection is a rich and fascinating chapter of that larger history. As a country open to diverse traditions and committed to liberty, America has been fertile ground for expressions of individual conscience. Unfortunately, Americans have not always been as tolerant of such expressions as our professed ideals call us to be.

The original Americans whose tribal society existed here for centuries are often thought of as a warring people. Most Native Americans believed it one's duty to fight back if attacked, but many tribes maintained nonviolent behavior within the tribe, between tribes, and even in response to invading Europeans. Historian George Catlin, observing Indian culture in the central and southern parts of North America, wrote, "and thus in these little communities, strange as it may seem, in the absence of all systems of jurisprudence, I have often beheld peace and happiness and quiet, reigning supreme, for which even kings and emperors might envy them."[1]

Indian tribes generally engaged in battle when provoked, and there is no written record of consistent objection to such violence from any tribe, individual or group.

Many of the first Europeans who came to America did so to escape forced military service against their beliefs. These were mainly pacifist religious sects, the largest being the Society of Friends (Quakers), the Mennonites and the Church of the Brethren. As colonial America took shape, these groups stood out as active, law-abiding segments of society that were unshakably committed to nonviolence. The Friends, Mennonites, Brethren, Shakers, Christadelphians and other small sects would not drill with local militias or join fellow settlers in building forts and battling Indians.

Members of the Church of the Brethren were known to follow the anabaptist principle of nonresistance even in the face of Indian attacks, to the exasperation of their neighbors. A Pennsylvania historian records one such occasion: "After the massacre of thirty of them in less than 48 hours, Colonel Piper . . . made a stirring appeal to them. But it was of no avail; they were nonresistants, and evidently determined to stay such."[2] So strong was Brethren opposition to violence that when one member of their sect killed two Indians who attacked him in his mill, his fellow Brethren boycotted the mill thereafter in protest.

The Friends were perhaps the most visible of these pacifist groups, and made public statements of conscientious objection even before the Revolutionary War. In 1672 a group of New York Friends informed colony officials that "being in a measure redeemed of wars and stripes we cannot for conscience' sake be concerned in upholding things of that nature."[3]

The experience of these early conscientious objectors and society's response to them reflected what was to become a recurring pattern in American history. At first Quakers and others were persecuted for refusing to fight; cursed as heretics, whipped and required to pay stiff fines for not joining militias. Gradually, as religious objectors remained firm in their nonviolence and it became evident no persecution could induce them to fight, society grew more tolerant. Citizens came to respect the pacifist position, and by the mid 1700s most colonies had laws exempting "men of tender conscience" from any requirement to bear arms.

This tolerance decreased as the American colonies began the Revolutionary War. Most colonists were ardent to free themselves from England by military means, and patriotism was interpreted as service in the local militia; this too would become a recurring pattern. While members of the pacifist sects may have been equally eager for freedom, they did not compromise their nonviolent stance. The historic peace churches and smaller groups remained firm in their refusal to fight. The Friends explained, "... we would have joined with our fellow citizens in peaceful legal resistance to them [England] and have suffered ... for the principles of liberty and justice. But we do not believe in revolutions and we do not believe in war."[4]

In the heat of war this conscientious stand was perceived as cowardice, and was punished. An accusation which conscientious objectors would face repeatedly through the next centuries was expressed by officials of Philadelphia; "That People sincerely and religiously scrupulous are but few in Comparison to those who upon this Occasion, as well as others, make Conscience Convenience."[5] Those who would not fight were required to pay an annual fee for this privilege—and the amount went up as the war escalated. Objectors who could not or would not pay had lands and property seized. In a few cases, pacifists were dragged bodily from their homes into military units, and in one instance 14 Quakers so taken had muskets tied to their bodies.[6]

War fever eventually ebbed as America went about the business of building a new nation. America's conscientious objectors continued their quiet, firm witness and once again gained an increased measure of acceptance. Most of the state constitutions that took shape included exemption from military service for those religiously opposed, although paying a fee or hiring a substitute to fight was often required.

Many groups and individuals considered paying such fines aiding the military, and as immoral as fighting. The Church of the Brethren discussed these type of fines at their Annual Conference of 1815 and agreed to support any of their members who refused to pay for the privilege of following their conscience. The Shakers officially protested the practice of fines in a document submitted to the legislature of New Hampshire in 1818:

> In all free governments it is acknowledged as a self-evident truth that the liberty of conscience is an inalienable right; consequently no human authority has a right to claim any jurisdiction over the conscience ... We therefore ... do exhibit our consciencious[sic] scruples and objections to bearing arms, hiring substitutes, paying fines or rendering any equivalent whatever in lieu thereof, since all contribute to support the same cause.[7]

Concern for rights of conscience was not limited to pacifist religious groups. Many governing officials of early America supported conscientious objection. It is a significant, though generally overlooked fact that near-successful attempts were made to include a conscientious objection clause in the Bill of Rights.[8] Opposition to conscription was strong within the first Congress, as was evidenced when Secretary of War James Monroe proposed a national military conscription bill. Even in the midst of the War of 1812 and continued threats from Britain, Congress rejected this measure. Daniel Webster, speaking to the House of Representatives in 1814 insisted that the "abominable doctrine" of conscription "foully libelled" the Constitution:

> Where is it written in the Constitution, in what article or section is it contained, that you may take children from the parents and parents from their children and compel them to fight the battles of any war in which the folly or the wickedness of Government may engage it? Under what concealment has this power lain hidden ... to trample down and destroy the dearest rights of personal liberty?[9]

Webster's plea was based not on pacifism but "the dearest rights of personal liberty," reflecting a broadening of the concept of conscientious objection which took place in 19th-century America. In early America conscientious objection had been a religious phenomenon, limited to small groups who asked only that their members' scruples be honored. In the mid-1800s individuals outside peace churches voiced conscientious objection for ethical reasons, with the intent of influencing society.

One voice which stimulated this shift to conscientious objection as a means of social change was that of Henry David Thoreau. Thoreau was a New England naturalist, writer, tax resister and outspoken critic of the 1846 Mexican War. His "Essay On Civil Disobedience," maintaining it is an individual's duty to society to resist immoral laws, proved a major influence on conscientious objection.

Into this context of broadening conscientious objection came the outbreak of civil war, and the first national draft. The outrage at conscription Webster had expressed proved to be present among the American population in 1863 when the "Enrollment Act" was passed. Mass protests occurred, including three days of intense "draft riots" in New York City. Nevertheless conscription of eligible men began in both North and South. No provision was made in the draft law for exemption on the basis of conscience; those called had only the option of paying a fine for a substitute.

Quakers and other pacifist groups had been working nonviolently to end slavery for decades, and were not about to compromise their nonviolence because the government had decided on a military response. Most peace groups objected even to paying fines for substitutes. Resistance was strong enough that in 1864 Congress provided that members of established peace churches could perform service in hospitals or for freed slaves in lieu of fighting.

This exemption was frequently ignored, and pacifists were forcibly taken into military units, particularly in the South as the need for soldiers grew desperate. But even where the provision of alternative service was honored, this service violated the conscience of many objectors, for it was always under military command in military hospitals. The "absolutists," individuals who could not in conscience accept any options offered by the conscription system, made up a large proportion of the total group of COs. They represented a type of conscientious objection which would emerge even more strongly in future American drafts.

The peace sects supported the absolutist position as one conscientious response, but the general public was unsympathetic towards absolutists and conscientious objectors in general. Although President Lincoln was extremely sympathetic towards COs—he told Secretary of War Stanton that unless these people's religious scruples were respected the Union could not expect the blessing of heaven[10]—the tide of popular opinion had again turned hostile in the heat of war.

It is during this period that truly brutal treatment of COs first became frequent. Both COs who were forced into the army and absolutists who would not do alternative service were subjected to imprisonment and torture. This treatment came at the hands of men within the military who vented their frustration at being drafted on those who for conscience' sake would not fight.

An example of the harsh treatment COs received is found in the diary of a Quaker, Cyrus Pringle, who was drafted into the Union Army, but would not fight, obey military orders, or serve in a military hospital. Pringle and two other Friends were repeatedly threatened, tied spread-eagle to the ground for hours, and kept in the guard house without food. He wrote, "Here we are in prison in our own land for no crimes, no offense to God nor man; nay, more we are here for obeying the commands of the Son of God and the influences of his Holy Spirit."[11]

Another Quaker objector, Seth Laughlin, was tortured brutally by soldiers for a week, and finally sentenced to death by a military firing squad. As twelve soldiers pointed their guns at him and the officers who had ordered the execution looked on, Laughlin asked for one final prayer, and calmly said, "Father, forgive them, for they know not what they do." Historian Fernando Cartland records the executioners' response:

> Strange was the effect of this familiar prayer upon men used to taking human life and under strict military orders. Each man, however, lowered his gun, and they resolutely declared that they would not shoot such a man, thereby braving the result of disobeying military orders. But the chosen 12 were not the only ones whose hearts were touched. The officers themselves revoked the sentence.[12]

Dramatic incidents like this reveal that although COs were small in number (an estimated 1,500 at most throughout the Civil War) their witness had a profound effect. It is also significant that during the Civil War we find the first public statement—from conservative *Harper's Weekly,* oddly enough—that members of "peace churches" should not be given special treatment over COs from other denominations.[13] Officially, the CO exemption was still limited to those from traditional peace sects, but clearly conscientious objection was broadening, and outgrowing the laws.

The gaps between official laws governing conscientious objection and the actual state of conscience in America widened as the country approached World War I. In the early 1900s pacifism was a strong philosophy supported by much of the American public. Even as America entered World War I pacifist voices protested from positions of influence. Some of the strongest protests came from leaders in the Women's Suffrage Movement. Jeannette Rankin, the first woman elected to Congress, nearly ruined her political career by voting against America's declaration of war, accompanying her vote with a statement for peace.

Jeannette Rankin

    Much of the public may have silently agreed with Ms. Rankin. Historians have speculated that both the decision to enter World War I and the conscription act of 1917 would have been defeated if submitted to a public referendum. And while many peace groups, both secular and religious, remained strong opponents of the draft and the war, official sentiment ran high for the fighting, dissent was attacked, and the public once again caught war fever. The Selective Service Act was passed, providing only a narrowly defined exemption for conscientious objectors from established peace churches to perform noncombatant service.
    These provisions proved drastically inadequate for the depth and diversity of conscientious objection which existed in America by 1917. Men and women from many traditions—peace churches, major Christian denominations, eastern religions and obscure sects, Humanitarianism, the International Workers of the World (I.W.W.) and other political groups—were prepared to resist war for diverse reasons, and with varying goals. And resist they did, in creative ways that challenged the system and caused controversy in society far out of proportion to the actual number of objectors.
    Resistance began with draft registration, as many individuals privately said "no" and groups like the I.W.W. and Christian Molokans

publicly refused. The pacifist Molokans, who had emigrated from Russia to escape conscription, held worship services outside registration offices as a witness to their religious nonregistration.

Those conscientious objectors who did register and were drafted found themselves in military camps under military direction, even if granted CO status. Many individuals could not in conscience perform noncombatant service, so the camps were full of "absolutist" objectors who were treated very harshly. Selective Service eventually appointed a three member Board of Inquiry to travel around the camps judging the situation of "uncooperative" objectors, but the Board proved unequal to this sensitive task. One objector was told by the Board he must "stand up and fight or be shot."[14]

Some absolutist objectors were granted farm furloughs or relief services in France. Also, the Government *unofficially* broadened CO policy to include ethical objectors outside religious traditions. But these measures were inadequate; many men whose consciences fell outside the law remained subject to brutal treatment in military camps and inhumane conditions in military prison.

More than 500 conscientious objectors spent time in the military prisons of Fort Jay, Alcatraz and Leavenworth, and accounts of their treatment represent some of the most shameful brutalities in American history. Intense beatings, hangings from the ceiling, and confinement in "the hole" (solitary) without food or water were common measures. Those who refused prison orders were, as a regular practice, manacled to their cells in a standing position and fed only bread and water. Four Hutterians at Alcatraz were kept manacled, unclothed, in the "dungeon" for rejecting military uniforms, but remained steadfast in their refusal, as did many of the large group of imprisoned Mennonites. Two of these youths contracted pneumonia and died; one's body was shipped home in military uniform.[15]

These WW 1 prisoners for conscience' sake represented incredibly diverse backgrounds, yet the men fraternally supported and encouraged each other. When the Molokans at Leavenworth were confined in solitary, Evan Thomas, a philosophical objector, initiated a work strike in solidarity with the Molokans, and soon all solitary cells were filled with striking objectors.

A survey of the sentences COs received reveals the excessively vindictive view the government developed in this period: 86 jail terms of more than 24 years, 142 life sentences, 17 sentences of execution.[16] Government action became extreme and absurd—one conscientious objector quipped to his friend who had received a 25 year sentence, "Oh, man! You are no C.O. *I* was sentenced to be *shot by musketry!*"[17]

In the face of subhuman treatment during this period conscientious objectors displayed an amazingly strong nonviolent spirit, which could not be broken by threats, torture or isolation. A letter from an objector at Camp Pike forced to haul rocks while his feet were in iron shackles, expressed this spirit: "They will never know where I get my strength, but it comes, and that freely. They think they can break me, but the more they lay on me the stronger that inner man gets and the happier I become.[18]

This spirit of resistance remained strong in the interim between the "War to End all Wars" and America's next war. Although conscientious objectors moved out of the public eye, they continued witnessing to society, often through the courts. A political objector and atheist Louis Fraina challenged the narrow view that conscientious objection must stem from traditional religion, asking the Court of Appeals, "since when must a man necessarily belong to a church . . . before he can have a conscience?"[19] Another objector, Hungarian pacifist Roszika Schwimmer, protested the American policy that forbade her to become a U.S. citizen because she would not swear to bear arms for her country.

In 1940, America's youth were again asked to bear arms for the country. With the brutal treatment of COs during the last conflict in mind, pacifist and civil liberties groups sought to secure basic rights of conscience before a draft began. At hearings on the "Burke-Wadsworth" conscription bill, groups ranging from the Socialist Workers Party to major Christian denominations testified that conscientious objectors must be respected and provided for justly. It was at this time that the historic peace churches, urging other religious bodies to join them, formed the National Service Board for Religious Objectors. The *raison d'etre* of NSBRO was to serve and protect the rights of conscientious objectors, as remains true today for NSBRO's successor NISBCO.

Voices of conscience were heard protesting America's entry into World War II, among them the voice of Rep. Jeannette Rankin. As the sole member of Congress to vote against declaring war after Pearl Harbor Day, Ms. Rankin was politically ostracized and publicly insulted. Other individuals and groups who stood by pacifist principles through America's most popular war, such as Dorothy Day and the Fellowship of Reconciliation, were similarly maligned.

Americans wanted to believe the country was unanimously behind the war effort, and the 75,000 men who contradicted this claim by filing for CO status were viewed with hostility. The draft law did provide exemption for COs, and due to the efforts of NSBRO and other groups, objectors were treated more justly than during World War I, but it was still an uphill struggle for rights of conscience. CO status was granted only to those opposed to all war on the basis of "religious training and belief" and COs were assigned to restrictive camps to perform service which "would further the general war effort."[20]

Resistance to war emerged in the same strong spirit of World War I, encompassing an even broader array of religious and political viewpoints. Christian, ethical and political objectors, even many with automatic draft exemptions, such as Lutheran minister Jim Bristol, refused to register and willingly faced jail. Altogether there were 15,758 convictions of draft law violations throughout the war. These included objectors drafted and denied CO status who refused to fight, and those classified "IV-E" (conscientious objector) who would not violate their beliefs by working for the war effort in their assigned camps.

Minister's White House demonstration — October 16, 1946

It is not surprising that many COs objected on principle to the Civilian Public Service (CPS) camps. Although facilitated by the historic peace churches the camps were under government authority, and while the work was technically noncombatant, to many it was perceived as part of the war effort.

Catholic CO Gordon Zahn described how the CPS "chain of authority" stretched from camp directors to NSBRO and Selective Service in

Washington, where the "civilian nature of the direction was diminished if not lost altogether."[21] NSBRO's role in administering alternative service was controversial, for many felt the agency was too accommodating to Selective Service, and that the CPS arrangement represented a "sell-out."

There was no question that life in CPS camps was rigid and oppressive, involving long hours of manual labor under discipline that matched the military's. Throughout the country 11,950 CPSers fought fires, planted trees, built dams and roads, dug ditches, and filled other needs. If the Government had paid the workers by military standards it would have given $18,000,000. But even CPSers with families to support received no wages, a policy which Selective Service admitted was designed to discourage people from being COs.

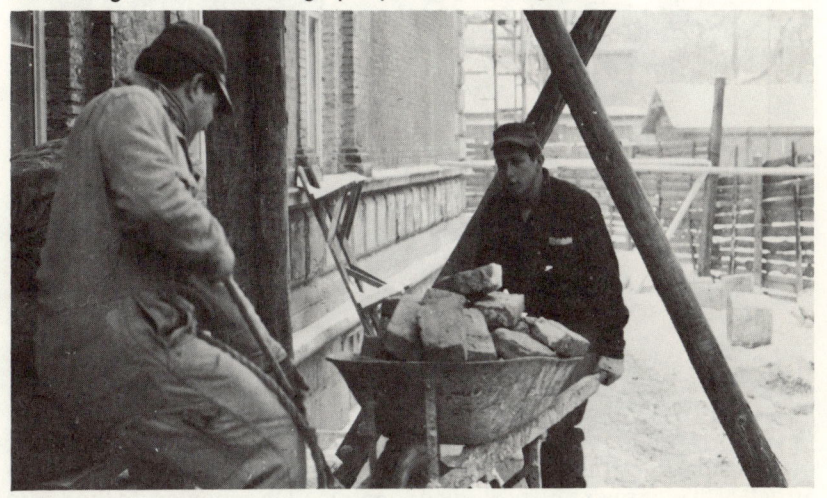

Conscientious objectors work on a construction project

Some objectors felt the best way to witness to their beliefs was by serving in the camps with a willing spirit, but others saw CPS as an immoral extension of the military system which must be resisted. Camp officials called cooperators "second mile men" and resisters "men against the state."

Many men with the latter label went beyond the absolutist position of refusing to work and developed active resistance movement within the camps, with the stated goal of abolishing CPS. Their tactics included public statements, a resistance conference in Chicago, and a mass work strike. Objectors also used similar measures to seek reforms in the camps. Resistance became so widespread and effective that the government developed a special camp, Germfask, for "troublemakers."

While resisting war, conscientious objectors made many positive contributions to society beyond their 8 million-man-days of work on CPS projects. Objectors who provided desperately needed care in mental hospitals helped expose inadequacies and enact needed reforms in the treatment of mentally ill persons. The National Mental Health Foundation was established by conscientious objectors. Noncombatant COs gave invaluable medical aid, and one received a Congressional Medal of Honor for brave service.

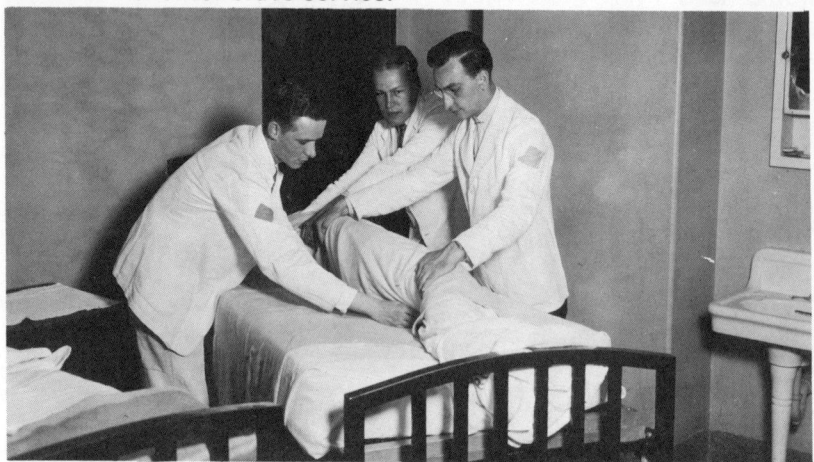

Conscientious objectors in Civilian Public Service working in a hospital

Unfortunately these selfless actions were not appreciated until long after WWII was over and prejudices against COs subsided. In the years following the war's end conscientious objectors were misunderstood and discriminated against, as states tried to pass laws forbidding COs from holding public office or owning property.

But the witness against war strengthened in the latter half of the 1900s. Traditional peace churches remained at the forefront, joined by social, political and philosophical movements, Christian and Jewish denominations, and individual women and men who spoke out for conscience' sake. In 1948 the Central Committee for Conscientious Objectors was formed to assist COs whose beliefs fell outside the legally proscribed category of conscientious objection.

A. J. Muste of the Fellowship of Reconciliation was an extremely influential voice, particularly in his essay *Of Holy Disobedience,* urging total resistance to the military system. Muste went beyond Thoreau's view of civil disobedience as a societal duty to describe "holy disobedience" which, in the face of an evil like conscription, "becomes a virtue and indeed a necessary and indispensable measure of spiritual self-preservation."[22]

Muste's timely essay was published in 1952 when conscientious objectors again faced demands to serve the state. From 1948 to 1952 COs were allowed total exemption from service, but in 1952, as the Korean "police action" raged, conscription again required alternative service of those exempted. The CPS experience must have warned Selective Service against trying to control conscience, for alternative service was handled much more liberally from 1952 to 1972. Generally, COs chose their own placements, subject to approval by SSS, and so performed work meaningful and morally acceptable to the individual.

This alternative service arrangement, and the fact that the Korean "conflict" was never a declared war probably decreased war resistance, for although key groups and individuals opposed the fighting, the numbers of men heeding Muste's advice were not large. At least 1% of men drafted for Korea were classified COs, but nonregistration was fairly low.

The following decade brought an upsurge of war and draft resistance which rocked society and made conscientious objection a position more were proud to claim. Opposition to nuclear weapons, which groups like Fellowship of Reconciliation had carried bravely through cold war years, blossomed into a popular movement. Rumblings for peace came from many sources, but it was America's participation in the Vietnam War, from 1959 to 1972 which was the catalyst of widespread war resistance, particularly among young people. This unpopular war drew a conscientious "no" to fighting not only from religious pacifists and political liberals but from "mainstream" American youth—"conservative", nonreligious, and apolitical—and from minority and disadvantaged groups, and those within military ranks.

Conscientious expression went beyond the thousands who acquired CO status and performed alternative service. Many individuals took an absolutist approach by not registering or resisting the system at other points. In the spirit of Thoreau, conscientious objectors used creative means to dramatize war resistance and move popular sentiment: burning of draft cards, protest rallies, civil disobedience, public worship. Objectors and resisters were not limited to those subject to a draft; women and men of all ages, clergy, veterans and public officials joined in supportive actions against more war.

Leadership in this struggle came from familiar sources like pacifist churches, long-time peaceworker Jeannette Rankin and other feminists, and from new sources—student leaders, Dr. Benjamin Spock, Catholic priests Phil and Daniel Berrigan and many other places of prominence. Civil rights leaders Julian Bond and Martin Luther King, Jr., encouraged young men, particularly blacks, to resist the war; for this action Bond was nearly barred from the Georgia legislature.

This broadbased movement brought together people from farranging religious political and social perspectives, and conscientious objection was finally officially broadened to include objectors outside traditional religion. The Supreme Court's 1965 decision in *U.S. v Seeger,* reinforced by the 1970 Welsh decision, defined "religious" beliefs as any sincere conviction of ultimate importance in one's life.

The Vietnam War also brought an increase in the number of "selective objectors," people conscientiously opposed to a particular conflict, but not necessarily to all war. Since they were given no legal recognition many resorted to "draft dodging" techniques rather than act against their beliefs or lie to get CO status. Three U.S. Army privates brought suit against Secretary of Defense McNamara, claiming they would serve anywhere but in the "illegal and immoral" conflict of Vietnam.

Since the Vietnam War, the drama of the 60s peace movement has died down but the firm witness against war continues. The Vietnam experience has removed much of the stigma from conscientious objection and made people more ready to question and resist the government's military measures. While the American government seems committed to a massive military posture and a violent response to international conflicts, in the past decades, American people have begun waking up to the practical and moral error of this approach and are exploring nonviolent alternatives. Conscientious objection now includes opposition to America's nuclear policy, and conscientious objectors from all walks of life are expressing their opposition in creative ways. Tax resistance, protests and civil disobedience, disarmament studies and increased involvement of major churches are all facets of conscience in America today.

In 1980, the government again demanded that young men register for a draft, and again young people of conscience, in greater numbers than ever before, are saying "no" to this first step toward conscription. Conscientious objection in America has come a long way since the first Brethren settlers refused to kill their Indian neighbors. But it is the same commitment to conscience Americans show today—only broader and stronger for the history behind it.

—Naomi Thiers

NOTES

[1] Forbes, Jack D., ed., *The Indian in America's Past* (Englewood Cliffs, NJ: Prentice-Hall, Inc., 1964), pp. 23-34.
[2] Jones, U.J. quoted in *Selective Service Special Monograph No. 11, Part I: Conscientious Objection* (Washington, DC: Government Printing Office, 1950), p. 33.
[3] Schlissel, Lillian, ed., *Conscience in America* (New York: E. P. Dutton & Co., Inc., 1968), p. 29.
[4] *Ibid.*, p. 30.
[5] *Ibid.*, p. 31.
[6] *Ibid.*, p. 32.
[7] *Ibid.*, p. 74.
[8] *Selective Service Special Monograph No. 11, Part I*, p. 38.
[9] *Schlissel, pp. 67-68.*
[10] *Selective Service Special Monograph No. 11, Part I*, p. 43.
[11] Schlissel, p. 104.
[12] *Ibid.*, p. 119.
[13] *Ibid.*, p. 94-95.
[14] Thomas, Norman, *The Conscientious Objector in America* (New York: B. W. Huebsch, Inc., 1923), p. 113.
[15] Thomas, pp. 197-200.
[16] *Ibid.*, p. 179.
[17] Thomas, p. 180.
[18] Thomas, p. 148.
[19] Schlissel, p. 182.
[20] *Selective Service Special Monograph No. 11, Part I*, p. 171.
[21] Zahn, Gordon, *Another Part of the War: The Camp Simon Story* (Amherst, MA: University of Massachusetts Press, 1979), p. 39.
[22] Muste, A. J., *Of Holy Disobedience* Wallingford, PA Pendle Hill, 1952), p. 30.

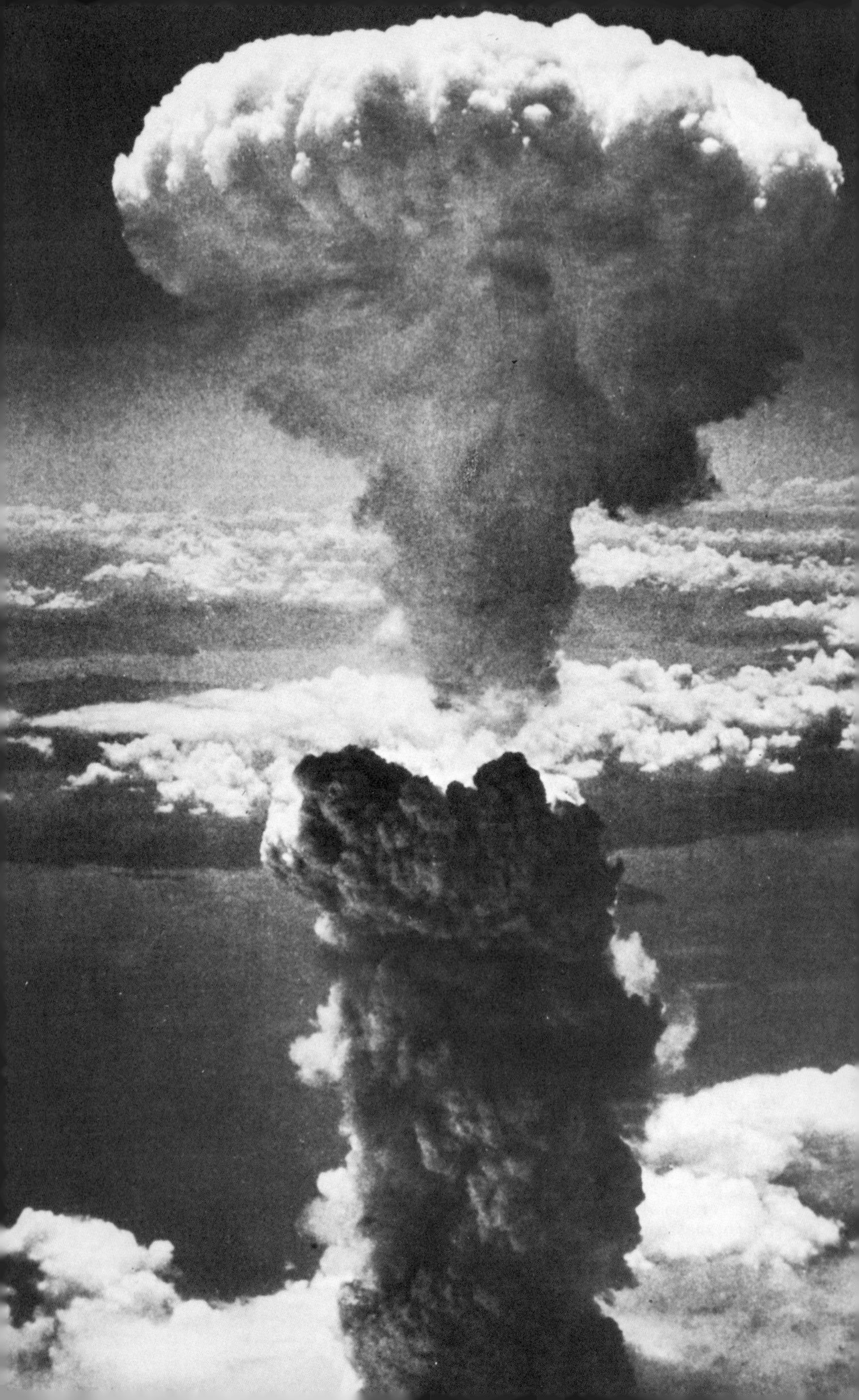

Conscience in the Current Age: The Birth of Nuclear Pacifism

In recent years concern over nuclear weapons has caused many who did not consider themselves pacifists to reconsider their position on war in the modern era. The following three statements reflect this emerging type of conscientious objection.

Mushroom cloud from atomic bomb dropped on Nagasaki, August 9, 1945, killing 36,000.

Pope John Paul II
*World Day of Peace Homily, January 1, 1980**

The truth (to) which we refer in this year's message for the first of January, is in the first place a truth about man. Man always lives in a community, in fact he belongs to various communities and societies. He is a child of his nation, an heir to its culture and a representative of its aspirations. He depends in various ways on economic, social and political systems. Sometimes he strikes us as being so deeply involved in them that it seems almost impossible to see him and reach him in person, so many are the factors that condition and determine his earthly existence.

And yet we must do so, we must try to do so continually. We must return constantly to the fundamental truths about man, if we wish to serve the great cause of peace on earth. Today's liturgy refers precisely to this fundamental truth about man, in particular by means of the strong and concise reading from the letter to the Galatians. Every man is born of a woman, just as the Son of God, the man Jesus Christ, was also born of a woman.

Man is born in order to live!

War is always made in order to kill. It is a destruction of lives conceived in mothers' wombs. War is against life and against man. The first day of the year, which with its liturgical content concentrates our attention on the Motherhood of Mary, is already for that very reason a proclamation of peace. Motherhood, in fact, reveals the desire and presence of life; it manifests the holiness of life. War, on the contrary, means the destruction of life. War in the future could be an absolutely unimaginable work of destruction of human life.

The first day of the year reminds us that man is born to life in the dignity that is due to him. And the first dignity is the one that derives from his humanity itself. On this basis rests also that dignity which the Son of Mary revealed and brought to man: "when the time had fully come, God sent forth his Son, born of woman, born under the law, to redeem those who were under the law, so that we might receive adoption as sons. And because you are sons, God has sent the Spirit of his Son into our hearts, crying, Abba! Father! So through God you are no longer a slave but a son, and if a son then an heir" (Gal. 4:4-7).

Pope John Paul II

The great cause of peace in the world is outlined, in its very foundations, by these two values: that of man's life and that of his dignity. We must refer to these incessantly, serving this cause...

I have recently received from some scientists a concise forecast of the immediate and terrible consequences of a nuclear war. Here are the principal ones:

—Death, by direct or delayed action of the explosions, of a population that might range from 50 to 200 million persons;

—A drastic reduction of food resources, caused by residual radioactivity over a wide extent of arable land;

—Dangerous genetic mutations, occurring in human beings, fauna and flora;

—Considerable changes in the ozone layer in the atmosphere, which would expose man to major risks, harmful for his life;

—In a city stricken by a nuclear explosion the destruction of all urban services and the terror caused by the disaster would make it impossible to offer the inhabitants the slightest aid, creating a nightmarish apocalypse.

Just two hundred of the fifty thousand nuclear bombs, which it is estimated already exist, would be enough to destroy most of the large cities in the world. It is urgent, those scientists say, that the peoples should not close their eyes to what an atomic war can represent for mankind.

These few reflections are enough to raise the question: can we continue along this way? The answer is clear.

The Pope discusses the subject of the danger of war and the necessity of saving peace with many men and on various occasions. The way to safeguard peace lies through bilateral or multilateral negotiation. However, at their basis we must find again and reconstruct a principal factor, without which they will not yield fruit in themselves and will not ensure peace. We must find again and reconstruct mutual trust! And this is a difficult problem. Trust cannot be acquired by means of force. Nor can it be obtained with declarations alone. Trust must be won with concrete acts and facts.

"Peace to men of goodwill." These words once uttered, at the moment of Christ's birth, continue to be the key to the great cause of peace in the world. Those in particular on whom peace depends most must remember them.

Today is the day of great and universal prayer for peace in the world. We connect this prayer with the mystery of the Motherhood of the Mother of God, and Motherhood is an incessant message in favour of human life, since it speaks, even without words, against everything that destroys it and threatens it. It is impossible to find anything that is in greater opposition to war and slaughter than Motherhood.

In this way therefore, let us raise our great universal prayer for peace on earth, drawing inspiration from the mystery of the Motherhood of her who gave the Son of God human life. . .

*Excerpted from the Weekly English edition of *L'Oservatore Romano*, January 27, 1980.

Billy Graham

Rev. Billy Graham

*A Change of Heart**

Sojourners: When you were in Poland at Auschwitz last year, you said, "The present insanity of the global arms race, if continued, will lead inevitably to a conflagration so great that Auschwitz will seem like a minor rehearsal." Would you share further your feelings about the nuclear arms race?

Billy Graham: The present arms race is a terrifying thing, and it is almost impossible to overestimate its potential for disaster. There is something ironic about the fact that we live in a generation which has made unprecedented advances in such fields as public health and medicine, and yet never before has the threat of wholesale destruction been so real—all because of human technology.

Is a nulear holocaust inevitable if the arms race is not stopped? Frankly, the answer is almost certainly yes. Now I know that some people feel human beings are so terrified of a nuclear war that no one would dare start one. I wish I could accept that. But neither history nor the Bible gives much reason for optimism. What guarantee is there that the world will never produce another maniacal dictator like Hitler or Amin?

As a Christian I take sin seriously, and the Christian should be the first to know that the human heart is deceitful and desperately wicked, as Jeremiah says. We can be capable of unspeakable horror, no matter how educated or technically sophisticated we are. Auschwitz is a compelling witness to this.

I know not everyone would agree with this, but I honestly wish we had never developed nuclear weapons. But of course that is water under the bridge. We have nuclear weapons in horrifying quantities, and the question is, what are we going to do about it?

Sojourners: How does your commitment to the lordship of Christ shape your response to the nuclear threat?

Graham: I am not sure I have thought through all the implications of Christ's lordship for this issue—I have to be honest about that. But for the Christian there is—or at least should be—only one question: what is the will of God? What is his will both for this world and for me in regard to this issue?

Let me suggest several things. First, the lordship of Christ reminds me that we live in a sinful world. The cross teaches me that. Like a drop of ink in a glass of water, sin has permeated everything—the individual, society, creation. That is one reason why the nuclear issue is not just a political issue—it is a moral and spiritual issue as well. And because we live in a sinful world it means we have to take something like nuclear armaments seriously. We know the terrible violence of which the human heart is capable.

Secondly, the lordship of Jesus Christ tells me that God is not interested in destruction, but in redemption. Christ came to seek and to save that which was lost. He came to reverse the effects of the Fall. Now I know there are mysteries to the workings of God. I know God is sovereign and sometimes he permits things to happen which are evil, and he even causes the wrath of man to praise him. But I cannot see any way in which nuclear war could be branded as being God's will. Such warfare, if it ever happens, will come because of the greed and pride and covetousness of the human heart. But God's will is to establish his kingdom, in which Christ is lord.

Third, of course, Christ calls us to love, and that is the critical test of discipleship. Love is not a vague feeling or an abstract idea. When I love someone, I seek what is best for them. If I begin to take the love of Christ seriously, then I will work toward what is best for my neighbor. I will seek to bind up the wounds and bring about healing, no matter what the cost may be.

Therefore, I believe that the Christian especially has a responsibility to work for peace in the world. Christians may well find themselves working and agreeing with non-believers on an issue like peace. But our motives will not be identical. The issues are not simple, and we are always tempted to grasp any program which promises easy answers. Or, on the other side, we are tempted to say that the issues are too complex, and we cannot do anything of significance anyway. We must resist both temptations.

Sojourners: How would you describe the changes in your thinking on the nuclear arms question, and what factors would you cite as important in prompting those changes?

Graham: It has only been relatively recently (sort of a pilgrimage over the last few years) that I have given as much attention to this subject as it deserves. I suppose there have been a number of reasons why I have come to be concerned about it. For one thing, during my travels in recent years I have spoken to a number of leaders in many countries. Almost to a person they have been concerned and pessimistic about the nuclear arms race.

Second, I think also that I have been helped by other Christians who have been sensitive to this issue. I guess I would have to admit that the older I get the more aware I am of the kind of world my generation has helped shape, and the more concerned I am about doing what I can to give the next generation at least some hope for peace. I have fourteen grandchildren now, and I ask myself, "What kind of world are they going to face?"

Third, I have gone back to the Bible to restudy what it says about the responsibilities we have as peacemakers. I have seen that we must seek the good of the whole human race, and not just the good of any one nation or race.

There have been times in the past when I have, I suppose, confused the kingdom of God with the American way of life. Now I am grateful for the heritage of our country, and I am thankful for many of its institutions and ideals, in spite of its many faults. But the kingdom of God is not the same as America, and our nation is subject to the judgment of God just as much as any other nation.

I have become concerned to build bridges of understanding among nations and want to do whatever I can to help this. We live in a different world than we did a hundred years ago, or even a generation ago. We cannot afford to neglect our duties as global citizens. Like it or not, the world is a very small place, and what one nation does affects all others. That is especially true concerning nuclear weapons...

*Excerpted from *Sojourners* Magazine, August 1979.

Rabbi Isidor B. Hoffman

Rabbi Isidor B. Hoffman

Judaism and Nuclear War

By reason of their values, their experiences and their temperament Jews have placed a major emphasis on peace. Violence and war are to be avoided even at great loss and risk. This is a basic teaching of Judaism. Those who believe and practice Judaism have thought of themselves and have been regarded by others as the people of the book, not as the wielders of the sword. Throughout almost all of the 4,000 years of their existence Jews have been devoted more to moral and intellectual concerns than to physical prowess. Their heroes have been lawgivers, prophets, scholars, scientists, such as Moses, Isaiah, Hillel and Einstein. Their Bible and the Talmud refrain from praising David and the Maccabees for their military leadership but underscore their eminence as psalmist and as upholders of religious freedom.

A large part of the explanation for this phenomenon is the high value Judaism attaches to the sanctity of life. Jews have had a tremendous zest for living. God and nature intend and provide for humans to find joy and fulfillment both in the spiritual and physical aspects of life. It follows that life must be preserved, not destroyed. War is planned demolishing of life.

At the present time acceptance of war as a means of settling disputes between nations requires the expenditure of vast funds on armaments, especially nuclear bombs and delivery systems. This diminishes the resources of substance and scientific attention necessary for the quantity and quality of life of hundreds of millions who need help with food, education, and health.

In our nuclear age the risk of any war escalating into nuclear war is very high. Our military and scientific leaders are almost unanimous in their opinion that there is no defense against nuclear attack. There would be no real winner of such a war. The losses on both sides would involve the annihilation of a large part of their populations, and most of the survivors would be in a pitiful condition.

It is understandable, therefore, that Judaism, which has always warned against war, should now oppose nuclear war as an impermissible horror. The two largest rabbinical organizations in the United States are on record that conscientious objection to war and military service is in accord with the highest ideals of Judaism.

*Written for WORDS OF CONSCIENCE by Rabbi Isidor Hoffman, Honorary Chairman of the Jewish Peace Fellowship.

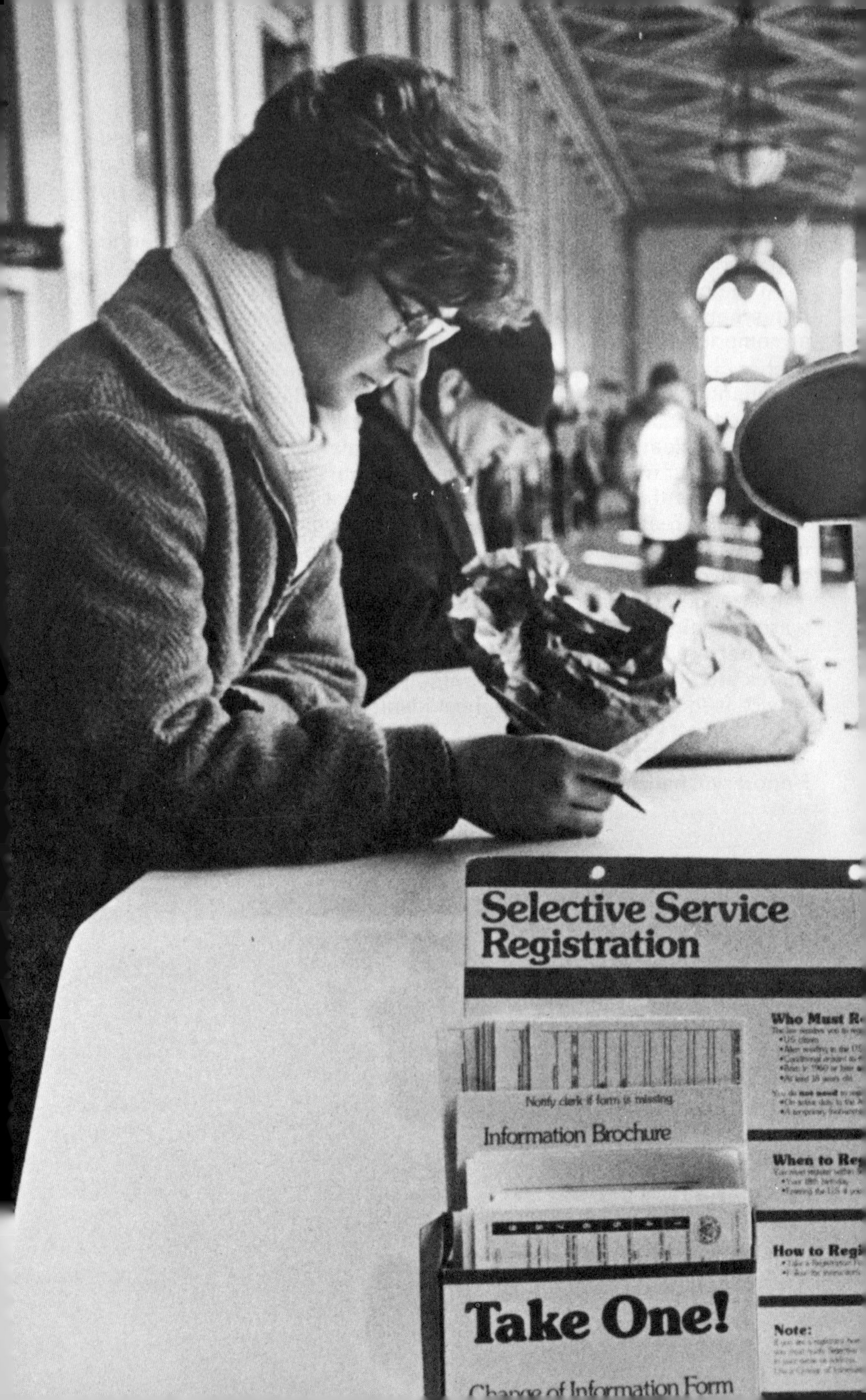
Selective Service Registration
Who Must Re
Notify clerk if form is missing
Information Brochure
When to Reg
How to Regi
Take One!
Note:
Change of Information Form

Am I a Conscientious Objector?

It is important to carefully consider what you believe about participation in war. A decision about this matter is not a simple one, but involves careful thought and soul-searching. It is not a decision to be taken lightly.

You should consider and explore your own beliefs about war and conscientious objection, so that you would be prepared to respond if the draft were resumed. If war were declared, draft inductions would immediately begin, and after receiving an induction notice you would have a *very short time* to decide whether to report for induction or file a claim for conscientious objection. In making your own decision, it is helpful to be aware of different kinds of conscientious objection.

Conscientious Objection

What is conscientious objection? Generally, conscientious objection is a deep personal conviction motivated by beliefs that prevent someone from taking part in armed combat.

Currently, federal law recognizes as conscientious objectors those who by reason of religious training and belief are conscientiously opposed to participation in war in any form. Section 6(j) of the Military

Selective Service Act provides exemption for conscientious objectors to war. It reads in part:

> Nothing contained in this (Act) shall . . . require any person to be subject to combatant training and service in the armed forces of the United States who, by reason of religious training and belief is conscientiously opposed to participation in war in any form. As used in this subsection, the term "religious training and belief" does not include essentially political, sociological, or philosophical views, or a merely personal moral code. Any person claiming exemption from combatant training and service because of such conscientious objection whose claim is sustained by the local board shall, if he is inducted into the armed forces under this (Act), be assigned to noncombatant service . . . or shall, if he is found to be conscientiously opposed to such noncombatant service, in lieu of induction, be ordered by his local board, subject to such regulations as the president may prescribe, to perform for a period (of two years) . . . civilian work contributing to the maintenance of the national health safety, or interest.

Under this law the basic standards are that a conscientious objector must be religious, object to all war, and be sincere in his application.

In *U.S. v. Seeger* (1965) the Supreme Court ruled that the phrase "religious training and belief" includes all sincere religious beliefs which are based on a power or being, or upon a faith, to which all else is subordinate or upon which all else is ultimately dependent . . . in other words, any sincere or meaningful belief that occupies a place in the life of its possessor parallel to that filled by an orthodox belief in God.

In the Welsh decision of 1970, the Supreme Court said that deeply held moral and ethical beliefs which are entirely "secular" may still be "religious" in the sense intended by law, if they are held with the strength of traditional religious convictions.

In summary, the Court said that the draft law exempts all persons "whose consciences, spurred by deeply held moral, ethical or religious beliefs, would give them no rest or peace if they allowed themselves to become a part of an instrument of war."

Within this definition, federal law recognized two kinds of conscientious objectors: 1) conscientious objectors—those who can not participate in the military in any way, and 2) noncombatants—those who do not object to performing noncombatant duties (such as being a medic) in the armed forces.

There are types of conscientious objection that are not recognized by federal law. These could be broken down into three major categories:

Selective Objection

Selective objectors are persons whose consciences would not permit them to participate in what they believe to be an "unjust" war. For example, many people who were conscientiously opposed to the Vietnam War because they believed it was unjust, said that they would have fought in World War II.

Most of the major religious bodies of the Western world have traditionally held this position based on the just-war theory. What are the conditions of the just war theory? Traditionally, they have been regarded as the following:

1. The war must be undertaken for a "just cause" and declared by a legitimate authority, such as a government.
2. The war must be undertaken for the "right intention" of securing peace and reconciliation.
3. Going to war must be the "last resort" after all other avenues for correcting the problem have failed.
4. There must be a "probability" that going to war will successfully bring about the just end desired, rather than produce needless bloodshed in a hopeless cause.
5. The damage inflicted in the war must be "proportional" to the good accomplished so that tremendous destruction and loss of life do not occur in reaching the "just end."
6. "Just means" must be used in fighting the war. No civilians may be killed.

Federal law does not recognize the selective objector, because according to the law conscientious objectors must object to participation in war in any form. Many people do not believe that in the age of nuclear weapons that there can be a just war.

Nuclear Pacifism

Nuclear pacifists are persons whose consciences would not permit them to participate in a nuclear war, or what they believe would likely become a nuclear war. Some nuclear pacifists are opposed to all war because of their belief that any war fought today would lead to the use of nuclear weapons.

As such this belief could possibly be recognized by the federal government as conscientious objection to war in any form in the future. It has not yet been tested in the courts.

Noncooperation

Noncooperators are persons whose consciences do not permit them to cooperate with the draft agency, Selective Service System. Noncooperators refuse to register for the draft, or if registered, may refuse/fail to inform Selective Service of address changes or to respond to induction. Some may also attempt to thwart the draft through legal or procedural maneuvers; Some may choose to go "underground" or move to another country.

Nonregistration is currently illegal. Federal law stipulates that those who fail to register, when required by the President, are subject to criminal penalties of up to 5 years in prison, and/or a $10,000 fine. The possible consequences of noncooperation make this a position which must be carefully considered.

Certainly there are broad definitions of general categories, and though your conscience must chart its own course irrespective of formal definitions, these explanations may assist you in understanding what conscientious objection is. Following are some questions to help you in determining what you believe:

---

1. If a war were declared today, what would you do?
2. What does it mean to be conscientiously opposed to all war?
3. Could you perform noncombatant duties in the armed forces during a war?
4. Why do some people say that they would fight in one kind of war, but not others?
5. If a person objects to participating in any war that might lead to the use of nuclear weapons, are there any wars that would be fought today in which he or she could participate?
6. Is it right for someone to refuse to register?
7. Are you a conscientious objector? Why? Why not?
8. How did you acquire those beliefs?
9. How do these beliefs affect the way you live?

If you decide you are a conscientious objector, you may find that many of your friends, family members, neighbors and teachers disagree with your decision. They, as well as your draft claims board, may ask questions which test and challenge your belief. It is wise to be aware of and consider the answers to these questions you may be asked.

1. Is your objection to killing or being killed?

2. Why did Christ say, "He that hath no sword, let him buy one," "Render unto Caesar that which is Caesar's..." and "I came not to bring peace, but a sword"?
3. How about the Christian doctrine of approval for just wars?
4. How do you explain all of the wars in the Old Testament?
5. Do you think that combat soldiers who believe they serve God in serving their country are misled?
6. Can you say that a medic helping a dying soldier is performing an immoral act and can never be an expression of God's love?
7. Do you honestly think the Armed Forces should be abolished?
8. What method would you use to resist evil?
9. Would you use force to prevent someone from killing an innocent person? From killing you? From killing himself?
10. If someone were attacking your mother, would you try to stop the person?
11. Didn't Jesus use violence in driving the money changers from the temple?
12. If everyone believed the way you do, wouldn't the Communists take over the country?
13. Do you think that the authority of your conscience is more reliable than the consciences of most Americans?
14. Aren't you being unrealistic? Haven't we always had wars?
15. What will you do if your application for CO is denied?

These are tough questions. We present them not to discourage but to prepare the conscientious objector. These challenges should help you think through your position.

Peacemaking

Conscientious objection is often viewed as a negative position because it seems to be based on the refusal to do something. But it is important to know that most COs today see this position as more than a refusal to perform combatant military service. COs are workers for peace. Many COs become devoted peacemakers for their entire lives.

If you are considering conscientious objection you have started down a path that should lead you to work positively for peace. Simple refusal will not put an end to war, anymore than it will put an end to violence in our communities.

Active peacemakers are needed if there will be an end to war and violence. Conscientious objection can be the start of the peacemaker's life-long pilgrimage.

—Shawn Perry and Beth Ellen Boyle

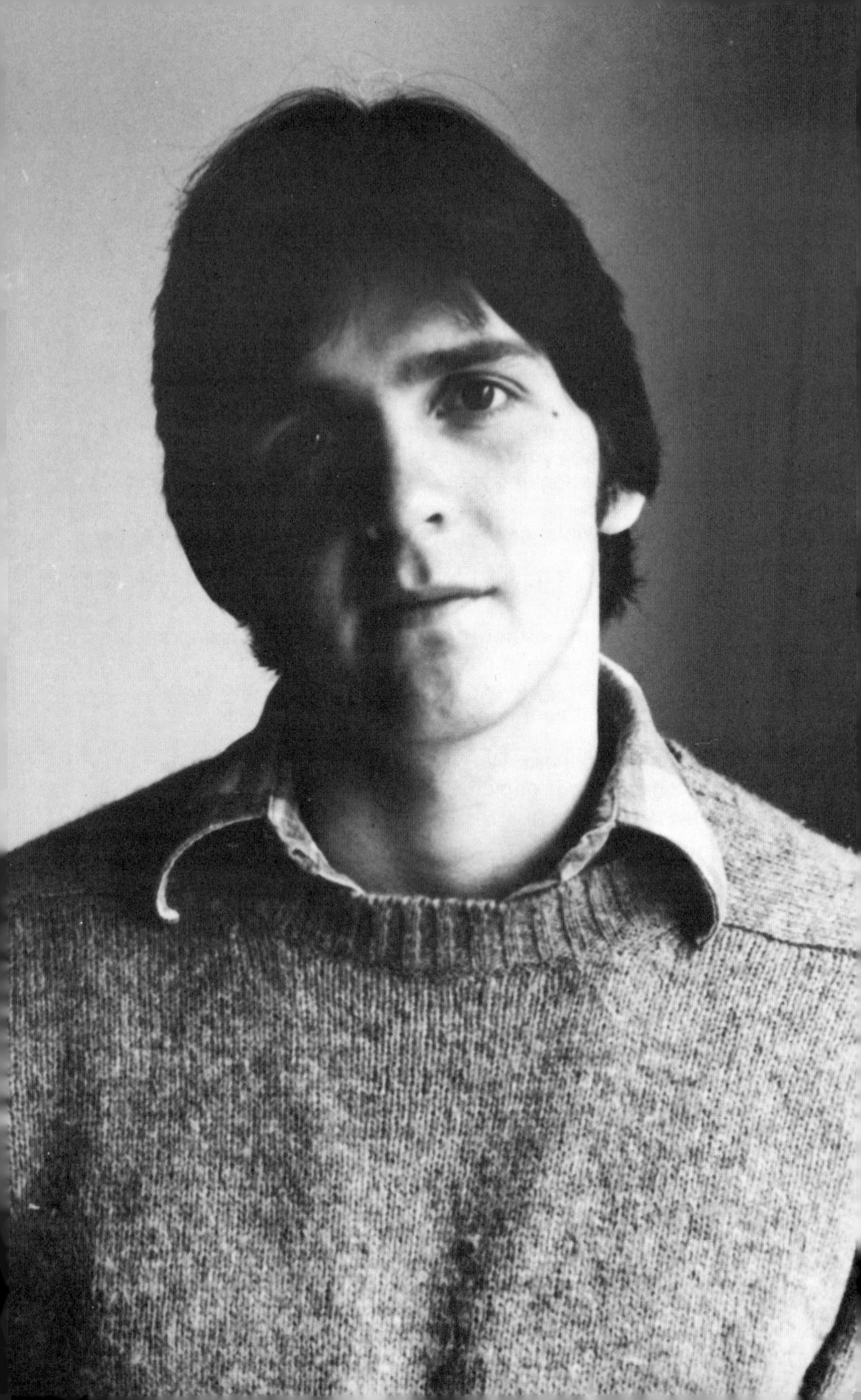

Where Do I Go From Here?

When you have concluded that you are a conscientious objector, a number of questions then arise. One of the most important questions to consider is, "What opportunities are available to me to demonstrate my beliefs?" Such specific opportunities as "peace" conferences, church activities, political work, writing articles and demonstrating are a few obvious ones, but there are some not-so-obvious choices of simple living, peaceful relationships, responsible investment, and environmental responsibility which are signs that a person's conscientious beliefs are influential in all areas of his or her life.

How far may a conscientious objector go in complying with the Selective Service System? The answer to this question will depend upon the individual conscience. Many conscientious objectors, while deploring preparations for war, will acknowledge that the government has the right to require them to register for the military draft. They will do so, intending to apply for classification as conscientious objectors.

Others will find themselves deciding that they cannot participate in preparations for war, and they will refuse to register for the military draft. This is an illegal act, for which the person may be brought to trial.

Those who register may find that they are not awarded the conscientious objector classification, and refuse to accept induction; this is also an illegal act.

In any case, whether or not you have decided to comply with the requirement to register for the draft, your beliefs about conscientious objection should be documented. Such documentation will serve as evidence, either for the local board who would hear and decide one's claim to classification as a conscientious objector, or in any trial or hearing resulting from a violation of the Military Selective Service Act.

For many people, such documenting is a useful exercise for exploring and clarifying their beliefs. Those approaching draft age are very often unaccustomed to speaking about their beliefs to those who may believe differently. Those who are beginning to counsel conscientious objectors will also find clarifying and documenting their own beliefs helpful.

Selective Service uses Form 150, Special Form for Conscientious Objector, as the basis of a CO (conscientious objector) application. In general, the questions on this form ask the applicant to describe his or her beliefs, whether they are religious, moral, or ethical in nature, how these beliefs have been acquired, why these beliefs do not allow participation in war, and how the applicant can demonstrate that he lives by these beliefs.

Answers to all of these questions are involved, and may overlap frequently. For many young people, especially, the answers to "How did you acquire your beliefs?" may seem quite similar to the question, "How do you lead your life by these beliefs?", since the answers to both questions will involve a review of their upbringing.

According to the Selective Service Local Board Member Trainer's Manual, local board members will be looking for four components in every CO claim: "Registrant must demonstrate *opposition to war in any form;* for 1-O claim (note: 1-O conscientious objectors object to all forms of military service, and must serve in *alternative* service, while 1-A-O conscientious objectors serve in *noncombatant military* service), registrant must demonstrate opposition to any type of military training and service; registrant's opposition must be based on religious training and belief, strictly religious beliefs, ethical or moral beliefs that are strongly held; registrant must be sincere."

In documenting your beliefs, it is always helpful to include evidence which would support the claim you are making. Letters of support are very effective as evidence. These letters can and should be obtained from a representative sample of the people who know you well and can attest to your conscientious sincerity. They could be written by your friends, family, church, school, and place of employment. It is helpful if at least one of the letters is written by a professional person, a teacher or a doctor, for example, who knows you well.

Other kinds of written evidence could be articles and essays you've written; photographs or other evidence of participation in peace activities and demonstrations; or church statements which support conscientious objection or which were influential in the formation of your conscience. In submitting letters of support as evidence of your sincerity, it may prove important to notarize the writer's signature.

Statements, letters of support, and other evidence, if compiled in advance of your claim or your trail, *should be placed on file with a local, permanent, draft counseling agency,* such as a church. The agency should be *permanent* because the CO claims and trials in which they would be needed might not take place for years after the file is begun. The agency should be *local* because the time allowed for you to present your claim to a local board may be as little as two weeks, which may not allow enough time for a national counseling agency to respond to a request for a file.

The "mobilization draft," which is the kind of draft the current regulations call for, requires that all men register for the draft within 30 days of their eighteenth birthday, unless they are incarcerated, hospitalized, or in the military, in which case they are required to register upon their release.

When inductions are requested by the President and approved by the Congress, Random Sequence Numbers will be awarded in the draft lottery, and induction orders will be sent out by mailgram. These mailgrams inform the recipient that he has been classified 1-A, available for military service, and that he is to report to a Military Entrance Processing Station within ten days, at an address given in the mailgram. "If you believe you qualify for postponement or reclassification, you may apply to Selective Service in the way noted," the mailgram/induction order states; it continues, "Go to a U.S. Post Office for a copy of the Selective Service Classification Information Booklet and application forms." The completed forms are to be mailed to the Selective Service Area Office with jurisdiction over the inductee, and the address for that office is given in the mailgram.

The Classification Information Booklet contains SSS Form 9, Claim for Postponement or Reclassification. After filing a Form 9 the applicant will be provided with the forms necessary to apply for the classifications in which he or she is interested, the reporting date mentioned in the mailgram is cancelled, and the CO claimant is scheduled to appear before the local board.

The CO would then prepare the claim by responding in writing to the SSS Form 150 questions, and by gathering any new letters of support and other supportive evidence, including the file from the local draft counseling agency. He would submit this material in advance of his hearing date, if at all possible. At the hearing, the CO would be allowed three witnesses, as well as an advisor. In most cases, the local board will arrive at a decision at the time of the hearing. An affirmative decision would make the CO responsible to perform alternative service; negative decisions may be appealed to the SSS District Appeal Board.

—Charles Maresca

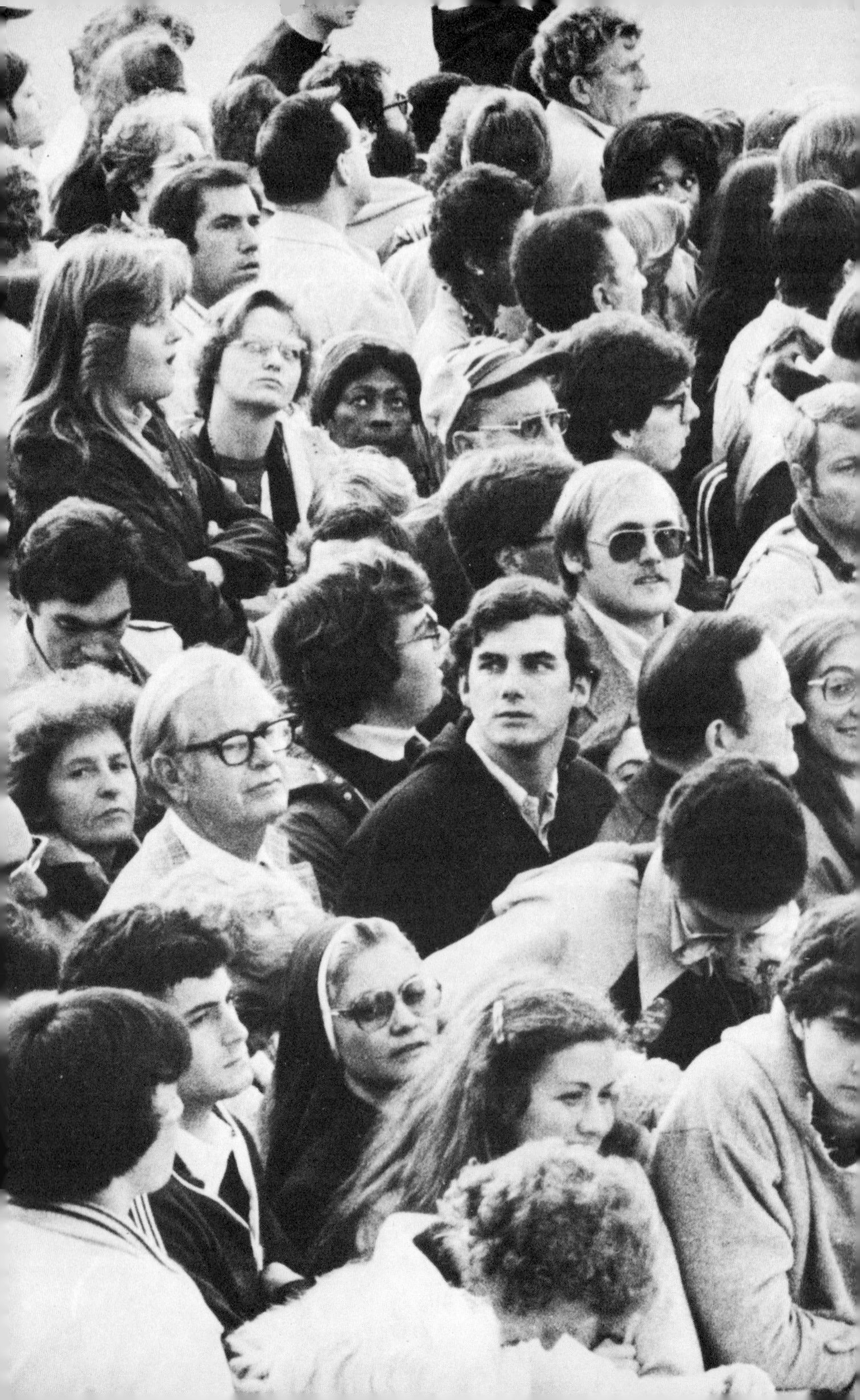

Resources

War and Peace

Christian Attitudes Toward War and Peace by Roland Bainton. (Abingdon Press, 1960, 299 pp.) Bainton examines the writings of the church fathers and provides a helpful typology of evolving Christian attitudes toward war, pacifism, the just war, and the crusade.

The Fight Against War by Albert Einstein. Edited by Alfred Lief. (John Day Co., 1933)

If the War Goes On . . . Reflections on War and Politics by Hermann Hesse. (Farrar Straus, and Giroux, 1971) These essays present the pacifist position of the Nobel-Prize-winning novelist.

It is Not Lawful for Me To Fight by Jean Michel Hornus. (Herald Press, 1980, 384 pp.) An extremely thorough study of the early church attitude toward war, violence, and the state.

Neither Victims Nor Executioners by Albert Camus (World Without War, 1972, 60 pp.) Camus' expresses his philosophical views on violence and war.

War: Four Christian Views edited by Robert Clouse. (InterVarsity Press, 1981, 208 pp.) Four prominent Christian scholars present essays on their varying positions —pacifism, nonresistance, defensive war and crusade-type war.

War and Peace by Leo Tolstoy. (available in numerous editions and translations) This novel is commonly recognized as one of the greatest classics written. An account of Napoleon's invasion of Russia, the story delves deeper into reflection on war and peace and the fate of man in history.

Biblical Studies

Christ and Violence by Ronald J. Sider. (Herald Press, 1979, 108 pp.) Three lectures by Sider on the biblical call to peace and justice.

New Call for Peacemaking by Maynard Shelley. (Faith and Life Press, 1979, 109 pp.) A study guide on peace including biblical references, bibliography and a list of peace-making agencies.

New Testament Basis of Peacemaking by Richard McSorley. (Center for Peace Studies, Georgetown University, 1979, 167 pp.) Addresses the question of war in the modern age, discussing New Testament texts that support pacifism as well as those used to justify militarism.

The Politics of Jesus by John Howard Yoder. (Eerdmans, 1972, 260 pp.) Presents a pacifist understanding of Jesus' relationships to the political realm and explores relationship between Christian ethics and New Testament scholarship.

War and the Gospel by Jean Lasserre. Translated by O. Coburn. (Herald Press, 1962, 243 pp.) This French Reformed Pastor gives a theological defense of pacifism with a penetrating analysis of the New Testament.

Conscience and War in History

Another Part of the War: The Camp Simon Story by Gordon Zahn. (University of Massachusetts Press, 1979) Zahn gives a history and personal account of a CO camp in World War II and reflects on the meaning of his experience.

Chance and Circumstance: The Draft, The War and The Vietnam Generation by Lawrence M. Baskir and William A. Strauss. (Vintage, 1978, 312 pp.) Documents the history of the Indochina war draft and the birth and breadth of protest to it.

Conscience in America edited by Lillian Schlissel. (Dutton, 1968, 444 pp.) A careful history of conscientious objection in America which includes a rich collection of historical documents.

Men Against War by Barbara Haberstreit. (Doubleday Books, 1973, 216 pp.) A concise history of pacifism in America, highlighting some of the most active pacifists.

The Path of Most Resistance by Melissa Miller and Phil Shenk (Herald Press, 1982, 242 pp.) A history in story form of ten Mennonite Vietnam draft resisters, showing the varied experiences resistance brought for each of them.

Peace Be With You by Cornelia Lehn. (Faith and Life Press, 1980, 126 pp.) A story book for the whole family, compiling 60 accounts of "peace heroes" primarily from the Anabaptist and particularly, Mennonite heritage.

The Power of the People by Robert Conney and Helen Michalowski. (Peace Press, 1977, 240 pp.) A powerful and comprehensive illustrative history of nonviolence in the United States from colonial days to the present.

Nonviolence

Dwell in Peace: Applying Nonviolence to Everyday Relationships by Ronald C. Arnett. (Brethren Press, 1980) A study in applying nonviolent peacemaking and creative dialogue to interpersonal relationships.

The Kingdom of God is Within You by Leo Tolstoy. (Farrar, Straus and Cudahy, 1961) Tolstoy's interpretation of the Sermon on the Mount and a major statement of his belief in nonviolence.

Of Holy Disobedience by A. J. Muste. (Pendle Hill, 1952, 36 pp.) The classic advocating noncooperation with conscription.

The Roots of Jewish Nonviolence. (Jewish Peace Fellowship, 1981, 64 pp.) A collection of articles on Jewish opposition to war.

Conscience and War Taxes

Affirm Life: Pay for Peace - A Handbook for World Peace Tax Fund Educators edited by Maynard Shelley and Ron Flickinger. (Faith and Life Press, 1981 86 pp.)

Ain't Gonna Pay For War No More by Robert Calvert (War Tax Resistance, 1970)

Guide to War Tax Resistance edited by Ed Hedeman (War Resisters League, 1981, 120 pp.)

Handbook on Nonpayment of War Taxes (Peacemakers, 1981, 64 pp.)

People Pay for Peace edited by William Durland. (Center Peace Publishers, 1982, 103 pp.)

The Tax Dilemma: Praying for Peace, Paying for War by Donald Kaufman. (Herald Press, 1978, 102 pp.)

Groups Working For Peace
(other than those with statements in this book)

Clergy and Laity Concerned *(CALC)*, 198 Broadway, New York, NY 10038

Center for Defense Information, 122 Maryland Ave. N.E., Washington, D.C. 20002

Central Committee for Conscientious Objectors *(CCCO)*, 2208 South St., Philadelphia, PA 19146, or 1251 Second Ave., San Francisco, CA 94122.

Draft Action, 534 Washington Building, 1435 G Street, Washington, D.C. 20005

Friends Committee on National Legislation *(FCNL)*, 245 Second St., N.E., Washington, D.C. 20002

Midwest Committee for Military Counseling *(MCMC)* Suite 317, 343 South Dearborn St., Chicago, IL 60604

Mothers and Others Against the Draft, 6 Carey Rd., Great Neck, NY 11021

National Council for a World Peace Tax Fund, 2111 Florida Ave., N.W., Washington, D.C. 20008

SANE - Citizens Committee for a Sane World, 318 Massachusetts Ave., N.E., Washington, D.C. 20002

Sojourners Peace Ministry, 1321 Otis St., N.E. Washington, D.C. 20017

War Resisters League, 339 Lafayette St., New York, NY 10012

Women's International League for Peace and Freedom *(WILPF)*, 1213 Race St., Philadelphia, PA 19107

World Peacemakers, 2852 Ontario Rd., N.W. Washington, D.C. 20009

Worksheet on War

QUESTION 1: DESCRIBE THE BELIEFS WHICH ARE THE BASIS FOR YOUR CLAIM FOR CLASSIFICATION AS A CONSCIENTIOUS OBJECTOR, AND WHETHER THOSE BELIEFS WOULD PERMIT YOU TO SERVE IN A NONCOMBATANT POSITION IN THE ARMED FORCES.

This question asks you to describe, in detail and as forthrightly as possible, the basic principles by which you insist on guiding your life. You should describe those values which are of utmost importance to you such as God, love, truth, etc., and why these beliefs are in conflict with military service. This question asks you to formulate your own statement of conscientious opposition to war. You should begin by saying that you are conscientiously opposed to war, and then describe why.

The second part of this question seeks to determine whether you seek noncombatant status or a full exemption from military service. You should specify what it is about noncombatant service which would violate your conscience, if this is the exemption you seek.

IMPORTANT: Remember that at this time federal law does not recognize selective objection or nuclear pacifism, and does not allow exemptions for people in these categories. This should not stop you from filing such statements of belief, however. In the event of your beliefs or the law should change, your statements could prove invaluable.

If your convictions lead you to be a noncooperator you may wish to record those convictions here. Nonregistration is currently *illegal*.

QUESTION 2: **DESCRIBE HOW YOU ACQUIRED THESE BELIEFS.**

In answering this question, you should include any formal religious training you have had if you feel such training has helped you arrive at your position. If you feel you believe as you do with no help from your formal training, there is no need to mention it. The influence of clergy, teachers, family members, books, membership in organizations, are essential to list. Be specific; you must show that strong influences in your life have stimulated you to think seriously and clearly about participation in war.

Specific incidents can be included, such as demonstrations, seminars, or assemblies you have attended, to show that you believe as you do. Be careful not to give the impression that your beliefs are mainly "political."

QUESTION 3: **DESCRIBE HOW YOUR BELIEFS AFFECT THE WAY YOU LIVE, AND THE TYPE OF WORK YOU DO OR PLAN TO DO.**

This is sometimes a difficult question for the young objector, since he or she has not had experiences which can show deeply held beliefs. Such a person should discuss how his or her future plans are deeply affected by a commitment to those beliefs. Describe kinds of employment you have had or plan to have which reflect your commitment. Discuss any public expression, written or oral, you have given to your beliefs.

Describe your lifestyle, mention your life's goals as you have set them, and show how they are an outgrowth of your beliefs.

After completing this worksheet, prepare your own statement of your beliefs in final form (preferably typewritten) and your answers. Keep the original for your own records and send a copy to NISBCO, to your religious body, or to a local church or counseling agency. It is preferable to deposit your statement with a local group, since this will provide more immediate access to your statement in case of draft inductions.

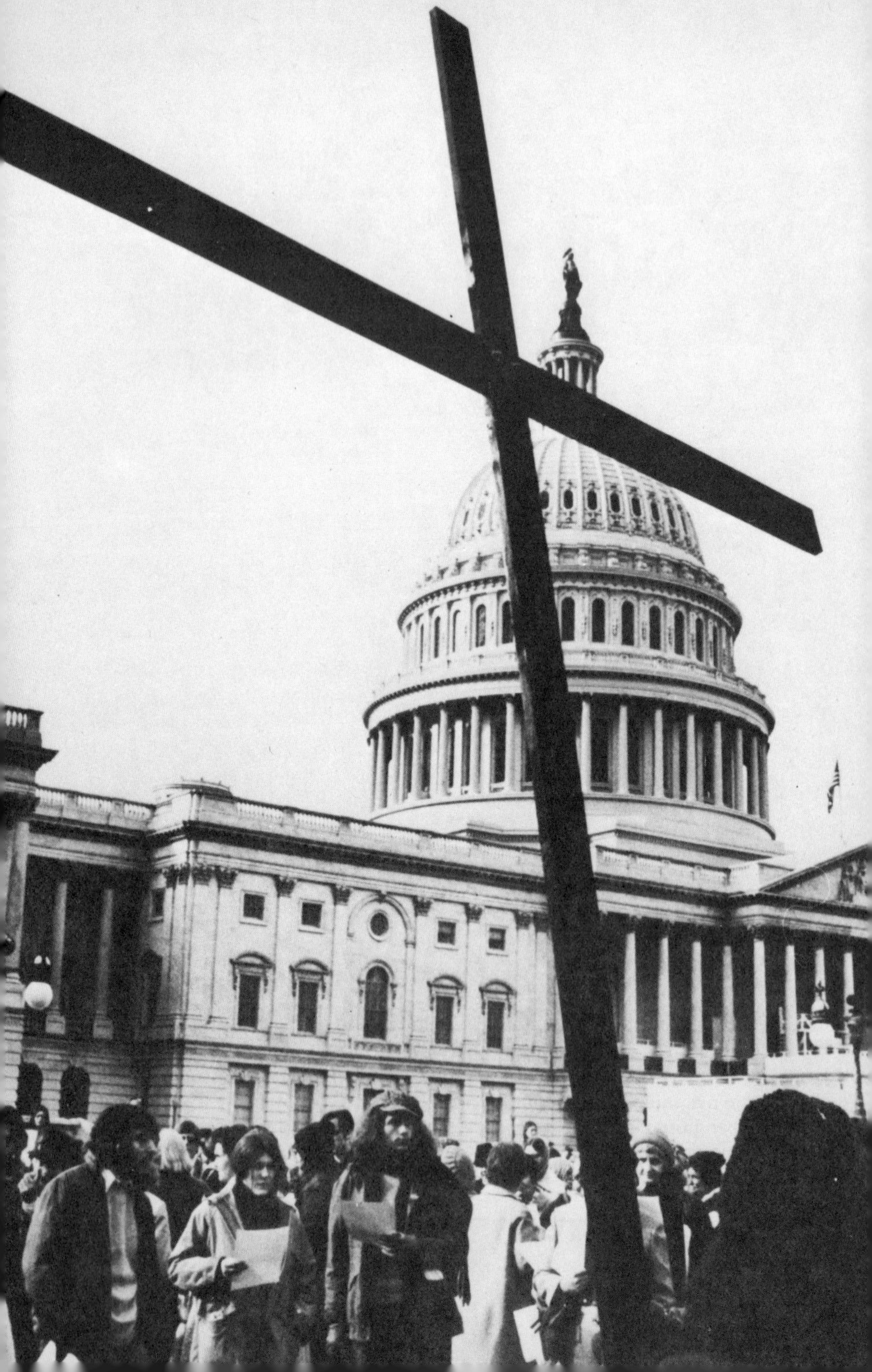

Words of Conscience:

Official Statements by Religious Bodies

"Do you know, Fontanes, what astonishes me most in this world? The inability of force to create anything. In the long run the sword is always beaten by the spirit."

—Napoleon

AMERICAN ETHICAL UNION

Resolution, For Protection of Rights of Moral-Ethical Conscientious Objectors:

WHEREAS, the American Ethical Union has, in the last decade, consistently opposed all statutory and administrative restrictions which granted conscientious objector status only to registrants holding traditional religious beliefs; and

WHEREAS, our representatives in concert with representatives of other organizations have been successful before congressional committees, in the Supreme Court, and with the previous administration of the Selective Service System, to have such restrictions lifted; and

WHEREAS, the valid legal standard as construed by the Supreme Court now does grant moral-ethical conscientious objectors equality with their religious counterparts; and

WHEREAS, the present administration of the Selective Service System disregarding such legal standard and, under its own self-promulgated restrictive rules, continues the administrative denial of such equality;

THEREFORE, BE IT RESOLVED, that the American Ethical Union deplore the continuing administrative deprivation of moral-ethical conscientious objectors of their rights to exemption from military service, assured them by the law of the land, and we instruct our appropriate agencies to continue their intervention at every opportunity to the end that such deprivation come to an early end.

Should any form of selective service be reinstituted, the American Ethical Union supports the exemption of conscientious objectors. For this purpose, conscientious objectors include those who object to war in any form and those who object to wars they consider unjust, whether their objection is based on belief in a Supreme Being or on dedication to ethical values.

Resolution approved by 1972 Assembly, reworded and reaffirmed by 1979 Assembly.

FOR FURTHER INFORMATION: Write to the American Ethical Union, 2 West 64th Street, New York, N.Y. 10023.

AMERICAN HUMANIST ASSOCIATION

Many humanists have reached the conclusion that any war and the participation in any armed conflict is morally unjustifiable. Others have concluded that only wars of aggression must be opposed. The American Humanist Association believes that both are equally entitled to exemption, and is prepared to provide limited counseling to interested persons.

SUPPORT FOR THE RELIGIOUS HUMANIST OBJECTOR: The Board of Directors of the American Humanist Association declares its support of those young men of Humanist belief, and especially those who are members or of member families of our Association, who by reason of Humanist religion and belief are conscientiously opposed to participation in war in any form. We support the right of such young men to be treated as Conscientious Objectors under the provision of Selective Service Law.

SUPPORT FOR ALL SINCERE CONSCIENTIOUS OBJECTORS: The Board of Directors of the American Humanist Association declares its support of all youth of Humanist belief, and especially those who are members or of member families of our Association, who are committed to the substance of a Humanist non-violent belief, but who interpret their obligation in other than formal religious terms. We believe that the substance of such a conscientious commitment should be the prevailing consideration in determining a registrant's qualification as a Conscientious Objector rather than the merely verbal terms in which his faith or belief may be expressed.

(Statements of AHA Board of Directors, October 12, 1969.)

We support the young people protesting President Carter's call for renewal of draft registration. Peace-time conscription is unconstitutional, war is unconscionable. Freedom cannot be preserved by denying freedom to youth and forcing them to a service they don't want to perform. The lives and futures of our young citizens are too precious to be left to chance in a draft lottery . . .

We call on the President, our legislators, and our fellow citizens to listen to the young protestors and to heed their objection. As Humanists we pledge to them our dedication to their right to options to military service and mastery of their own fates, and invite them to join with us is building a world community.

(Statement of the Western Regional Conference of Humanists, San Diego, January 1980.)

FOR FURTHER INFORMATION: Write to the American Humanist Association, 7 Harwood Dr., Amherst, NY 14226.

ASSEMBLY OF COVENANT CHURCHES

As Christians, we are called to be a people who do not support war as the proper way to resolve conflicts of interest, questions of sovereignty, differing methods of government, or questions of honor. Rather, so far as possible, we are called to be peacemakers and thereby reflect our identity as sons and daughters of God. Our ministry of reconciliation has practical application in the arena of world politics as an attitude towards the resolution of conflicts between nations.

We realize that there are differences among Christians, even in our churches, as to whether such a stand means that there is never any justification for war. We do affirm, however, that pacifism is a valid Christian ethical option, that is, that a proper outworking of a theology of reconciliation can lead to pacifism as one of its results.

Therefore, we commend and support those within our churches who are genuine pacifists. (This must be adequately demonstrated to their church government.) We furthermore ask the governing authorities of this nation to grant conscientious objector status to those who take such a stand.

(1980 Statement)

FOR FURTHER INFORMATION: Write to Rev. Ernesto M. Obregon, Assembly of Covenant Churches, 3512 Archwood Ave., Cleveland, OH 44109.

ASSEMBLIES OF GOD—GENERAL COUNCIL

As a movement we affirm our loyalty to the government of the United States in war or peace.

We shall continue to insist, as we have historically, on the right of each member to choose for himself whether to declare his position as a combatant, a noncombatant, or a conscientious objector.

(From Bylaws of the Church, Article XX, Military Service)

FOR FURTHER INFORMATION: Write to Joseph R. Flower, General Secretary, General Council of The Assemblies of God, 1445 Boonville Avenue, Springfield, MO 65802.

ASSOCIATION OF BIBLE STUDENTS

"WHEREAS the Congress of the United States has enacted a conscription law and this law affects the young men and the young women of our fellowship who adhere to the context of the resolution and the teaching of Jesus Christ our Lord, we in General Convention assembled at Chautauqua, Ohio, as representatives of the various Bible Student congregations of the United States, take this opportunity to clearly state our position regarding participation in military service and training in time of peace or time of war.

"For the past sixty years the teachings of Pastor Russell in the six Volumes of 'Studies in the Scriptures', 'Tabernacle Shadows', and his other writings, have and do still represent the convictions of all those in our fellowship and service.

"Our convictions are the same today as they were during World War I and World War II. We believe that we as Christians should not engage in military service and training. This conviction is based upon our belief that we are children of God, whose laws forbid participation in war.

"Further, we recognize the individuality of every Christian in the exercising of his conscience in harmony with the obligations or vows he has made to his Creator.

"It is moved that we, The Bible Students General Convention, assembled at the Miami Valley Chautauqua, Chautauqua, Ohio, August 1-8, 1948, declare the above statement is a proper expression of our conscientious convictions."

(Statement of Bible Students General Conference, 1948 and reaffirmed 1965, 1970, 1978 and 1982. Amended 1978.)

FOR FURTHER INFORMATION: Write to Bible Students National Committee, Leo B. Post, 24 Lexington Rd., New City, NY 10956.

BAHÁ'Í

In view of the importance of a clear understanding of the details of the Bahá'í teachings relating to military service, the National Spiritual Assembly of the Bahá'ís of the United States presents the following statement of general principles for the information and guidance of the members of the Bahá'í Community in the United States and others who may have an interest in the Bahá'í viewpoint.

The Bahá'í teachings require that followers of the Faith obey the laws of the government under which they live. However, Bahá'ís are also required to apply for noncombatant service whenever the opportunity to do so is legally provided by their government on the basis of religious training and belief.

While the religious convictions of Baha'is require them to seek whatever exemption from combatant duty may be granted by their government on the grounds of religious belief, they definitely are not pacifists in the sense of refusal to cooperate with and obey the laws of their government. Thus Baha'is do not, on the grounds of religious conviction, seek to abandon their obligations as citizens. Baha'is who are citizens of the United States are able to reconcile their fundamental spiritual convictions and their civil obligations by applying for noncombatant service under the existing laws and regulations.

The members of the Baha'i Faith make no reservations in claiming that they are fully obedient to all provisions of the laws of their country, including the Constitutional right of the Federal Government to raise armies and conscript citizens for military service. Baha'is try to serve as members of the Armed Forces, in the Medical Corps, or in any capacity in which they may legally maintain a noncombatant status regardless of the effect which that may have on their personal safety, their convenience, the kind of activity they must discharge or the rank to which they may be assigned.

FOR FURTHER INFORMATION: Write to the National Spiritual Assembly of the Baha'is of the United States, 536 Sheridan Road, Wilmette, IL 60091.

BAPTIST

AMERICAN BAPTIST CHURCHES—U.S.A.

Resolution on Christian Conscience and Military Service

All persons are created in the image of God and owe their first allegiance to God. All persons have the responsibility to read and interpret the scriptures and to reflect on their religious experience in order to understand God's will for them and the world, and they are called in conscience to live out that understanding. The supreme responsibility of every person is to obey God's will above all human lives and directives.

In light of the continuing discussion concerning the possibility of reinstatement of registration for military service and in anticipation that the process for registering as a conscientious objector may be altered, the Board of National Ministries:

1. Reaffirms the public position consistently taken by this denomination of upholding the right of the individual to participate or to refuse to participate in military service on the grounds of conscience;
2. Urges that all American Baptists support the rights of those who take a position of conscientious objection to military service as well as the rights of those who take a position of conscientious acceptance of military service;
3. Encourages American Baptist youth and adults to think through their positions with regard to military service in order that their acceptance or rejection of the possibility of service in the military be made on the basis of conscience;
4. Urges that persons who come to the conclusion that their position must be one of conscientious objection to military service advise National Ministries through a declaration of their conviction so that an official record will be created and maintained;
5. Requests that if the draft is reinstated at any time in the future, that persons granted conscientious objector status have the right to choose alternate service under voluntary agencies.

(General Board, December 1979.)

FOR FURTHER INFORMATION: Write to National Ministries, American Baptist Churches—U.S.A., Valley Forge, PA 19481.

SEVENTH DAY BAPTIST GENERAL CONFERENCE

Seventh Day Baptists believe that the first responsibility and supreme right of everyone is to seek and obey God's will for his life as he understands it. This duty takes precedence over all laws of merely human origin. Much as we love liberty, and loyal as we are to our nation, and willing as we are to give our lives, if need be, for her and the ideals for which she stands, we hold even more precious our relationship with God, and our duty to Him to obey His commands, and in case of conflict between these two duties, we say with the apostles of old, "We must obey God rather than men."[1]

Seventh Day Baptists realize that individuals, by reason of conscience select a variety of positions regarding military service. Recognizing the responsibility of the individual for his own actions and the right of governments to exact penalties for refusal to comply with civil law, Seventh Day Baptists encourage people to follow their religious convictions concerning military service. We urge that prayer be made for all who struggle with the question of conscientious participation or conscientious objection to military service.

(Statement adopted by the Seventh Day Baptist General Conference, August 1974; reaffirmed in August 1980.)

[1] *This portion of the statement was first adopted in 1940.*

FOR FURTHER INFORMATION: Write to Rev. Dale D. Thorngate, Secretary, Seventh Day Baptist General Conference, P. O. Box 1678, Janesville, WI 53547.

SOUTHERN BAPTIST CONVENTION

Baptists have always believed in liberty of conscience and have honored men who were willing to brave adverse public opinion for the sake of conscientious scruples. A considerable number of members of churches of our Convention, through their interpretation of the moral teachings of Christ, have reached the position of a conscientious objection to war that prohibits them from bearing arms.

The Convention ought to accord to them the right of their convictions as it accords to others the right to differ from them, and ought to protect them in that right to the extent of its ability. Therefore,

Be It Resolved, That the Convention go on record as recognizing such right of a conscentious objection, and that the Convention instruct the Executive Committee to provide facilities for their registration with the denomination, in order that the Executive Committee may be able to make accurate certification to the government concerning them at any time it should be called for.

(Resolution of Southern Baptist Convention, 1940.)

FOR FURTHER INFORMATION: Write to Dr. Harold C. Bennett, Executive Secretary, Southern Baptist Executive Committee, 460 James Robertson Parkway, Nashville, TN 37219.

BRETHREN

CHURCH OF THE BRETHREN

Reaffirmation of Opposition to War and Conscription for Military Training

The Church of the Brethren Annual Conference views with concern the ongoing Selective Service System registration of young men. The reintroduction of registration in 1980 was opposed by our church since we do not concede to the state the authority to conscript citizens against their conscience . . .

. . . We again affirm these two positions — (1) alternative service as conscientious objectors engaging in constructive civilian work, or (2) open, nonviolent noncooperation with the system of conscription—to be in keeping with the mind of Christ.

The Selective Service System on June 7, 1982, proposed new guidelines for alternative service work in the event of a future draft. These proposed regulations, as they now stand, would make it extremely difficult for the Church of the Brethren to cooperate with the Selective Service System in carrying out an alternative service program. The delegate body of this Annual Conference requests our government to:

1. Allow the Church of the Brethren to provide alternative work assignments for our members desiring to use them.

2. Provide civilian administration of the alternative service program rather than requiring conscientious objectors to be assigned and evaluated by military personnel.

3. Allow the Church of the Brethren to provide the orientation for alternative service workers assigned to our programs.

4. Provide adequate safeguards to prevent arbitrary job assignments and reassignments of alternative service workers.

5. Allow an alternative service worker to seek employment with any approved agency rather than making work options such as civil defense a top priority.

6. Allow alternative service workers to be assigned overseas.

(Excerpted from Reaffirmation adopted by the General Board, Church of the Brethren Annual Conference, Wichita, Kansas, July 1982.)

The Church and War

The Church of the Brethren, since its beginning in 1708, has repeatedly declared its position against war. Our understanding of the life and teachings of Christ as revealed in the New Testament led our Annual Conference to state in 1785 that we should not "submit to the higher

powers so as to make ourselves their instruments to shed human blood." In 1918 at our Annual Conference we stated that "we believe that war or any participation in war is wrong and incompatible with the spirit, example and teachings of Jesus Christ." Again in 1934 Annual Conference resolved that "all war is sin. We, therefore, cannot encourage, engage in, or willingly profit from armed conflict at home or abroad. We cannot, in the event of war, accept military service or support the military machine in any capacity." This conviction, which we reaffirmed in 1948 and now reaffirm again, grew out of the teachings of Christ.
(Statement approved by 1968 Annual Conference)

The Church and Conscience

The church has stood likewise for the principle of freedom of worship and freedom of conscience. The church itself respects the right of the individual conscience within its membership and has never set up an authoritative creed. Instead, it accepts the entire New Testament as its rule of faith and practice and seeks to lead its members to comprehend and accept for themselves the mind of Christ as the guide for their convictions and conduct.

We believe that no government has the authority to abrogate the right of individual conscience. "We must obey God rather than men" (Acts 5:29).

The official position of the Church of the Brethren is that all war is sin and that we seek the right of conscientious objection to all war. We seek no special privileges from our government. What we seek for ourselves, we seek for all — the right of individual conscience. We affirm that this conscientious objection may include all wars, declared or undeclared, particular wars, and particular forms of warfare. We also affirm that conscientious objection may be based on grounds more inclusive than institutional religion.
(Statement approved by 1968 Annual Conference)

The Church and Conscription

The Church of the Brethren feels constrained by Christ's teachings to lead its people to develop convictions against war. The church cannot concede to the state the authority to conscript citizens for military training or military service against their conscience.

The church will seek to fulfill its prophetic role in this matter in two ways: by seeking to change political structures and by influencing individual members.

The church will seek to use its influence to abolish or radically restructure the system which conscripts persons for military purposes.

The church pledges its support and continuing fellowship to all of our draft-age members who face conscription. We recognize that some feel obligated to render full or non-combative military service and we respect all who make such a decision.

We commend to all of draft age, their parents, counselors and fellow members, the alternative position of (1) Alternative Service as conscientious objectors engaging in constructive civilian work, or (2) Open, non-violent non-cooperation with the system of conscription. The church pledges itself to renew and redouble its effort to interpret to the membership of the church at all levels of the church's life these positions which we believe are in harmony with the style of life set forth in the gospel and as expressed in the historic faith and witness of our church.

The church extends its prayers, spiritual nurture and material aid to all who struggle and suffer in order to understand more fully and obey more perfectly the will of God.

(Statement approved by 1970 Annual Conference)

The Church and Alternative Service

The church pledges its support to the draft-age member facing conscription who chooses to engage in constructive alternative service civilian work as a conscientious objector. Such service might include participation in relief and rehabilitation in war or disaster areas anywhere in the world; technical, agricultural, medical, or educational assistance in developing countries; service in general or mental hospitals, schools for the handicapped, homes for the aged, and kindred institutions; and medical or scientific research promising constructive benefits to mankind.

The church will seek to establish, administer, and finance to the extent of its resources, projects for such service under church direction or in cooperation with other private civilian agencies.

(Statement approved by 1970 Annual Conference)

The Church and Noncooperation

The church pledges its support to the draft-age member facing conscription who chooses open noncooperation with the system of conscription as a conscientious objector. Individuals who follow the lead of their conscience to this position will need the support of the church in many ways. The church will seek to meet these needs, to the extent of its resources, by providing such ministries as legal counsel, financial support, and prison visitation. To demonstrate a sense of community and fellowship with the noncooperator, congregations are encouraged to offer sanctuary and spiritual support. All members of the church who take the position of noncooperation should seek to exhibit

a spirit of humility, goodwill, and sincerity in making this type of courageous witness most effective, non-violent, and Christian.
(Statement approved by 1970 Annual Conference)

The Church and Support of National Defense

We declare again that our members should not participate in war, learn the art of war, or support war.

Although recognizing that almost all aspects of the economy are directly or indirectly connected with national defense, we encourage our members to divorce themselves as far as possible from direct association with defense industries in both employment and investment.

While recognizing the necessity of preserving academic freedom, we find recruitment by the armed forces on Brethren college campuses inconsistent with the church's position.
(Statement approved by 1970 Annual Conference)

The Church and Taxes for War Purposes

While the Church of the Brethren recognizes the responsibility of all citizens to pay taxes for the constructive purposes of government, we oppose the use of taxes by the government for war purposes and military expenditures. For those who are conscientiously opposed to paying taxes for these purposes, the church seeks government provision for an alternative use of such tax money for peaceful, non-military purposes.

The church recognizes that its members will believe and act differently in regard to their payments of taxes when a significant percentage goes for war purposes and military expenditures. Some will pay the taxes willingly; some will refuse to pay all or part of the taxes as a witness and a protest; and some will voluntarily limit their incomes or use of taxable services to a low enough level that they are not subject to taxation.

We call upon all of our members, congregations, institutions, and boards to study seriously the problem of paying taxes for war purposes and investing in those government bonds which support war. We further call upon them to act in response to their study, to the leading of conscience, and to their understanding of the Christian faith. To all we pledge to maintain our continuing ministry of fellowship and spiritual concern.
(Statement approved by 1968 Annual Conference)

FOR FURTHER INFORMATION: Write to World Ministries Commission, Church of the Brethren, 1451 Dundee Avenue, Elgin, IL 60120.

DUNKARD BRETHREN

We believe that the principle of nonresistance is clearly taught in the Scriptures, and therefore has been accepted as a doctrine of the church. In support of our position we give the following: Christ is the Prince of Peace (Isa. 9:6); his kingdom is not of the world and nis servants do not fight (John 18:36); the weapons of our warfare are not carnal (II Cor. 10:4); but we are to love our enemies (Matt. 5:44); overcome evil with good (Rom. 12:21), and pray for them which despitefully use and persecute us (Matt. 5:44). Learning the art of war and participating in carnal warfare or service in any branch of military establishment at any time is forbidden by the Scripture; and the boy and girl scout movements and any other movement requiring a uniform, or having any military features, fall under the same condemnation.
(Dunkard Brethren Polity, page 13, Section 2, 1980.)

As a Christian people, throughout more than two hundred years, we have maintained nonresistance as an integral part of our faith. Therefore, we petition that we may be granted exemption from any and all forms of military service, in case this country becomes involved in war.

Since the National Constitution grants freedom of religious worship, and since we have no code or confession of faith other than the New Testament, we follow its teachings. "If any man have not the Spirit of Christ, he is none of His." "Recompense to no man evil for evil" (Romans 8:9, and 2:17). "Dearly beloved, avenge not yourselves, but rather give place unto wrath: for it is written, Vengeance is mine; I will repay, saith the Lord. Therefore, if thine enemy hunger, feed him; if he thirst give him drink; for in so long thou shalt heap coals of fire on his head. Be not overcome of evildoing, but overcome evil with good." (Romans 12:19-21). The Savior said, "My kingdom is not of this world. If my kingdom were of this world, then would my servants fight" (John 18:36). Romans 13:9 renewed the command "Thou shalt not kill." "Ye have heard that it hath been said, Thou shalt love thy neighbor and hate thine enemy. But I say unto you, Love your enemies, bless them that curse you, do good to them that hate you, pray for them which despitefully use you, and persecute you; That ye may be the children of your Father which is in Heaven: for He maketh His sun to rise on the evil and on the good, and sendeth rain on the just and on the unjust." (Matthew 5:43-45).

"And behold, one of them which were with Jesus stretched out his hand, and drew his sword, and struck a servant of the high priest's, and smote off his ear. Then said Jesus unto him, put up again thy sword into his place: for all they that take the sword shall perish with the sword.

Thinkest thou that I cannot now pray to my Father, and He shall presently give me more than twelve legions of angels?" (Matthew 26:51-54).

(Approved by General Conference, Quinter, Kansas, 1940.)

FOR FURTHER INFORMATION: Write to Howard J. Surbey, Executive Secretary, Dunkard Brethren Civilian Service Board, 749 West King St., Littlestown, PA 17340.

OLD GERMAN BAPTIST BRETHREN

The convictions of the Old German Baptist Brethren are based on the fundamental belief in a Supreme Being. The New Testament which is the inspired word of God, teaches that the destruction of human life and property is wrong. It exhorts us to "love our enemies" and to "live peaceably with all men," that we should not "kill", or "resist evil" but "rather overcome evil with good." To these and many other Scriptures she has strictly adhered from the beginning, and even though we are living in changing times and beliefs, we base our opposition to participation in all wars on the Word of God which changeth not. Following are some of the decisions of her Yearly Meetings:

Article 3, Whereas, our beloved Fraternity, as well as other historic peace churches, is not facing a crisis, as the church has at intervals for hundreds of years of her history, with regard to her position on nonviolence and nonresistance as taught by the Scriptures, as understood and applied by the fathers of our Fraternity, and interpreted and recorded by our various annual councils, as follows:

1781. "Exhort in union all brethren to behold themselves guiltless, and take no part in war or bloodshedding."

1785. "First, we do not understand at all that we can give ourselves up to do violence . . . We cannot see or find any liberty to use any carnal sword."

1917. Article 3 which reads as follows: "Inasmuch as our country has gone into warfare and has taken up the draft law in order to raise its armies, will not this Yearly Meeting advise our dear members, especially, the young, their duty as nonresistant and noncombatant followers of our Lord and Savior Jesus Christ who has given us a pattern that we should follow after in our pilgrimage here below?

And is it deemed advisable to abide by the law so far as to register when the census is taken of the men that come under the draft age? Answer: We, your sub-committee, agree to grant the request in the forepart of this query. As to the latter part of the query, we think it necessary to register as demanded by the law. Passed."

We, therefore, pray this Yearly Meeting of 1941 to reaffirm and thereby strengthen all the above minutes referred to as well as all others that bear directly upon the issue, and advise our brethren against combatant and noncombatant service inasmuch as other provisions are offered by our government; and may the united conclusion of the brethren assembled in the fear of the Lord exhort all members to faithfully adhere to the injunction to "Pray for kings and all that are in authority" (I Tim. 2:2).
(Statement of Yearly Meeting, 1941.)

Not to participate in war in any form has been one of the fundamental principles of our Fraternity ever since its organization, and is one of the conditions upon which we receive applicants for baptism. Therefore, it is the united mind of this Service Committee that any members who enter the Armed Forces of our government as combatant or noncombatants, have broken their baptismal vow and cannot be held as members.
(Statement of Yearly Meeting, 1946)

The above conference, and brotherhood position and decision we feel are in full harmony with the New Testament teaching according to Matt. 5:44, Acts 5:29 and many other Scriptures.

We ask for no special privileges, but what the Old German Baptist Brethren seek for themselves we seek for all others, that they may be granted the liberty to obey the teaching of God as they interpret it, and to obey the civil law insofar as it does not conflict with the divine law, and we pray to be granted liberty of conscience.

We reaffirm the above statements and state further that we do not take part in nor do we support any acts of civil disobedience or war-resisting demonstrations. We continue to recognize the biblical separation of church and state and feel kindly toward our good government and pray earnestly for them in these perilous times. "Let every soul be subject unto the higher powers. For there is no power but of God; the powers that be are ordained of God. Whosoever therefore resisteth the power, resisteth the ordinance of God: and they that resist shall receive to themselves damnation," Romans 13:1, 2.
(Statement of Brotherhood Service Committee, 1978.)

FOR FURTHER INFORMATION: Write to Carl W. Bowman, Secretary, 4065 N. State Route 48, Covington, OH 45318.

BRETHREN IN CHRIST CHURCH

The Brethren in Christ church stated its position on peace in detail at the General Conference of 1976 when it adopted a "Position Paper on Church, War and Respect for Human Life." Following is an excerpt from that paper:

Responsible Citizenship and Military Service

The church is in the world, yet not of the world. Christians, while being part of the body of Christ, are also part of one of the nations of the world. We are called to pray for rulers, respect them, honor them, and be obedient (Romans 13:lff). Christians can be good citizens of this world's nations to the extent that good citizenship is defined in unselfish terms. Jesus calls us to be salt to the earth and light to the world. (Matthew 5:13-14). We obey laws, respect authority and encourage the development of constructive ways to meet the needs of all the people in our society regardless of race, origin, or economic status.

We recognize the need for the place of civil government. The Scriptures teach that government is "ordained of God" (Rom. 13:1ff), because it is necessary for the direction and control of civil affairs.

How do we relate to government and express ourselves? We obey laws to the limit of conscience, we express ourselves by voice or letter to those who are making laws, letting them hear our concerns. We pray for them as persons, under God, needing wisdom, forgiveness, humility, insight, and divine help (1 Tim. 2:1-2).

Christians are concerned with loyalties; therefore we must be aware of the dangers of idolizing the state. Nationalism was evident in Israel which expressed itself in national pride, ethnocentricity and religious bigotry. The classic illustration is the patriot prophet, Jonah, who first refused to preach judgment and repentance to a pagan nation, but who, when forced to preach, and Ninevah repented, was upset at a forgiving God (Jonah 4:1ff). For Jonah, feelings regarding nation superseded obedience to God, love and forgiveness.

The church lost much of its dynamic vitality under Constantine, when the government determined what was Christian, who was Christian and what was the role of the church.

One of the unfortunate miscarriages of the Reformation was that the church used the state to its advantage, but was also dominated by the state. This led to great abuse and persecution of Pietists, Anabaptists, and minority groups.

In the twentieth century, we do well to remember the errors of Jonah, Constantine, and some of the reformers. Are not those who advocate a kind of nationalistic Christianity falling into the same snare? The church is not called to promote or protect any political system.

There can be appreciation for one's country or nation without the need to idolize it. When the state becomes the object of highest loyalty, this is a form of idolatry.

The call to responsible citizenship is not a call to compromise Christian convictions (Acts 5:29). It is rather to lend support to constructive and unselfish goals in service to mankind. At this point in history, some governments make way for expression of Christian conviction in some form of alternative service in lieu of military service.

When Peter and Paul found themselves in conflict with the existing powers, they both in similar ways expressed the reason for a particular point of view and each of them spent time in prison for his faith (Acts 16). Our own history has shown that the way of expressing a position and taking the consequences has been a significant stance. The church is not called to spearhead revolution nor is it called to protect any political system. It has a higher calling.

It has been our position that we cannot participate in military service in any form. The outworkings of this conviction in history took men to prison, some to constructive alternative service work ministering to the needs of others in various ways. Voluntary Service through the Mennonite Central Committee or Mission Board or similar church agency has been a significant way to say we are concerned about preserving the resources God gave. It has been a good way to say that our human resource, our time, our ability and our substance must be devoted to the great purpose of helping rather than destroying.

The calling in Christ is a call to constructive service. It is a call to bring food to the hungry, clothes to the naked, healing to the sick, encouragement to the distressed and oppressed, peace and redemption to the guilty and sinful (Romans 5:1). This calling includes all of life. We cannot compartmentalize Christian conduct and declare that at a given time we are representing Jesus Christ and at another time we represent the state (Matthew 25:34).

War is also a major exploiter of resources. Mechanized warfare uses large quantities of fuel. Valuable ores are mined and sent to battlefields as weapons to destroy and to be destroyed. A nation in which war is fought experiences great loss of property, resources, and the demoralizing insecurity war causes. Another nation, participating in that destruction, may, back home be experiencing prosperity because of the material demands of war.

Our call to follow Christ is a call to serve Him by using our material possessions to demonstrate His Spirit and compassion in the world.

Even though it may be impossible to be completely separated from the prosperity of war economy, we would be deeply concerned about profiteering because of war. Since we believe participation in war is not in keeping with our Christian commitment, we also believe that vocational activity which creates and produces weapons of destruction should be avoided. Neither can those who believe that participation in war is wrong support war by the payment of taxes without earnest searchings of conscience. We encourage the avoidance of war tax payment by giving maximum charitable contributions to reduce tax liability.

We cannot ignore the moral decay of society produced by war. Practices accepted in wartime (spying, deceitfulness, sexual immorality, etc.) become accepted in peacetime. These corrupting effects are seen not only at the time and place of war but reach deeply into the life of society.

We believe that peace-practicing Christians have a responsibility to the larger Christian community. We need to share the good news of the way of peace with the unconvinced. We commend such efforts at dialogue as the Seminar on Christian Holiness and the Issues of War and Peace (June 1973 at Winona Lake, Indiana). We also commend the service of peace teams in churches and colleges, and grass roots emphasis of congregational peace meetings, and Sunday School literature which creates wholesome opportunity to communicate alternatives to participation in war.

FOR FURTHER INFORMATION: Write to John Stoner, Brethren in Christ Church, P.O. Box 27, Mt. Joy, PA 17552.

BUDDHIST

WHEREAS, The Buddha-Dharma (Teachings of Buddha) teaches that each person possesses the potentiality to develop his unique personality to Perfect Enlightenment, each according to his innate capacity; and

WHEREAS, the Buddha-Dharma teaches that all life is sacred; and

WHEREAS, the Buddha-Dharma thus recognizes the freedom of each person to make decisions according to his conscience and religious convictions; and

WHEREAS, the Buddha-Dharma thus teaches the interdependence of all things in the universe, an awareness of which leads one to the feeling of gratitude to one's country; now Therefore be it

RESOLVED, that the Buddhist Churches of America will give moral and spiritual support and counsel to any young Buddhist who chooses to serve his country; and be it

RESOLVED FURTHER, that the Buddhist Churches of America will give the same support and guidance to those who, according to their conscience and personal religious conviction, choose not to participate in war in any form.

(Resolution passed by the National Council, Buddhist Churches of America, February 28, 1971, San Francisco, California.)

FOR FURTHER INFORMATION: Write to Buddhist Churches of America, 1710 Octavia Street, San Francisco, CA 94109.

CHRISTADELPHIANS

Christadelphians are a religious people who are looking for the personal advent of the Lord Jesus Christ to set up His divine government over all the earth. They were organized as a religious sect and became known as Christadelphians during the Civil War. Their existing belief, which is expressed in their Statement of Faith, and their principles, forbid its members to participate in war in any form* and their religious convictions are against participation therein, in accordance with such belief and principles. These religious and conscientious objections apply to military and naval service in any and every capacity*, and have always been principles of the Christadelphians since the beginning of their existence as an organized religious sect.

*Includes combatant and noncombatant service.

(From Certificate of Membership filed by Registrants with the Selective Service System, 1940.)

FOR FURTHER INFORMATION: write to H. Blair Smith, 214 Canterbury Road, Richmond, VA 23221, or John S. Peake, 47 Pheasant Lane, No. Oaks, White Bear Lake, MN 55110, or William Winfree, 3930 Providence Place, Fairfax, VA 22030, or Glen L. Johnson, 1421 Belmont Boulevard, Rockford, IL 51103, or Wallace M. Scott, 11 Franklin Woods Drive, Somers, CT 06071, or Douglas R. Egles, 546 Plymouth Street, Holbrook, MA 02343.

CHRISTIAN CHURCH (DISCIPLES OF CHRIST)
Resolution Concerning the Reinstitution of the Compulsory Draft in Peacetime

WHEREAS, the Lord said, "live at peace with everyone. Don't plot harm to others" (Zech. 8:14-17); and

WHEREAS, we must strive for peace if we are called the sons and daughters of God (Matt. 5:10); and

WHEREAS, the historical Christian perspective has affirmed human dignity and value and worth; and

WHEREAS, the Christian Church (Disciples of Christ) historically has opposed military conscription except in time of great national emergency and so declared its opposition in resolutions as follows:

> "We affirm our opposition to the enactment of any legislation during the present war providing for compulsory military training and service in peace time." (1944)

> ". . . that this International Convention of Disciples reaffirm our opposition to conscription for military training or service in time of peace . . ." (1946)

> ". . . that we call upon the Congress and the President of the United States to procure the necessary armed forces through voluntary enlistment." (1948)

> "That we express again our opposition to 'Universal Military Training' in the United States in whatever form since it tends to fasten upon our people a concept of the state totally foreign to our American tradition and a spirit of futility with regard to the possibility of peace which may turn out to be one of the chief blocks to its achievement . . ." (1954)

> ". . . reaffirms its opposition to conscription except in time of great national emergency and commends President Nixon for his decision to seek an end to the draft after the Vietnam war . . ." (1969); and

WHEREAS, mandatory conscription into military or civil service during peacetime is a violation of an individual's right under the Constitution of the United States which prohibits involuntary servitude, except as a punishment for crime, and

WHEREAS, in recent months the military and the Congress of the United States have been debating the reinstatement of the compulsory draft in order to conscript persons into military service during a time of peace;

THEREFORE, BE IT RESOLVED, that the General Assembly of the Christian Church (Disciples of Christ) meeting in St. Louis, Missouri, October 26-31, 1979, reaffirm its historic stance against involuntary military conscription during peace time, and make known to the public its opposition to the compulsory draft of males and females during peacetime (a time when the United States has not officially declared war on a country or countries); and

BE IT FURTHER RESOLVED, that congregations and individuals secure resource materials from the Department of Church in Society of the Division of Homeland Ministries for use in education and advocacy programs, and

BE IT FURTHER RESOLVED, that this resolution be transmitted to the President of the United States and the appropriate Congressional committees by the General Minister and President of the Christian Church (Disciples of Christ), and

BE IT FURTHER RESOLVED, that members of the Christian Church (Disciples of Christ) be urged to transmit copies of this resolution to their representatives in the Congress of the United States.

(Resolution No. 7943 adopted by the General Assembly, October 1979)

Resolution Concerning Support for the Conscientious Objector to War

WHEREAS, human rights are basic to our Christian faith and to the Christian Church (Disciples of Christ), and

WHEREAS, the right to refuse to participate in war is a basic human right, and

WHEREAS, the Christian Church (Disciples of Christ) is called to support the rights of conscience for those who are conscientious objectors as they do those who by conscience feel compelled to serve, and

WHEREAS, our churches are also called to support the peace testimony of the Christian Church,

THEREFORE, BE IT RESOLVED, that the General Assembly of the Christian Church (Disciples of Christ), meeting in Anaheim, California, July 31-August 5, 1981, call upon all our members and churches to support fully all our members and non-members who are conscientious objectors to war, with our prayers, our love and with any other support we can give these young people of draft age, and to encourage our churches and communities to offer opportunities for youth who are unsure and who wish to explore their alternatives.

(Resolution No. 8120 adopted by the General Assembly, July-August 1981)

FOR FURTHER INFORMATION: Write to Joanne Kagiwada, Department of Church in Society, Christian Chuch (Disciples of Christ), P.O. Box 1986, Indianapolis, IN 46206.

CHRISTIAN REFORMED CHURCH

Guidelines for Ethical Decisions About War
A. We believe that the following statements express biblical principles and should underlie all decisions about war:
(1) All wars are the result of sin and though God may use wars in his judgment on nations, it is his purpose to make all wars to cease.
(2) The supreme standard of all moral decisions is the will of God. When Jesus said, "Love your enemies," he taught that there are no exceptions to God's command to "love your neighbor as yourself." In all circumstances the Christian believer must live by the law of love enunciated by the sovereign Lawgiver and Judge and exemplified in his Son.
(3) The Christian should obey the state when it orders him to act within the framework of righteousness. Conversely, he should disobey every order of the state to perform acts contrary to the will of God, and he may not obey such demands of government as require him to sin. The Christian must obey God rather than men.

B. Careful distinction must be made between *basic biblical principles* and the *guidelines* set forth to assist Christians in living by those principles. All Christians must surely agree that the root cause of all war is sin; that God "makes wars cease to the end of the earth"; that

Christians are called to be peacemakers. But there have been and probably will continue to be significant differences among Christians on how to implement these principles in the real world of hate and violence . . .

C. In his unrelenting opposition to all war, the committed pacifist may not despise and reject a fellow-Christian whose conscience persuades him of the legitimacy of his nation's armed response to aggression. Nor should the Christian, whose conscientious patriotism readies him to take up arms against aggression, scorn and condemn the Christian pacifist whose conscience forbids him to engage in or encourage any act of violence. The Bible in a number of places approves passive resistance, and, although this report concludes that war is sometimes necessary and participation therein justified, we do not hesitate to point out that Christian pacifism has a long and respected history. The difficulties inherent in the problem of war and Christian participation therein, together with the imperfect moral state and limited wisdom of every Christian, summon all members of the church to mutual understanding and tolerance of the conscientious convictions of one another.

GUIDELINES
In fulfillment of our mandate and in the name of the Prince of Peace the committee submits to synod the following guidelines for making ethical decisions about war in the hope that with the indispensable guidance of the Holy Spirit, they will be useful to all who seek to do the will of God in matters involving war.
1. Christians faced with problems concerning war should respect their need of the communion of saints, remembering the affirmation of Scripture: "You are a chosen race, a royal priesthood, a holy nation, God's own people, that you may declare the wonderful deeds of him who called you out of darkness into his marvelous light". (I Peter 2:9). By divine grace Christians are bound to God in holy covenant, and by faith are united to Christ in one body. Therefore they should realize that weighty moral decisions are made responsibly before the face of God only if the prayers and counsel of the covenant fellowship are sincerely sought and lovingly offered.
2. If the nation has or is about to become involved in a war or in any military action against another nation, Christians, as morally responsible citizens of the nation and of God's kingdom, should evaluate their nation's involvement by diligently seeking the answers to questions like the following, drawing on the counsel of fellow-members with special qualifications as well as pastors and the assemblies of the church:

a. Is our nation the unjust aggressor?

b. Is our nation intentionally involved for economic advantage?

c. Is our nation intentionally involved for imperialistic ends, such as the acquistion of land, natural resources, or political power in international relations?

d. Has our nation in good faith observed all relevant treaties and other international agreements?

e. Has our nation exhausted all peaceful means to resolve the matters in dispute?

f. Is the evil or aggression represented by the opposing force of such overwhelming magnitude and gravity as to warrant the horrors and brutality of military opposition to it?

g. Has the decision to engage in war been taken legally by a legitimate government?

h. Are the means of warfare employed or likely to be employed by our nation in fair proportion to the evil or aggression of the opposing forces? Is our nation resolved to employ minimum necessary force?

i. In the course of the war has our nation been proposing and encouraging negotiations for peace or has it spurned such moves by the opposing forces or by neutral nations or international organizations?

3. If a Christian cannot conscientiously engage in a given war or in alternate service, his refusal must be within the framework of law. He must expose himself to the due process and even the penalty of the state whose laws he has knowingly, publicly, and conscientiously broken. He should not "go underground" or flee the country except under conditions of extraordinary oppression or intolerably brutal tyranny.

4. If an individual must make a personal decision about involvement in war, he should seek the prayers and guidance of his parents and other members of his family group. The family, in turn, should provide such guidance and prayer support. If there are continuing disagreements within the family, the various members should exercise mutual respect, forbearance and charity.

5. A Christian who believes it is sinful for him to serve in a given war, or who conscientiously objects to serving in any war, should notify his church and be open to its counsel. . .

(Excerpted from Synod Decision of 1977.)

Guidelines for Justifiable Warfare—Just War Implications

In the Christian view the ultimate purpose of a just war is the establishment of a lasting peace upon the foundation of justice. Its final end is the achievement of a righteous and stable political order within which concrete human values are preserved and a well-ordered human society can flourish.

No war may be considered just which, while visiting destruction upon all that is bad, destroys every living human witness to that which is good; no war can be considered an allowable remedy for evil which destroys, together with this evil, all or almost all of history's accumulated goods; no war can be considered a fit political instrument for the establishment of peace which brings no peace but the peace of death.

Although a just war is in principle thinkable, and in the past was concretely possible, it is at least questionable whether, in view of the destructive power of modern weapons, it can any longer become actual. Any war which would scorch the earth, destroy all or the major part of the technical, cultural, and spiritual treasures of mankind, and annihilate the human race, or leave alive only a maimed and wounded fragment of it, lies outside the traditional concept of a just war and must be judged morally impermissible . . . .

(Excerpted from 1982 Synod position on Justifiable Warfare.)

CHRIST'S SANCTIFIED HOLY CHURCH

It is the faith and belief of Christ's Sanctified Holy Church that its members should take "No Part" in war, but endorse the peace treaty, and believe that all controversies and difficulties between nations should be settled by counsel and arbitration.

(From Church Discipline, 1893.)

Under no circumstances should one of our members take up arms or train with same. The teachings of the Holy Scriptures together with the Holy Spirit has caused us to take this position. For Jesus himself says in Matthew, 5th Chapter, 38th and 39th verses, "Ye have heard it hath been said an eye for an eye and a tooth for a tooth; but I say unto you that ye resist not evil, but whosoever shall smite thee on thy right cheek, turn to him the other also." Now again in Ephesians, 6th Chapter, 11th and 12th verses, "Put on the whole armour of God, that ye may be able to stand against the wiles of the devil; for we wrestle not against flesh and blood, but against principalities, against powers, against the rulers of the darkness of this world, against spiritual wickedness in high places." Romans, 12th Chapter, 19th verse, "Dearly beloved, avenge not yourselves but rather give place unto wrath; for it is written, vengence is mine, I will repay saith the Lord." II Corinthians, 3rd and 4th verses: "For though we walk in the flesh we do not war after the flesh; for the weapons of our warfare are not carnal, but mighty through God to the pulling down of strongholds." St. John, 18th Chapter, 36th verse, "Jesus answered, my kingdom is not of this world; if my kingdom were of this world then would my servants fight, that I should not be delivered to the Jews. But now is my kingdom not from hence."

Under the first covenant before Christ's time the people of God fought army against army with carnal weapons but Christ came to do away with the thing that causes war on the inside—"For what the law could not do in that it was weak through the flesh, God sending his own son in the likeness of sinful flesh, and for sin, condemned sin in the flesh" (Romans 8:13).

Christ's Sanctified Holy Church believes that because of the transgression of our first fathers in the Garden of Eden right after He made man, sin entered into the world. All are sinners in the sight of God until they are regenerated, which we believe takes place instantaneously as the Apostle Paul did when he was converted on his way to Damascus.

Of course, environment and training educates or teaches the conscience to what is right or what is wrong. We do teach and train our people on this doctrine concerning opposition to war in any form.

But, we feel in early life as young people start out in life, they may deviate from the way they have been trained and taught because of the nature of sin in their heart and life. We believe that they may become convicted of sin and repent and have a change of life take place and cause them to "walk in newness of life." We feel this should be given much consideration, as the desire to conform to the Divine will comes only when we become a Christian.

FOR FURTHER INFORMATION: Write to Rev. E. Joseph Clelland, 1024 Seminole Drive, West Columbia, SC 29169, or Ben Jernigan, Rt. 2, Box 130-E, Evans, GA 30809.

CHURCH OF CHRIST

In 1971 and early 1972 the members of 252 local congregations of the Church of Christ (located in 31 states) signed letters designed to tell those who may be concerned how we feel that it is wrong for us to sanction war. Furthermore, it was brought out in these letters that we are anxious to upbuild this nation and those in need.

The letters stated:

"This is to certify that we, the undersigned members of the Church of Christ are conscientiously opposed to carnal warfare. Our belief in the Supreme Being (God) involves duties superior to those arising from any human relation. The basis of this faith is found in a multitude of Holy Scriptures, some of which follow: Matthew 26:48-52; Acts 5:29; Rom. 12:9; 2 Cor. 10:3-5; Eph. 6:10-17; Matt. 5:21; Rom. 12:19-21; Rom. 13:9; Luke 3:14; 1 Thess. 5:22.

"Our position on this vital subject has been set forth many times in this country by our ministers across the nation. In sermons and writings made public throughout the 1800s American Bible pioneers of our faith set forth this conviction as one of the integral parts of our faith. "The Christian and Carnal Warfare" by Paul O. Nichols published in 1945 in the Old Paths Pulpit was a more recent pronouncement of this faith.

"We do not know of an active minister in these Churches of Christ who does not oppose war and urge those that make the laws of this land and those that govern to seek peaceful means to settle world problems. These Churches of Christ are not to be confused with many which wear the same name; due to fundamental differences **we constitute a distinct fellowship.**

"We wholeheartedly endorse the civilian work programs whereby conscientious persons may serve the national health and interests in a civilian capacity... such as in hospitals, institutions, and rehabilitation work.

"We submit this that all may know our position relative to our opposing war, and that we might be recognized **as a distinct group or fellowship** which now is and in the past history of this country has been a "peace church", to use modern terminology.

We have assembled and set down together these principles, statements, and references so that all may know our position and that we stand behind those of our young people who because of their strong faith and dedication to the betterment of mankind seek to serve in hospitals, institutions, and rehabilitation work rather than to violate Christian principles they hold dearer than their own lives. Each member studies the Scriptures for himself and takes his or her own stand based upon faith and conviction.

FOR FURTHER INFORMATION: Write to Nelson Nichols (Evangelist), Church of Christ, Park Street, P.O. Box D, Anderson, MO 64831.

CHURCH OF CHRIST, SCIENTIST

Statement on Pacifism

The Church of Christ, Scientist, is deeply committed to the establishment of peace on earth and to unceasing search for pacific methods of settling national differences. It is not a pacifist church, however, as the term is applied to such religious bodies as the Quakers and the Mennonites. It does not enjoin on its members either support of or opposition to military action as an instrument of national policy.

This does not mean that it is indifferent to the moral issues of war and peace. Its Founder, Mary Baker Eddy, writes in **The First Church of Christ, Scientist, and Miscellany** (p. 278), "War is in itself an evil, barbarous, devilish." But she indicated in related passages that it may sometimes be the lesser of two evils and that armaments may be necessary for the prevention of war and the preservation of peace.

Christian Scientists are expected to fulfill the duties of responsible citizenship either through accepting military service in combatant or noncombatant status, or through choosing the alternative civilian service provided for those whose conscience will not allow them to serve under arms. The church includes within its membership both professional military personnel and committed pacifists. While differing in their views of temporary means and necessities, all Christian Scientists are committed to the increasing establishment of the kingdom of heaven on earth through prayer, spiritualization of thought, Christianization of motive, and elimination of those elements of the carnal mind which cause and constitute war. The healing of the nations is no less imperative a demand than the healing of individuals.

Conscience and National Service

Many countries conscript citizens for a period of national service. The draft laws of a number of these countries recognize that the individual's conscience and religious convictions play a determining part in his response to this obligation. Accordingly, these laws provide several ways by which the citizen can fulfill his service. The three most prevalent are:
- (a) he can be ordered to armed combatant training and duty in the armed forces; or
- (b) he can be ordered to noncombatant training and duty in the armed forces, but is exempted from bearing arms; or

(c) he can be ordered to alternative civilian service in the national interest, under government regulation, but is exempted from service in the armed forces.

The Church of Christ, Scientist, respects the right of each member or adherent to request any of the classificiations provided in the laws of his country and to reach his own decision according to his highest sense of right and the dictates of his conscience. It does not tell him which course to follow, but strongly encourages him to seek God's guidance throgh prayer and through study of the Bible and the writings of Mary Baker Eddy, the Discoverer and Founder of Christian Science.

Individual Christian Scientists have had each of the classifications described above granted to them by the appropriate government agencies.

A man seeking any one of these classifications will encounter certain procedures and requirements that specifically concern him as a Christian Scientist.

The Christian Scientist who is facing his national service obligation should obtain current and accurate information about each classification well before he reaches the age for registering.

FOR FURTHER INFORMATION: Write to: The First Church of Christ, Scientist, Christian Science Activities for Armed Services Personnel, Christian Science Center, Boston, MA 02115.

CHURCH OF GOD (ANDERSON)

Like all true Americans, we as members of the General Assembly of the Church of God, view with deep concern the military involvement and the conscription of our youth for military service. We believe that war represents our moral failures. We abhor war and the causes that lead to it. We stand by the teaching and example of our Lord who taught us and showed us the way of radical, sacrificial love.

We are thankful to God that we live in a land of basic freedoms whose law makes provision for alternative service by those "who, by reason of religious training and belief, are conscientiously opposed to participation in war in any form." We encourage our young men who conscientiously object to war and participation in it to engage in such civilian work which contributes "to the maintenance of the national health, safety or interest."

We respect the right of each person to arrive at his own convictions. We believe in the principle of freedom of worship and freedom of conscience. We respect the rights of the individual conscience within our fellowship. We have not set up an authoritative creed. Instead, we accept the entire New Testament as our rule of faith and practice. We seek to lead every member of our fellowship to full comprehension and full acceptance of the Spirit of Christ as the guide for all conduct. What we seek for ourselves we seek for every citizen of our land—the right of individual conscience which no governmental authority can abrogate or violate.

We believe that the cause of Christ is best served when the Christian of draft age responds freely to his own conscience. Because we believe this, we support those who take the position of the conscientious objector, at the same time we insist that the conscientious military person has similar privileges and responsibilities before God. We also support that person who differs with our position regarding conscientious objectors and participates in military service. We seek to follow all persons with a ministry of help and guidance, but this is not to be construed as approval of war.

We fervently pray for the leaders of our nation and of other nations, many of whom we believe to be sincerely striving for peace. We pray that efforts by negotiation among countries, through the United Nations, and every possible channel may succeed in bringing peace to our troubled world. We pray for the Church all over the world to continue her rightful role in peacemaking.

Let this statement of conviction be construed by any and all to mean that we fully support young men of the Church of God who sincerely and conscientiously are opposed to participation in military service. We encourage them to seek constructive alternatives intended to bring health, healing, and understanding, and which serve the highest interests of our beloved country and of the whole world.

FOR FURTHER INFORMATION: Write to Division Church Service, Box 2420, Anderson, IN 46011.

CHURCH OF GOD (OKLAHOMA)

The ministers of the Church of God assembled at the Annual National Campmeeting (July 21-30, 1961) of the Church of God at Neosho (Monark Springs), Mo., being aware of the present critical world situation and the urgent need for the Church to reaffirm its position in regard to participation in war, approved and adopted the resolution which had been approved by the ministers of the Church of God at the Oklahoma State Campmeeting, Guthrie, OK, on August 13, 1948, which reads as follows:

Whereas: The Holy Scriptures teach us that our first duty is to God, namely, "Thou shalt love the Lord thy God with all thy heart, soul, mind, and strength," and the second is like unto this, "Thou shalt love thy neighbor as thyself." Furthermore, Jesus taught His followers to love their enemies, do good to them that hate you and pray for them which despitefully use you and persecute you that you may be the children of your Father which is in heaven (Matt. 5:39, 44-48);

And Whereas: There are many other scriptures such as John 18:36; Matt. 26:52; Rom. 12:14, 17, 19-21; Luke 6:31, which definitely forbid us to take up arms to fight or defend ourselves; and whereas, because of the teaching of such Scriptures, we are conscientiously opposed to accept noncombatant service in warfare or to work in any factory or plant which is directly engaged in producing instruments and/or munitions for the destruction of human life and happiness;

And Whereas: We are conscientiously opposed to participation in war in any form at any time, whether civil, political, or religious;

And Whereas: We are conscientiously opposed to the purchase of defense or war bonds and stamps for the prosecution of war;

And Whereas: We are citizens of the U.S. of America in all things willing to live honestly, believing that our Government is ordained of God and praying for our President and for all that are in authority, that we may lead a quiet and peaceful life in all godliness;

Now, Therefore Be It Resolved: That the above statement be adopted as a uniform teaching and practice of the Church of God, a copy of which is on file with the Secretary of the National Campmeeting.

The foregoing resolution was concurred in and approved by the ministers of the Church of God at the National Campmeeting on July 25, 1961.

FOR FURTHER INFORMATION: Write to Bob Stover, Secretary, The Church of God, 6304 S. 97th Ave., W., Tulsa, OK 74107.

CHURCH OF GOD (SEVENTH DAY)

A Christian is to love and work for the salvation of all mankind. Since this includes his enemies, a Christian will not participate in carnal warfare.

Article No. 28 of the revised Articles of Belief adopted by the North American Ministerial Council of the Church of God (Seventh Day), October 14, 1974.

FOR FURTHER INFORMATION: Write to Church of God (Seventh Day), P.O. Box 33677, Denver, CO 80233.

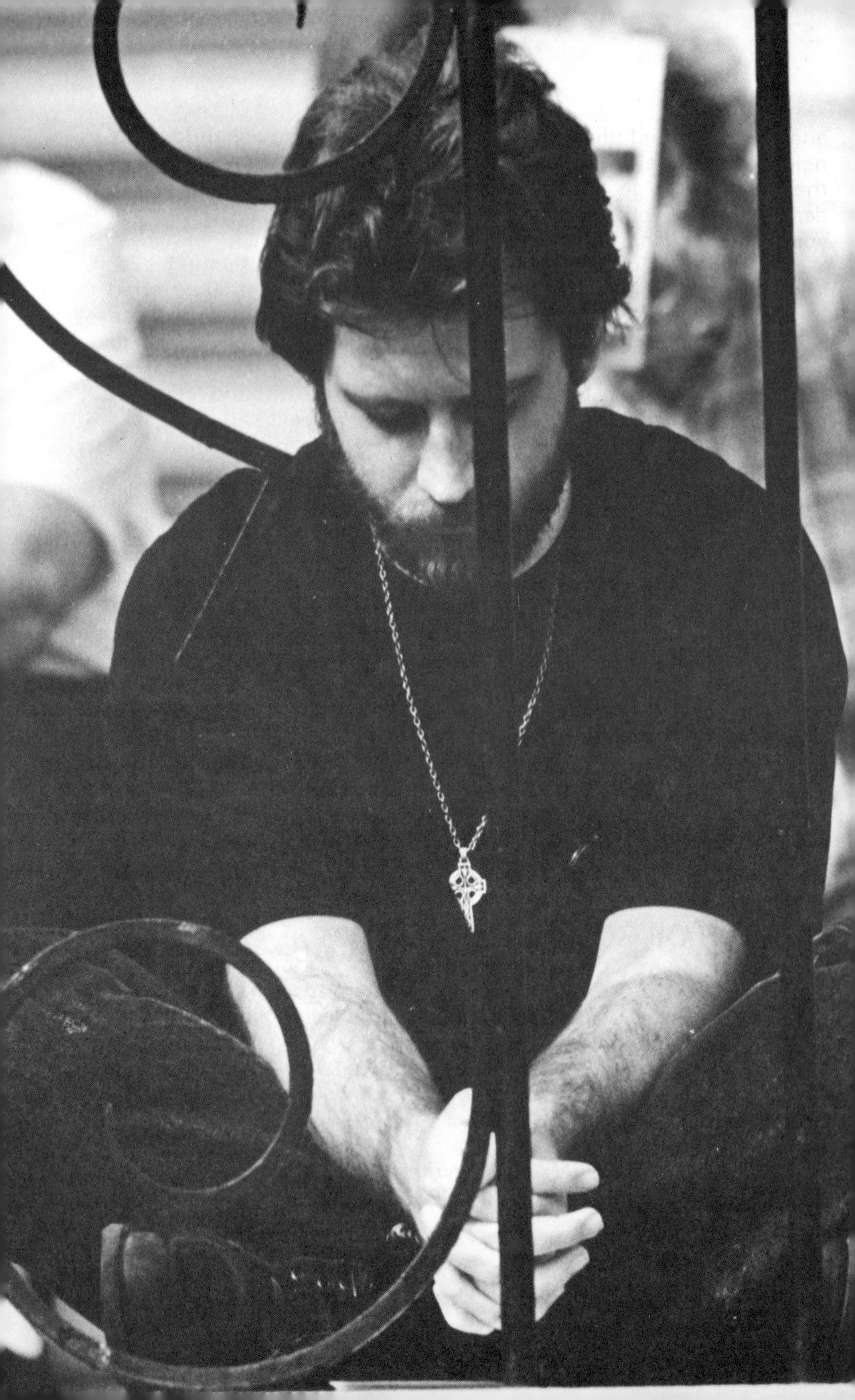

CHURCH OF GOD (7TH DAY, SALEM, W.VA.)

According to our earliest constitution the Church of God (Seventh Day) has always stood against its membership engaging in carnal warfare.

Article 23, of the Constitution, and the same numerical number in our Doctrinal Beliefs states: "That all carnal warfare, and the participation therein is condemned, as declared in our earliest constitution and belief" (Ex. 20:13; Matt. 5:21, 22; Rom. 13:8-10; Matt. 26:52; Rev. 13:10).

According to our "Bible Home Instructor," a book published for our membership, which is a grouping together of Bible Testimony on all subjects of sacred interest, the members are to abstain from engaging in carnal warfare. This is one of the evidences that they are Children of God and of their acceptance by God if they live in peace and do not kill any human being. (Pages 330, 331).

FOR FURTHER INFORMATION: Write to Chris W. Royer, P.O. Box 328, Salem, WV 26426.

CHURCH OF GOD OF THE ABRAHAMIC FAITH
(Roll, IN; Miami, FL; Perryville, KY; and Salem, OH)

The Church of God of the Abrahamic Faith is a religious community which looks for the personal return of the Lord Jesus Christ to reestablish the Kingdom of God over Israel and finally, the whole earth. This is based upon the promises made to Abraham, David, and Mary. (1 Chr. 28:5; Acts 1:6; Gen. 17:4-8; 2 Sam. 7:12-16; Luke 1:30-33).

We believe that the members of the Body of Christ must not participate in war. Therefore, we whose names appear upon the membership rolls of the Churches of God of the Abrahamic Faith subscribe to the following as stated in our Confession of Faith, page 28, Item III (d):

(d) Prohibit participation in war (Matt. 26; 52; Rev. 13:10; Matt. 5:39-41; John 6:15; Luke 12:13, 14; 1 Pet. 2:21, 23; Isa. 53:9; Jas. 5:6; 2 Cor. 11:20; Rom. 12:19-21; 1 Thess. 5:15; Heb. 12:14).

We are living in perilous times specifically pointed out by the sure word of prophecy. This unerring prophecy points with unmistakable certainty to the fearful doom which shall come upon this world resulting eventually in the battle of Armageddon. (Rev. 16:14-16; Zech. 14:1-3).

It is apparent that the governments of the present time are making unparalleled preparation for war under the guise of defense or balancing of powers. The governments of this world are established and maintained by the sword and will so continue during this dispensation. At the Lord Jesus Christ's return they will openly oppose his Kingdom. (Psa. 2:1-9). However, this Kingdom of God will bring righteousness and peace upon the earth. (Jer. 23:5, 6; Dan. 7:13, 14, 27; Rev. 5:9, 10; Rev. 11:15).

We, as children of God, are forbidden to avenge ourselves of any wrongs that have been committed against us. (Rom. 12:19). Those who live by the sword will also perish by the sword. (Matt. 26:52; Rev. 13:10).

All our actions must be in accordance with scriptural teachings, (Matt. 5:39-41; 1 Thess. 5:15) and those of our Lord and Saviour, Jesus Christ (Isa. 53:9), and we must practice love (1 John 4:10-11).

We cannot enter the military services of any country. We are willing to pay taxes, custom and honour and whatever does not conflict with the Law of God until the establishment of the Kingdon of God upon the earth, when and where righteousness will prevail. We cannot serve two masters. (Acts 5:29; Luke 1:31-33; Isa. 11:1-10; Matt. 25:31-34; Rom. 13:1-10).

—*January, 1979*

FOR FURTHER INFORMATION: Write to Mr. Ernest R. Rek, 161 Mill Creek Road, Niles, OH 44446.

CHURCH OF GOD, GENERAL CONFERENCE

Whereas, There are many of the members of the Church of God who, as individuals, sincerely and earnestly believe that military service, like similar activity in private life, is, in principle, contrary to the principles of forgiveness and love as taught by Jesus, and later by His apostles, and is, therefore, unchristian; and,

Whereas, Many of said Church of God believe, as is reported to have been stated during the administration of ex-president Wilson, that "there is no non-combatant service," but that what is called non-combatant service is a necessary part and parcel of any and every military campaign; that the participant therein is a contributor to the main service, and, as such, is in harmony with common law and practice of holding one who aids and abets another in the commission of unlawful deeds, a participant and an offender with the instigator and executor of the offense; and,

Whereas, The Government of the United States has from its beginning recognized the right of every person to exalt service unto God and His Son above the service to country and to flag (and this without in any manner manifesting disrespect to one's country) in that it has provided, by its Constitution, in Amendment I, Article I—

"Congress shall make no law respecting an establishment of religion or prohibiting the free exercise thereof";—and, Article 1, Section 9, Paragraph 2,

"The privilege of the writ of habeas corpus, shall not be suspended, unless when in cases of rebellion or invasion the public safety may require it";—and, further, Article 6, Paragraph 2,

"This Constitution...shall be the supreme law of the land"; and,

Whereas, the Government has continuously sought to execute the spirit of these constitutionally recognized duties and provisions respecting all persons who furnish conclusive evidence that they, as avowed followers of Christ, are conscientiously opposed to military service; and,

Whereas, This Church of God does not profess a creed, other than the Bible, by or according to which it receives or controls its members, and therefore cannot declare, as a matter of denominational creed, as to military service of its membership; therefore,

Be It Resolved, That this General Conference of the Church of God, in Conference assembled at Oregon, Illinois, August 17, 1922—

(1) Urge each individual member of its number to at all times, in military and all other matters, continue true and faithful in the performance of Christian duty according to personal conviction as to what constitutes faithful and loyal service to God through His Son;

(2) Open a book of registration for the use of each and every one of its members, male and female, who may wish to register as one religiously and conscientiously opposed to military service, combatant, non-combatant, or both;

(3) Take steps to keep the government properly informed of those thus conscientiously opposed to military service;

(4) Use at all times its every good office with the Government in an effort to secure to each such registrant those exemptions from military service to which such persons are Constitutionally entitled.

(5) Cancel from the register the names of any and all persons who by habitual life prove lack of sincerity in their conscientious objection to individual military service; and,

(6) Be It Further Resolved, That nothing in this resolution shall be construed to constitute a cause for Christian fellowship with reference to such as do, or do not, register as personally opposed to military service, either in a combatant or non-combatant manner.

Resolution Passed by the General Conference of the Church of God, August 17, 1922, and published with the minutes of said Conference in a supplement to The Restitution Herald, September 12, 1922.

FOR FURTHER INFORMATION: Write to Dr. David Krogh, Executive Director, Box 100, Oregon, IL 61061.

CHURCH OF THE GOSPEL

Be it Resolved: That it is the mind of this Holiness Convention session at Pittsfield, Massachusetts, that war is unchristian, entirely opposed and foreign to the doctrine of Jesus Christ and the principles of the gospel of peace.

Be it further Resolved: That we as Christian believers connected with the Church of God (later changed to Church of the Gospel) and gathered together in convention November 14-16, 1924, do place ourselves on record as withholding ourselves from participation in ungodly warfare.

(Resolution of Convention, 1924.)

At the annual business meeting of the church held at Pittsfield, Massachusetts, January 19, 1925, it was unanimously voted that the above resolution be placed on the church records.

At the annual meeting of the church held at Pittsfield, Massachusetts, January 15, 1934, it was unanimously voted that this same resolution become a law of the Church of the Gospel.

The spirit of war is contrary to the spirit of the Gospel. For the Son of Man is not come to destroy men's lives, but to save them (Luke 9:56). John 18:36 reads, "Jesus answered, My kingdom is not of this world; if my kingdom were of this world, then would my servants fight, that I should not be delivered to the Jews; but my kingdom is not from hence." Read Matthew 5:38-48. We are not to return evil for evil, or railing for railing, but contrariwise blessing (1 Peter 3:9). We are to love our enemies and do all we can to win them to Christ. How could one with the love of God in their heart take the life of another? "If thine enemy be hungry, give him bread to eat; and if he be thirsty, give him water to drink; for thou shalt heap coals of fire upon his head, and the Lord shall reward thee." (Proverbs 25:21-22). The love of God in one's heart keeps them from harming their enemies and helps them to pray for them. A Christian could never fight and take the life of others, but show forth the love of Christ for them.

(1982 statement)

FOR FURTHER INFORMATION: Write to Lonnie R. Wyant, Rt. 2, Box 259, Woodford, Va. 22580.

CHURCH OF THE LORD JESUS CHRIST OF THE APOSTOLIC FAITH

Apostolic Standard on Conscientious Objection:
The Church of the Lord Jesus Christ is conscientiously opposed to participation in combat and non-combat service in any form. It is further opposed to the wearing of military and naval uniforms, taking oaths, pledging allegiance to any national state or flag. We do not involve ourselves in international political conflict. While we encourage all of the members of the Church of the Lord Jesus Christ to be loyal to the sovereign national state to which they have residence, we believe that there is an eternal law which supersedes any law of a given society, this being the Holy Scriptures. We take this position since we believe ourselves to be only pilgrims and strangers journeying in a strange land, having heavenly citizenship. We look for a better land and a better day when there will be no more wars nor personal conflict.

"For the weapons of our warfare are not carnal, but mightly through God to the pulling down of strongholds" (II Cor. 10:4).

Maltreatment:
In time of persecution or ill treatment at the hands of an enemy, we should not avenge ourselves but rather give place to wrath; for it is written, "Vengeance is mind; I will repay, saith the Lord" (Rom. 12:19; Deut. 32:35). Neither shall we take up any weapon of destruction to slay another, whether in our defense or in the defense of others, for it is written, do violence to no man (Luke 3:14; Matt. 26:52; John 18:36; John 15:18-19). We should rather suffer wrong than do wrong.

Civil Government
All Civil magistrates are ordained of God for peace, safety and the welfare of all people (Rom. 13:1-10). Therefore it is our duty to be in obedience to all requirements of the laws that are not contrary to the word of God and that do not force one to violation of the sixth commandment by bearing arms and going to war. It is our duty to honor them, pay tribute or such taxation as may be required without murmuring (Matt. 17:24-27, 22: 17-21) and show respect to them in all lawful requirements of the civil government.

FOR FURTHER INFORMATION: Write to Miss Velada Waller, Church of the Lord Jesus Christ, 1230 "C" Street, N.E., Washington, D.C. 20002, or The Apostolic Committee for the Oversight of Conscientious Objectors, on Apostolic at 22nd & Bainbridge Streets, Philadelphia, PA 19146.

CHURCH OF THE NAZARENE

War and Military Service

We believe that the ideal world condition is that of peace and that it is the full obligation of the Christian Church to use its influence to seek such means as will enable the nations of the earth to be at peace and to devote all of its agencies for the propagation of the message of peace.

However, we realize that we are living in a world where evil forces and philosophies are actively in conflict with these Christian ideals and that there may arise such international emergencies as will require a nation to resort to war in defense of its ideals, its freedoms, and its existence.

While thus committed to the cause of peace, The Church of the Nazarene recognizes that the supreme allegiance of the Christian is due to God and, therefore, it does not endeavor to bind the conscience of its members relative to participation in military service in case of war, although it does believe that the individual Christian as a citizen is bound to give service to his own nation in all ways that are compatible with the Christian faith and the Christian way of life.

We also recognize that, as an outgrowth of the Christian teaching and of the Christian desire for peace on earth, there are among our membership individuals who have conscientious objection to certain forms of military service. Therefore, the Church of the Nazarene claims for conscientious objectors within its membership the same exemptions and considerations regarding military service as are accorded members of recognized noncombatant religious organizations.

The Church of the Nazarene, through its General Secretary, shall set up a register whereon those persons who supply evidence of being members of the Church of the Nazarene may record their convictions as conscientious objectors.

(Statement of the General Assemblies, 1940, 1968, 1980.)

FOR FURTHER INFORMATION: Write to Leroy A. Bevan, Chaplaincy Coordinator, Pastoral Ministries, 6401 The Paseo, Kansas City, MO 64131.

CHURCHES OF CHRIST

Because of the autonomous nature of its organization, no man or group can speak authoritatively for Churches of Christ. Therefore, no formal declaration can be issued regarding a position occupied by Churches of Christ toward Conscientious Objectors.
In practice, Churches of Christ recognize the right of and accord full fellowship to its members who, for conscience' sake, refuse to engage in military service. Each member is accorded the right and freedom to decide the matter for himself.

FOR FURTHER INFORMATION: Write to Floyd Williamson, c/o Church of Christ, 3601 Southern Ave., S.E., Suitland, MD 20746.

DOUKHOBOURS

We triumphantly declare that we do not allow any force whatever by man over man and even more so the allowance of killing of man or of men by a man or men under any circumstances, causes or arguments whatsoever. Every individual, group of individuals, parties or governments of men, and anyone whoever they may be proclaiming their struggle against war and its non-allowance but at the same time agreeing and allowing to kill even one individual for the sake of any interests whatsoever—is a lie and a hypocrisy and nothing but a "leaven of the Pharisees." The life of one individual is of equal value to the lives of many individuals. The commandment of God states: "Thou shalt not kill." Christ explains and warns: "No murderer shall inherit Eternal life." War—mass slaughter is an item compiled, where the killing of one individual is allowed there the allowance of mass murder is inevitably admitted—which is war.

(From the Declaration of the second all-Canada conference of Named Doukhobours, Verigin, Sask., Canada, 1934.)

Based on the Christian commandment in "thou shalt not kill" all consientious objection to participation in war is a human right that demands recognition by all governments of man if there is sincerity in the belief that we all aspire to a "brotherhood of man under the fatherhood of God."

FOR FURTHER INFORMATION: Write to John J. Verigin, Box 760, Grand Forks, B.C., Canada, V0H 1H0.

EPISCOPAL

THE EPISCOPAL CHURCH

WHEREAS, the Bishops of the Anglican Communion affirmed at Lambeth in 1958, echoing similar words in 1930 and 1940, that "war as a method of settling international disputes is incompatible with the teaching and example of our Lord Jesus Christ"; and

WHEREAS, the House of Bishops of this Church, while recognizing a Christian's basic obligation to the State and for obedience to law, has affirmed on several occasions that in any conflict of loyalties he must still be guided by his conscience in obedience to God as revealed in Jesus Christ; and

WHEREAS, this Church by General Convention resolution in 1934 petitioned the Congress of the United States to recognize non-combatant status for those who by reason of conscience refuse to serve in the military forces of the United States, and in 1940 established for such persons a Register of Conscientious Objectors; and

WHEREAS, a fresh statement of the position of this Church with respect to conscientious objection against war is now needed to guide our clergy in their counselling task in the light of the Selective Service Act of 1967, such statement to serve also as a guide for those who must interpret this Church's position to inter-church, inter-faith and secular committees; therefore, be it

RESOLVED, the House of Deputies concurring that this Convention hereby recognizes the propriety both of non-combatant service with the military and of civilian alternative service as legitimate methods for discharging one's obligation of service to his country as a conscientious objector against war; and be it further

RESOLVED, that we urge Congress to broaden the Selective Service law, which presently restricts conscientious objection to those who do so for "reasons of religious training and belief," by extending this status also to those who would take the stand for other ethical and moral considerations not necessarily associated with traditional religious commitment; and be it further...

RESOLVED, that the several Dioceses and the staff of Executive Council be urged to provide counsel and legal advice to those members of our Church who have problems of conscience with regard to the prospect of the military draft, cooperating with and assisting wherever possible other community agencies engaged in this counseling service.

(Resolution of General Convention, September 1967.)

Selective Conscientious Objection

... RESOLVED, That we, as Bishops, recognize the right of a man to object, on grounds of conscience, provided he has made every effort to know all of the relevant factors involved, to participation in a particular war, even though he may not embrace a position of pacifism in relation to all war, and urges our government to enshrine such a right in the laws pertaining to Selective Service.

(Excerpted from Resolution of House of Bishops, Augusta, October 1968.)

RESOLVED, the House of Bishops, concurring, That this 66th General Convention encourages young Episcopalians who consider themselves to be conscientious objectors to war to register that belief with the Executive Council of the Episcopal Church in the Register maintained for this purpose since 1940 and with the National Interreligious Service Board for Conscientious Objectors; and be it further

RESOLVED, the House of Bishops concurring, That this 66th General Convention acknowledges this Church's ministry to provide pastoral draft counseling for young persons if faced with a resumption of the draft or draft registration; and be it further

RESOLVED, the House of Bishops concurring, That this 66th General Convention calls upon the Executive Council to provide adequate resources to implement and maintain an ongoing program of draft counseling for young people if faced with a resumption of the draft."

(Resolution of the General Convention, September 1979.)

RESOLVED, the House of Bishops concurring, that this 67th General Convention of the Episcopal Church reaffirms the statement made by the Anglican Bishops assembled at Lambeth in 1978 and adopted by the 66th General Convention of the Episcopal Church in 1979, calling "Christian people everywhere ... to engage themselves in non-violent action for justice and peace and to support others so engaged, recognized that such action will be controversial and may be personally very costly;" and be it further

RESOLVED, that this General Convention, in obedience to this call, urges all members of this Church to support by prayer and by such other means as they deem appropriate, those who engage in such non-violent action and particularly those who suffer for conscience' sake as a result; and be it further

RESOLVED, that this General Convention calls upon all members of this Church seriously to consider the implications for their own lives of this call to resist war and work for peace.

(Resolution of General Convention, September 1982.)

RESOLVED, the House of Bishops concurring, That this 67th General Convention of the Episcopal Church declares its belief that nonviolent refusal to participate in or prepare for war can be a faithful response of a member of this church and a decision to support or participate in war should be made only after careful and prayerful consideration, and be it further

RESOLVED, that a person making such a conscientious decision to participate or not to participate should have the respect and ministry of the Church.

(Resolution of General Convention, September 1982.)

FOR FURTHER INFORMATION: Write to Registrar for Conscientious Objectors, The Episcopal Church, 815 Second Avenue, New York, NY 10017.

EPISCOPAL PEACE FELLOWSHIP

Episcopal Peace Fellowship membership includes those who commit themselves to the following statement:

In loyalty to the person, teachings and Lordship of Jesus Christ, my conscience commits me to His way of redemptive love; to pray, study and work for peace, and to renounce, so far as is possible, participation in war, militarism, and all other forms of violence.

In fellowship with others of like mind, I will work to discover and practice alternatives to violence in the resolution of conflicts.

As a member of the Holy Catholic Church, I urge the Episcopal Church, in accordance with our baptismal vows, "to renounce the evil powers of this world which corrupt and destroy the creatures of God," and to wage peace across all boundaries, calling upon people everywhere to repent, to forgive, and to love.

FOR FURTHER INFORMATION: Write to Episcopal Peace Fellowship, Hearst Hall, Wisconsin Ave. & Woodley Rd., N.W., Washington D.C. 20016.

EVANGELICAL COVENANT CHURCH OF AMERICA

WHEREAS, The Evangelical Covenant Church of America, assembled in Annual Meeting, has by resolution previously taken action to affirm "the sacred privilege and obligation of each Christian to follow the dictates of his own conscience," to pledge "moral support and protection to those who follow the voice of conscience whether in personal participation or refusal to participate in war"; and

WHEREAS, There are, both within and without the fellowship of the Evangelical Covenant Church of America, individuals who are not conscientious objectors in the traditional sense of rejecting all war as immoral, but who are persuaded by their conscience, after serious and responsible grappling with evidence available to their conscience, that a particular war or war waged under particular circumstances is wrong, and who, therefore, in this instance or under these circumstances, feel that they cannot engage in military service; be it therefore

RESOLVED, That the Evangelical Covenant Church of America express its pastoral concern for, stand by and prayerfully uphold, those of its members who in conscience choose to serve in the armed forces as well as those who in conscience object to military service, including those who in conscience object to a particular war; and be it further

RESOLVED, That the Annual Meeting call upon pastors, congregations, Conferences, and officers of the Church, to provide information, assistance, and counsel for those who take this position in order that they may more clearly evaluate their convictions, maintain integrity of conscience and find suitable alternative means for discharging their obligation as citizens in a time of national emergency or danger; and be it further

RESOLVED, That the Annual Meeting remind those who are disposed to take this position that they ought not to do so lightly but only after careful examination and weighing of the facts and of their own motives, the moral issues at stake including their proper obligations to the nation as an instrument of justice and order, the social as well as personal consequences of their decision, and their readiness to accept non-combative or civilian service of equivalent time, risk, and personal inconvenience if afforded them or else such penalties as may be legally imposed; and be it further

RESOLVED, That the Annual Meeting urge the Congress of the United States to amend the Selective Service Act to provide suitable alternatives of military or civilian service for those who on grounds of conscience object to participation in a particular war.

FOR FURTHER INFORMATION: Write to Headquarters, Evangelical Covenant Church of America, 5101 North Francisco Avenue, Chicago, IL 60625.

THE FELLOWSHIP OF RECONCILIATION

The Fellowship of Reconciliation is a worldwide peace organization which was founded in 1914. The FOR in the United States has approximately 30,000 members and is affiliated with 16 religious peace fellowships, including the Catholic Peace Fellowship, the Jewish Peace Fellowship and a large number of Protestant peace fellowships, most of whose members also belong to the FOR.

"That all may live in peace together" is the central purpose of the FOR. Its members include men and women "who recognize the essential unity of mankind and have joined together to explore the power of love and truth for resolving human conflict." They are committed to "work to abolish war and to create a community of concern transcending all national boundaries and selfish interests; as an integral part of that commitment they refuse to participate personally in any war, or to give any sanction they can withhold from physical, moral or psychological preparation for war."

The Fellowship of Reconciliation, as a participating member of the National Interreligious Service Board for Conscientious Objectors and of the Central Committee for Conscientious Objectors, has a program of counseling with COs and would-be COs, through its draft counseling program. It also counsels military personnel who have become COs through their experience in the military. During and between the major world wars, the Fellowship of Reconciliation has sponsored actions and peace education work to oppose peacetime conscription as well as to secure for the CO his legal rights and his human consolations and associations. It was a major supporter of the National Council Against Conscription from 1944 until the Council's suspension in 1960.

FOR FURTHER INFORMATION: Write to Fellowship of Reconciliation, Box 271, Nyack, NY 10960.

FRIENDS

We utterly deny all outward wars and strife, and fightings with outward weapons, for any end, or under any pretense whatever; this is our testimony to the whole world. The Spirit of Christ by which we are guided, is not changeable, so as once to command us from a thing as evil, and again to move us unto it; and we certainly know, and testify to the world, that the Spirit of Christ, which leads us unto all truth, will never move us to fight and war against any man with outward weapons, neither for the Kingdom of Christ, or for the kingdoms of this world...Therefore we cannot learn war any more.

(From a statement by George Fox, founder of the Society of Friends, and others, in a declaration made in 1660.)

FRIENDS, THE RELIGIOUS SOCIETY OF (QUAKERS)

We feel bound explicitly to avow our unshaken persuasion that all war is utterly incompatible with plain precepts of our divine Lord and Law-giver, and the whole spirit of His Gospel, and that no plea of necessity or policy, however urgent or peculiar, can avail to release either individuals or nations from the paramount allegiance which they owe to Him who hath said, "Love your enemies."
(Statement from Declaration of Faith issued by the Richmond Conference of Friends in 1887.)

Friends are urged:
1. To support Young Friends and others who express their opposition to conscription either by nonregistration, or by registration as conscientious objectors. We warmly approve civil disobedience under Divine compulsion as an honorable testimony fully in keeping with the history and practices of Friends.
2. To recognize that the military is not consistent with Christ's example of redemptive love, and that participation, even in a noncombatant capacity, weakens the testimony of our whole Society. Nevertheless, we hold in respect and sympathetic understanding all those men who in good conscience choose to enter the armed forces.
3. To extend our religious concern and assistance to all conscientious objectors who may fall outside the narrow definition of the Selective Service Act of 1948.
4. To avoid engaging in any trade, business, or profession directly

contributing to the military system; and the purchase of government war bonds or stock certificates in war industries.

5. To consider carefully the implication of paying those taxes, a major portion of which goes for military purposes.

6. To ask our Quaker schools and colleges to refuse to accept military training units or contracts, or military subsidies for scientific research, and to advise Young Friends not to accept military training in other institutions.

7. To create a home and family atmosphere in which the ways of love and reconciliation are so central that the resort to violence in any relationship is impossible.

8. To help develop the institutions, methods, and attitudes necessary to a harmonious and peaceful world; to replace political anarchy, national sovereignty and war by law and government; to press for world disarmament beginning unilaterally with the United States, if necessary, instead of the present armament race; to work for the immediate repeal of draft legislation; and to share willingly and sacrificially our resources for the rebuilding of the world.

We realize that the basic task in peacemaking is to fill the spiritual void in our civilization by replacing the fear that now cripples all our efforts with a faith in the Eternal Power by which God unites and sustains those who pursue His Will; and we extend our fellowship to all those of other persuasions who share this faith.

In humility and repentance for past failures, we call upon all Friends to renew the springs and sources of our spiritual power in our meetings for worship; to examine our possessions, to see if there be any seed of war in them; and to live heroically in that life and power that takes away the occasion of all wars and strife.

(Statement of a Conference of All American Friends in Richmond, Indiana, 1948, Reaffirmed by the Friends Coordinating Committee on Peace, and by a number of Yearly Meetings, 1968.)

We, as members of Friends United Meeting, hereby reconfirm our historical stand in opposition to all forms of war and our belief in the peaceful solution to all occasions of conflict. We believe this position is in keeping with the teachings of our Lord Jesus Christ as recorded in the Holy Scriptures (Matt. 5:44; Luke 5:27; Isaiah 2:4; Micah 4:1-4).

Cognizant of the fact that the young men of the United States must now legally register with the Selective Service, we encourage Monthly Meetings to give counsel, information, and support to those involved. This should be done in keeping with the guidelines established by local Meetings or by their respective Yearly Meetings. We suggest that Meetings record in their Minutes the names of those who wish to declare that they are conscientious objectors to participation in war. Regardless of the choice made by the individual, he should be given all respect and encouragement to follow the inner leadings of his conscience. This choice may include one of the following forms:

First, to register according to the law, and to be recorded as a conscientious objector with his own Monthly Meeting.

Second, to refuse to register (in this case, the legal consequences must be carefully considered).

Third, to register with the intent of serving if drafted into the armed forces even though this diverges from the historic testimony of Friends.

We are saddened by the burden of these difficult decisions that face our young men. Whatever personal decision they may make, we in Friends United Meeting will hold them in our prayers and extend our love and concern to them and to their families.

We embrace in our concern the possibility that as a result of the workings of Christ in one's heart or through a change in other inward or outward circumstances, an individual's point of view may change after the initial occasion for registration or even after entry into the armed services.

(Statement accepted at Friends United Meeting Trienniel gathering, July 1981.)

FOR FURTHER INFORMATION: Write to Peace Board, Friends United Meeting, 101 Quaker Hill Drive, Richmond, IN 47374.

THE AMERICAN FRIENDS SERVICE COMMITTEE

Despite widespread political misgivings and principled opposition a system of mandatory draft registration will be in operation by mid-summer. Registration is the necessary first step for conscription into military service, a step that heightens preparation for war.

The American Friends Service Committee cannot approve this registration scheme. The steadfast Quaker testimony against war making and war preparation lies at the heart of our contemporary position. For over 300 years Quakers have sought to "live in that life and power that takes away the occasion of all wars." Each generation faces anew the challenge of faithfulness to this peace testimony. In January 1980 the Board of Directors of AFSC, consistent with the teachings of the Religious Society of Friends, stated its opposition to the current plan for military registration.

Reimposition of registration and the draft will result in violations of religious freedom and civil liberties. Historically the burden of service under the draft falls disproportionately upon poor and minority people. Conscription encourages militarism in national mood and government behavior. Registration is now proposed along with a Rapid Deployment Force and other elements of an interventionist policy that seeks dangerous military solutions to world problems. We reject such an approach based upon violence, coercion, and the armed power of nation states.

Our stand is strengthened by the circumstances of this particular call to register young Americans. The Carter administration acknowledges that registration in the summer of 1980 is a political gesture rather than a manpower procurement measure. The Director of Selective Service advised *against* starting registration. The current plan is of doubtful value to the military unless followed promptly by classification and actual draft calls. Instead the plan is presented as a necessary show of resolve and toughness in a time of crisis. We see this as a charade of readiness and belligerence.

This political posturing disturbingly adds to escalating tensions and the rising risk of hostilities between the United States and the Soviet Union. The deadly slide toward war must be stopped. The arms race must be halted. Nuclear catastrophe must be averted. In this perilous context we regard opposition to military registration as a vital endeavor to help take away "the occasion of . . . war."

Under the leading of our religious faith we reach out to be of service to all young people who face registration, assisting them to make informed decisions based on individual conscience wherever it leads. The American Friends Service Committee encourages young people to follow the dictates of their individual consciences, and supports both (1) conscientious refusal to register for the draft and (2) conscientious objection to military service within the law following registration. The American Friends Service Committee will do its utmost to assist nonregistrants and all conscientious objectors to participation in the military.

The goal throughout our commitment and our service associated with military registration is to oppose violence and war and to raise up the power of peace and life.

(Approved by the Board of Directors, July 2, 1980.)

FOR FURTHER INFORMATION: Write to American Friends Service Committee, 1501 Cherry Street, Philadelphia, PA 19102.

GREEK ORTHODOX

The abhorrence of war and its accompanying tragedies is wholly supported by the spiritual and moral tenets of the Orthodox Church.

Notwithstanding this, Orthodoxy has often, over its long history, found itself at the very crossroads of national and international turmoil and persecution which made war eventually inevitable. While the Church abhors the making of war it must consider the larger alternative of evil which history has proven time and time again cannot be averted. Therefore, with the exception of students preparing for the priesthood, the Church has never taken a position preventing its members from serving in the Armed Forces.

Those seeking to apply for the status of Conscientious Objector must do so on the basis of personal belief and conviction nourished on the highest ideals of the Christian Gospel. These do not only forbid participation in the taking of life—an action necessitated by war—but the desire to attain the highest possible spiritual perfection in and through Our Lord and Saviour Jesus Christ. A candidate for the status of conscientious objector must proclaim that any other classification would infringe upon and frustrate his spiritual aspirations, and that service to one's country in a humanitarian capacity is the preferred alternative.

Any request for a statement as to individual character and religious commitment must be acquired from the local Greek Orthodox Priest who is personally familiar with the life of the candidate.

Statement by the Greek Orthodox Archdiocese of North and South America:

FOR FURTHER INFORMATION: Write to Rev. Dr. M. B. Efthimiou, Department of Church and Society, Greek Orthodox Archdiocese of North and South America, 10 East 79th Street, New York, NY 10021.

HUTTERIAN BRETHREN, CHURCH OF CHRIST (HUTTERITES)

In the light of the principles of Scripture, we are constrained as followers of Christ to abstain from all means of support of war and must consider members who violate these principles as transgressors and not of fellowship with the Church. Specifically, our position entails the following commitments:

1. We can have no part in carnal warfare or conflict between nations

nor in strife between classes, groups or individuals. We believe that this means that we cannot bear arms personally nor aid in any way those who do so and that as a consequence we cannot accept service under the military arm of the government whether direct or indirect, combatant or noncombatant, which ultimately involves participation in any operation aiding or abetting war and thus causes us to be responsible for the destruction of life, health and property of our fellow men.

2. On the same grounds consistency requires that we do not serve during war time under civil organizations temporarily allied with the military in the prosecution of war, such as the Y.M.C.A., the Red Cross, and similar organizations which, under military orders become a part of the system in effect, if not in method and spirit, however beneficial their peacetime activities may be.

3. We can have no part in the financing of war operations through the purchase of war bonds and war taxes in any form or through voluntary contributions to any of the organizations or activities falling under the category described immediately above, unless such contributions are used for civilian relief or similar purposes.

4. We cannot, knowingly, participate in the manufacture of munitions and weapons of war either in peacetime or in wartime.

5. We can have no part in military training schools and colleges, or in any other form of peacetime preparation for service as part of the war system.

6. We ought carefully to abstain from any agitation propaganda or activity that tends to promote ill-will or hatred among nations which lead to war, but rather endeavor to foster goodwill and respect for all nations, peoples and races, being careful to observe a spirit of sincere neutrality when cases of war and conflict arise.

We hereby adopt the above statement as representing our position on peace, war and military service. We would likewise suggest to each of our District conferences that they endorse this statement of position and bring it to the attention of every congregation and all the members, individually, in order that our people may be fully informed of our position and may be strengthened in conviction that we may all continue in the simple, peaceful, nonresistant faith of Scriptures as handed down to us by our forefathers of former times.

(From a statement by Montana Hutterites, 1951.)

FOR FURTHER INFORMATION: Write to: Rev. Joseph J. Waldner, #1129, Havre, MT 59501; Rev. Joseph J. Hofer, Rim Rock Colony, Sunburst, MT 59482; Rev. Paul Stahl, Gilford Colony, Gilford, MT; Rev. Joseph D. Waldner, #34, Route 1, Sun River, MT 59483; Rev. Peter J. Hofer, Harlowtown, MT 59036; Rev. John J. Entz, Ulm, MT 59485; Rev. John J. Wipf, Box 417, Cut Bank, MT 59427; Rev. Paul P. Wipf, Chester, MT 59522.

HUTTERIAN SOCIETY OF BROTHERS

The Church-community life of the Hutterian Society of Brothers seeks the way of the early Christian Church in Jerusalem. As it was with them, we are brought into a new relationship with those who share our faith and total commitment to Christ. The fullest exercise of love as found in the Gospel is seen by the Society to exclude any use of violence or participation in war, and this Christian love demands of us an absolute commitment to a common life together in a religious community. We experience this life-commitment as the call of Jesus and therefore as our calling. This is why there has been no instance, in the history of the Hutterian Brethren since 1528, of a member serving in the armed forces of any country, either in a combatant or a noncombatant capacity.

It is our desire and intention in the Hutterian Society of Brothers to respect and obey the governments of the countries where we abide, insofar as our consciences and our belief in God's laws can allow. We have often had occasion to be grateful for the understanding, help, and consideration shown us. The Society is very grateful for the freedom in which we have been allowed to live our life here in the United States.

For over 450 years our Hutterian communities have existed as united groups of Christian believers pledged to a life of brotherly community in love, service, and peace, with total abstinence from participation in war. Through the centuries many have suffered death through persecution rather than violate their conscience and their belief in God, to whom they owed their first loyalty above all other powers and authorities.

We believe in the prophetic vision of Isaiah that the swords be beaten into ploughshares, lances into sickles and pruning hooks, that nation no longer lift up sword against nation nor learn war anymore. We seek a true Christian life as an expression of reverence, justice, love to men, and the expectation of the future in faith.

We, the members of the Hutterian Society of Brothers, wish to witness with our lives to the fact that it is possible for people to live together in harmony as brothers. This life is possible only on a basis of voluntary surrender to Christ. That means we can no longer place any trust in possessions or power, nor can we return violence with violence. Thus we are conscientiously opposed to participation in war in any form, including service of any kind under military authority.

FOR FURTHER INFORMATION: Write to Hutterian Society of Brothers, Rifton, NY 12471.

INTERNATIONAL SOCIETY FOR KRISHNA CONSCIOUSNESS

From the Vedas comes the phrase, **mahamsyat sarva bhutani,** which means "never commit violence to anyone." As Lord Krishna says in the **Bhagavad-gita**—

O Partha, how can a person who knows that the soul is indestructible, unborn, eternal, and immutable, kill anyone, or cause anyone to kill? (Bg. 2.21)

His Divine Grace, A.C. Bhaktivedanta Swami Prabhupada writes in this connection—

When an embodied being is hurt by fatal weapons, it is to be known that the living entity within the body is not killed. The spirit soul is so small that it is impossible to kill him by any material weapon. Nor is the living entity killable in any case, because of his spiritual constitution. What is killed is supposed to be the body only. This, however, does not at all encourage killing of the body...The understanding that a living entity is not killed does not encourage animal slaughter.

According to the law of Karma, killing is a serious offense, be it killing of humans or killing of animals. For those who must eat meat, it is enjoined that the meat-eater must himself kill the animal, and just previous to the act he must whisper in the ear of the animal, "In your next birth you can kill me." And for one who kills an animal for sport, it is said he must suffer as many violent deaths in future births as there are hairs on the body of the animal (Manu Smriti).

Reaction, although less severe, also awaits vegetarians who kill plants to eat them—plants are living entities, too. Such is the cruel material nature. In the **Gita,** Lord Krishna gives the solution—The devotees of the Lord are released from all sins because they eat food for personal sense enjoyment, verily eat only sin (3.13). If one offers Me with love and devotion a leaf, a flower, fruit, or water, I will accept it (9.26).

Therefore the principle of Krishna consciousness, or bhakti yoga, is to act—not to stop acting out of fear of the material world—but to act for Krishna, God. Then we are no longer in the material world. Devotional service is the same as the spiritual world. So Krishna says—

O son of Kunti, all that you do, all that you eat, all that you offer and give away, as well as all austerities that you may perform, should be done as an offering unto me. (Bg 9.27)

Krishna mentions non-violence three times in the **Bhagavad-gita**. Srila Prabhupada explains the principle thus in his purport to one of the verses (10.5)—

Non-violence means that one should not do anything that will put others into misery or confusion. The human body is meant for spiritual realization, and anyone who does not further this end commits violence on the body.

So there are many kinds of violence. It is clear that as long as we live in this material world, there must be violence. We must kill to eat, though we needn't kill animals. Within our bodies germs and corpuscles are battling; as we breathe, we kill tiny living entities in the air; as we walk we kill bugs and worms on the ground. But withal, "the human body is meant for spiritual realization," and a person who does not take up the process is called in the **Sri Isopanisad** an atma-hanah, or "killer of the soul." That is actual violence.

Considering all these points, it has been a practical consideration for students in Krishna consciousness to apply for I-O or or IV-D classification. It is not because being a military man is not Krishna conscious— Arjuna was a warrior, and Krishna recommended that he fight! The difference is that Arjuna was able to fight for Krishna, and thus he was practicing yoga by his fighting — whereas it is unlikely that we could do the same in the present world situation. In other words, students of His Divine Grace A.C. Bhaktivedanta Swami Prabhupada are ministerial students; they are serving God, and thereby serve all living things.

FOR FURTHER INFORMATION: Write International Society for Krishna Consciousness, 10301 Oaklyn Dr., Potomac, MD. 20854.

ISRAELITE HOUSE OF DAVID

WHEREAS, the bill known as the draft law, having become effective, viz. "Nothing in this act contained shall be construed to require or compel any person to serve in any of the forces herein provided for, who is found to be a member of any well organized religious sect or organization, at present organized and existing, whose creed forbids its members to participate in war in any form, and whose religious convictions are against war or participation therein in accordance with the creed of said religious organization," etc.;

THEREFORE, we the undersigned, members of the voluntary religious association, known as the Israelite House of David, Benton Harbor, Michigan, humbly represent that our faith and religious convictions on the subject of war have been for many years a matter of public record, filed in our Articles of Association and Bylaws with the Secretary of State at Lansing, Michigan, and in the County Courthouse, at St. Joseph, Berrien County, Michigan, in Promiscuous Records, Vol. 4, Page 490, Article IX, viz, "As a body of Christian believers who believe in the law of righteousness and the gospel of Jesus Christ, which we believe teaches life without death, we further make it known that we do not believe in capital punishment, nor do we believe in going to war with the carnal sword, as the commandment of the law says: Thou shalt not kill, and the righteousness of the law as well as the prophets teaches life. We believe in life, without death, to wit, and redemption of our body (Romans 8:23), and the law of the Spirit of life will set us free from the law of sin and death (Romans 8:2), and if we kill or go to war we could not hope for life—for no murderer can inherit everlasting life for the body. We believe rather in beating our guns into plowshares, and our war spears into pruninghooks, and learn war no more (Isa. 2:4; Micah 4:3). Jesus, our pattern and waymark and teacher said, Put up thy sword. He that takes the sword shall perish by the sword (Matt. 26:52; Rev. 13:10), and our faith is the life of the body, soul and spirit (I Thess. 5:23)— to love God with all our heart, soul, mind and strength; and the next like unto it, to love thy neighbor as thyself; therefore, we would no more think of taking the gun, or sword to our fellow man than we would to ourselves; we would not carry the gun in one hand to slay our fellow man, and in the other the Bible, which forbids the carnal weapon; and what is not of faith is sin" (Romans 14:23).

We further proclaim that our religious convictions as to war would not permit us to take part therein "in any form," (as stated in the law), and that we could not therefore be party to any war preparation, such as the manufacture of war munitions, or any war camp duties, hospital service (see Numbers, chap. 5; Leviticus, chap. 15), or any other work which might be considered as noncombatant, believing as Jesus said He that delivereth me unto them hath the greater sin (John 19:11); and like Paul, who condemned himself unto death for merely holding the garments of those who persecuted and killed their fellow man; that we would thereby be partakers and assistants in the act of killing our fellow man, and therefore could not inherit eternal life.

Your undersigned petitioner represents that the above article of faith clearly sets forth his religious convictions, and he hereby humbly claims complete exemption as fully complying with the law herein set forth, and prays that this petition may be filed with his application for exemption.

(From the Petition for Exemption from Military Duty to the Local Board

of Division No. 1, St. Joseph, Berrien Co., Michigan, to be used by registrants in seeking conscientious objector status.)

FOR FURTHER INFORMATION: Write to H. Thomas Dewhirst, House of David, Box 1067, Benton Harbor, MI 49022.

JEHOVAH'S WITNESSES

Jehovah's Witnesses are an international association of Christians who have been confronted with the issue of compulsory military service in many lands. They desire to follow Jesus' command to "pay back Caesar's things to Caesar, but God's things to God." (Mark 12: 17) Each one balances this command with his Christian obligation of neighbor love. Jesus said: "These things I command you, that you love one another... you are no part of the world." "You must love... your neighbor as yourself.'" (John 15:17-19; Luke 10: 25-27) When the issue of military service or participation in war is presented, each individual Witness makes his own decision as to his duty before God and men.

Historically, their decision has been to refrain from acts of violence against their fellowmen of other nations, for they regard these as their "neighbors" whom they should love. They have subscribed to the position of Isaiah's well-known prophecy: "They will have to beat their swords into plowshares and their spears into pruning shears. Nation will not lift up sword against nation, neither will they learn war any more."—Isa 2:4.

In the past, the Congress of the United States has provided exemption to registrants who entertain sincerely-held, religious objections to military service. Jehovah's Witnesses are conscientiously opposed to war and to their participation in such in any form whatsoever. For this reason they inform officials of the government that they conscientiously object to serving in the military, in any substitute service therefor or in any civilian capacity which fosters or supports the military. Moreover, they are willing to accept the consequences of their Bible-based, conscientious position.

This is not a new belief which sprang from the anti-war movements of recent history, but rather one that has long been adhered to by individual Jehovah's Witnesses. To maintain such neutrality, Jehovah's Witnesses have endured concentration camps, prison sentences, and many have given their lives. For example, during World War II in Germany at least 203 Witnesses, according to incomplete reports, were either beheaded or shot because of their neutral stand. This figure does not include those who died from starvation, disease and other brutal treatment in concentration camps.

In the United States thousands of Jehovah's Witnesses have been imprisoned for not 'taking the sword'. (Matthew 26:52) This is true of Witnesses in many other countries as well. Due to their strict neutrality they have never contributed to the slaughter of husbands, sons and loved ones of innocents in war. They have caused no bereavement for the surviving family and friends of war victims and casualties.

This does not mean that Jehovah's Witnesses are extreme pacifists. The Bible clearly teaches that "Jehovah has a day of vengeance" and that the King Jesus Christ will fight a righteous war from the heavens, in which he goes "forth conquering and to complete his conquest." (Isaiah 34:8; Revelation 6:2) Very soon, this battle of Armageddon will "bring to ruin those ruining the earth." (Revelation 16:14, 16; 11:18) However, Jehovah's Witnesses here on earth will not take part in the actual fighting. Their commission is simply "to proclaim. . . the day of vengeance on the part of our God" and "to comfort all the mourning ones."—Isaiah 61:2.

The only warfare in which Jehovah's Witnesses engage is a spiritual one. The apostle Paul said to his fellow Christians: "For the weapons of our warfare are not fleshly, but powerful by God for overturning strongly entrenched things. For we are overturning reasonings and every lofty thing raised up against the knowledge of God; and we are bringing every thought into captivity to make it obedient to the Christ." (2 Corinthians 10:4, 5) In maintaining their strict neutrality, Jehovah's Witnesses do not campaign against the war efforts of the nations in which they may find themselves. They are not political pacifists engaged in resisting war or interfering with the armed forces of any nation. The Bible forbids their meddling or taking part in the political affairs or controversies of nations.

Jehovah's Witnesses follow the admonition the apostle Paul gave to Timothy: "As a fine soldier of Christ Jesus take your part in suffering evil. No man serving as a soldier involves himself in the commercial businesses of life, in order that he may gain the approval of the one who enrolled him as a soldier." (2 Timothy 2:3, 4) They do not involve themselves in any way in the military affairs of the world, having already enrolled as soldiers of Jesus Christ. They know that they cannot serve two masters nor can they allow themselves to be distracted from the preaching activity earthwide.—Matthew 24:14; 28:19, 20.

These Christians await the time when Jesus Christ will rule the world as the Prince of Peace. (Isaiah 9:6) Meanwhile, they remain law-abiding and peaceable, cooperating with the governmental authorities in all things which do not conflict with God's law. In those few instances where there is a direct conflict between God's law and that of the state, they "obey God as ruler rather than men." (Acts 5:29) Nevertheless, in so doing they offer no active resistance to the constituted, legal authorities and are quite willing to accept the consequences of their conscientious objection.—Romans 13:1, 2; Titus 3:1; Isaiah 2:4; Matthew 22:39.

This briefly outlines the position that individual Jehovah's Witnesses have taken with regard to military service. In the final analysis each one makes his own conscientious decision based upon his appreciation of the Bible principles. (Galatians 6:5)

(1982 Statement)

FOR FURTHER INFORMATION: Write to Watch Tower Bible and Tract Society of Pennsylvania, 25 Columbia Heights, Brooklyn, NY 11201.

JEWISH

SYNAGOGUE COUNCIL OF AMERICA
(Orthodox, Conservative, Reform)

Policy Statement on Selective Conscientious Objection, 1971

Respect for law is deeply ingrained in the texture of Judaism. While fully aware of the transfiguring power of love in the affairs of men, Judaism has never accepted the thesis that love supersedes the law and that human society can dispense with the legal order in its search for justice. Cognizant of the potential for chaos and violence in the absence of governmental authority where each man does that which is right in his eyes, the Jewish tradition, from ancient times, called on its adherents to give thanks to God the Creator for the institution of government and for the rule of law that is thereby made possible. Consequently, Judaism cannot give blanket approval of those dissenters who feel it necessary to violate laws which do not meet with their approval. Judism recognizes the dangers to the democratic order should dissenters be given carte blanche to defeat the will of the majority by resorting to illegal procedures. It is clear that no system of law is possible where each man is obliged to obey only those laws that correspond to his views.

At the same time, Judaism considers each individual personally responsible before God for his actions. No man who violates the eternal will of the Creator can escape responsibility by pleading that he acted as an agent of another, whether that other be an individual or the state. It is therefore possible, under unusual circumstances, for an individual to find himself compelled by conscience to reject the demands of a human law which, to the individual in question, appears to conflict with the demand made on him by a higher law. Because the laws of most states in history have not made special provision for the conscientious objector, such individuals usually had to pay the price exacted of those who violated the laws of the state. It is one of the glories of American democracy that conscientious objection to war is recognized by the law as worthy of respect and that those who harbor such objections to all wars are permitted to fulfill their obligations by means that do not conflict with their consciences. So far, however, the law has not seen fit to bestow the same privilege on those who, on grounds of conscience, object not to all wars but to a particular war. It has been suggested that the law be altered to include safeguards, similar to those presently in effect, to exclude the insincere but to permit those who object to a particular conflict on genuine grounds of conscience, to be exempt from participating in it.

The Synagogue Council of America, representing the Orthodox, Conservative and Reform branches of Judaism in the United States, is fully aware that such an expansion of the concept of conscientious objection would probably be unprecedented in the annals of human government. It is also aware that objections to the justice of a particular war require the making of specific factual judgements such as, for instance, the identity of the aggressor and the means employed by one or another of the parties, which, because they are judgements of empirical fact, cannot be made on grounds of conscience alone. Nevertheless, the Synagogue Council, obedient to the moral teachings of the Jewish faith, supports such an extension of the concept of conscientious objection. While there is no absolute right for any man to be exempt from the demands of the law, the gravity of the moral issues in war are such that it behooves a government as committed to the dignity of the individual as that of the United States to pioneer in the area of respect for the conscience of man. It goes without saying that a corresponding obligation devolves on the individual to refrain from invoking such a right except on the clearest and most compelling grounds of conscience.

This statement is adopted on its merits and is not to be construed as a judgement for the justice of any particular conflict, past or present.

FOR FURTHER INFORMATION: Write to Rabbi Henry Michelman, 327 Lexington, Ave., New York, NY 10016.

CENTRAL CONFERENCE OF AMERICAN RABBIS
(Reform)

The Central Conference of American Rabbis reaffirms its conviction that conscientious objection to military service is in accordance with the highest interpretation of Judaism and therefore petitions the Government of the United States to grant to Jewish religious conscientious objectors to war the same exemption from military service as has long been granted to members of the Society of Friends and similar religious organizations.
(Statement of the Central Conference, 1936.)

Our conference, some years since, affirmed the right of the conscientious objectors to refuse, on religious and humanitarian grounds, to bear arms. The Conference does not recede from this attitude. This affirmation may still be invoked by those whose conscience will not allow them, under any circumstances, to bear arms. Nor must those who invoke it become the object of recrimination on the part of the many of us who will not agree with them.
(Statement of the Central Conference, 1940.)

Registration and the Draft
WHEREAS we have previously recognized the right of both conscientious objection and selective conscientious objection to war; and
WHEREAS registration at this time is unnecessary; and
WHEREAS, believing that the costs of such an action draw funds from needed social, educational and economic programs that will make for social betterment,
RESOLVED, that the Central Conference of American Rabbis opposes the inauguration or implementation by our government of any national draft at this time. Similarly, we oppose the idea of registering our youth at this time for some future draft. We believe that should there arise some national emergency necessitating the mobilization of our population, sufficient techniques exist by which to effect that mobilization.
FURTHER RESOLVED, that we urge our colleagues to provide counseling services to interested and affected individuals, and to advertise widely this service in and through the community, so that Jewish youth particularly might know where they might go for counseling that is based on the Jewish religious tradition.
(Resolution adopted at the 93rd Annual Convention, June-July, 1982.)

FOR FURTHER INFORMATION: Write to Rabbi Joseph B. Glaser, 21 East 40th Street, New York, NY 10016.

JEWISH PEACE FELLOWSHIP

The Jewish Peace Fellowship unites those who believe that Jewish ideals and experience provide inspiration for a non-violent philosophy of life. Stimulated by elements in traditional and contemporary Judaism which stress the sanctity of human life, the JPF promotes the attitude of respect for humanity and confidence in its essential decency. These attitudes it endeavors to incorporate in the personal relations of its members and friends. In striving to eliminate the causes of war, the JPF is also concerned with the advancement of freedom and justice for all people.

The Jewish Peace Fellowship provides an extensive draft counseling service and publications.

FOR FURTHER INFORMATION: Write to the Jewish Peace Fellowship, Box 271, Nyack, NY 10960.

RABBINICAL ASSEMBLY (Conservative)

"We recognize the right of the conscientious objector to claim exemption from military service in any war in which he cannot give his moral assent, and we pledge ourselves to support him in his determination to refrain from any participation in it."
(Adopted by the Rabbinical Assembly in 1934 and reaffirmed in 1941.)

FOR FURTHER INFORMATION: Write to Rabbinical Assembly, 3080 Broadway, New York, NY 10011

LUTHERAN

THE AMERICAN LUTHERAN CHURCH

Duties of Citizenship and Dictates of Conscience

Historically the teaching of the Lutheran Church, based on its understanding of the Bible, has been that a Christian, as a citizen, willingly should assume the duties of citizenship, including the bearing of arms and engaging in "just war."

However, the church recognizes that on the basis of their understanding of the total message of Scripture and the traditions of the early church some of its members arrive at the conviction that they cannot with good conscience bear arms. The American Lutheran Church therefore sustains the individual who reaches this conviction in the necessity of following the dictates of his conscience.

... The American Lutheran Church respectfully asks that the pertinent provisions for alternate service be applied to those of its members whose conscience impels them to refuse the bearing of arms and commends to its members who are conscientious objectors those alternatives for fulfilling the responsibility of citizenship. It recognizes its duty to minister spiritually to the conscientious objector as well as to him who for conscience' sake bears arms ...

(From **War, Peace, and Freedom,** *adopted by the Third General Convention of The American Lutheran Church, October 1966.)*

Patriotism, Those Who Serve, Those Who Don't

The American Lutheran Church urges its members, and especially its pastors, to counsel with and stand by those who conscientiously object to military service as consistently as they counsel with and stand by those who for equal reasons of conscience serve in the armed forces. It warns against attempts to judge a person's patriotism or his Christian faith by his willingness or unwillingness to render military service.

(From **Selective Conscientious Objection,** *adopted by the Fourth General Convention, October 1968.)*

Military Conscription Reform, Selective Objection

We believe that serious consideration should be given to the feasibility of providing for the regular military defense needs of the country through a voluntary defense force. We favor the use of additional incentives to attract the needed numbers of volunteers. At the same time, we support provisions for conscription as authorized by Congress in time of declared national emergencies. If the President and the Congress should determine that conscription is necessary that decision should be subjected to periodic public scrutiny as to its continued necessity.

. . . We believe it is time also to amend the [Selective Service Act] to provide alternate forms of national service to those who object on religious, moral, and philosophical grounds to participation in a specific war.

. . . The exercise of moral judgment accepts the legitimacy of service in the armed forces. The exercise of moral judgment also requires the acceptance of the principle of selective conscientious objection . . . The Christian is personally accountable to God for his moral judgments and actions on matters of public policy.

(From **National Service and Selective Service Reform,** *Fifth General Convention, October 1970.)*

Compliance with Registration Law

RESOLVED, that The American Lutheran Church urge compliance with the Selective Service registration legislation; and be it further

RESOLVED, that congregations of The American Lutheran Church be urged to make provision for maintaining a written record for those of their members who wish to declare themselves to be conscientious objectors or selective conscientious objectors; and be it further

RESOLVED, that congregations, pastors, and teachers of The American Lutheran Church help young people for whom the registration requirement is approaching to become familiar with the church's ethical teaching concerning peace, war, and conscience.

(From resolution adopted by the Tenth General Convention, October 1980.)

FOR FURTHER INFORMATION: Write to Office of Church in Society, The American Lutheran Church, 422 South Fifth St., Minneapolis, MN 55415.

ASSOCIATION OF EVANGELICAL LUTHERAN CHURCHES

Military Service: Conscientious Participation and Conscientious Objection

RESOLVED:
1. That the Association of Evangelical Lutheran Churches express its pastoral concern for, stand by, and prayerfully uphold those of its members who in conscience choose to serve in the armed forces, as well as those who in conscience object to war, including those who in conscience object to particular wars.

2. That we affirm our church's ministry to its members serving in the armed forces as expressed through our pastors serving as military chaplains and supported through the AELC Office for Military Ministries.

3. That we urge our pastors and congregations to provide information, counsel, and assistance to their young people, that they may evaluate their convictions and maintain integrity of conscience in arriving at decisions, whether for conscientious participation or conscientious objection.

(Resolutions Adopted by AELC Delegate Assembly, October 1980.)

FOR FURTHER INFORMATION: Write to Elwyn Ewald, Association of Evangelical Lutheran Churches, 12015 Manchester, Suite 80LL, St. Louis, MO 63131.

LUTHERAN CHURCH IN AMERICA

War and military service are and always have been a cause of division among men of conscience. Many choose to bear arms, recognizing that in a sinful world force is often required to restrain the evil. Others, unable to reconcile the inhumanity of war with the demands of love and justice, refuse to participate in particular wars or in any armed conflict. Still others either enter the military or seek deferred status without having resolved the basic ethical dilemmas facing them.

Lutheran teaching, while rejecting conscientious objection as ethically normative, requires that ethical decisions in political matters be made in the context of the competing claims of peace, justice and freedom. Consequently, a man need not be opposed to participating in all forms of violent conflicts in order to be considered a bona fide conscientious objector. It is in responsible grappling with these competing claims that he should consider participation or nonparticipation in the military.

Consistent with this, the responsible, conscientious choice of the individual to participate or not to participate in military service or in a particular war should be upheld and protected. The office of soldier, like all other temporal offices, is to be held in esteem by all. At the same time, the conscientious objector should be accorded respect and such freedom as is consistent with the requirements of civil order.

Governments have rightly seen fit to provide legal status for conscientious objectors, allowing them the privilege of performing alternative service in lieu of military duty. In granting such status, governments recognize that conscientious objectors may make a more valuable contribution to their nation in alternative service than they would if imprisoned or otherwise penalized.

Furthermore, the moral considerations which underlie the stand of the conscientious objector can have a salutary influence upon a nation. The ethical sensitivity and human concern represented in conscientious objection have a value that far outweighs any potential risk to security involved in granting legal exemption. It is better for the general well-being that the conscientious objector be given more than the stark choice between compromised integrity and imprisonment.

However, legal exemption for the conscientious objector is a privilege, not a right, which a just government grants in the interest of the civil good. This does not imply that governments are required to exempt men from any legal obligation. Governments must reserve the right not to grant, or to revoke, the privilege of legal exemption in situations of clear danger to the public order.

The fact that some persons may falsely exploit conscience to defend irresponsible disregard for the obligations of citizenship does not excuse the church from its responsibility of defending the bona fide conscientious objector. The church must exercise special care in judging the spirit and motives of those who may call upon the church for safe-guarding in such a position.

Recognizing both the heart-searching of many persons confronted with the possibility of military conscription and the broader considerations of justice and public order, the Lutheran Church in America adopts the following affirmations:

1. This church recognizes its responsibility of assisting its members in the development of mature, enlightened and discerning consciences. It calls upon its pastors and agencies of Christian education and social ministry to continue in their efforts to cultivate sensitive persons who can act responsibly amid the complexities of the present day.

2. This church stands by and upholds those of its members who conscientiously object to military service as well as those who in conscience choose to serve the military. This church further affirms that the individual who, for reasons of conscience, objects to participation in a particular war is acting in harmony with Lutheran teaching.

3. Governments have wisely provided legal exemption for conscientious objectors, allowing such persons to do other work of benefit to the community. While such exemption is in the public interest the granting of it does not imply any obligation on the part of government to provide legal exemption to anyone who finds a law to be burdensome.

4. In the best interest of the civil community, conscientious objectors to particular wars, as well as conscientious objectors to all wars, ought to be granted exemption from military duty and opportunity should be provided them for alternative service, and until such time as these exemptions are so provided, persons who conscientiously object to a particular war are reminded that they must be willing to accept applicable civil or criminal penalties for their action.

5. All conscientious objectors should be accorded equal treatment before the law, whether the basis of their stand is specifically religious or not. It is contrary to biblical teaching (cf. Romans 2:15f) for the church to expect special status for the Christian or religious objector.

6. This church approves provisions whereby persons in the military who become conscientious objectors are permitted reclassification and reassignment. This church urges that these provisions also be extended to the conscientious objector to a particular war.

Consistent with these affirmations, the Lutheran Church in America directs a member who is a conscientious objector to send a written statement of his convictions to his pastor and to the president of his synod and the secretary of the church. Pastors of the church are directed to minister to all in their care who are conscientious objectors. *(Adopted by the Fourth Biennial convention of the LCA, Atlanta, Ga. June 1968.)*

FOR FURTHER INFORMATION: Write to Board of Social Ministry, Lutheran Church in America, 231 Madison Avenue, New York, NY 10016.

LUTHERAN CHURCH—MISSOURI SYNOD

WHEREAS, The Holy Scriptures teach that "every person be obedient to the governing authorities" (Rom. 13:1) but recognize the right and duty of the individual to obey God rather than men when the civil authorities demand obedience contrary to God's will: "We must obey

God rather than men" (Acts 5:29); and

WHEREAS, The Lutheran Confessions teach that Christians may without sin engage in just wars and as soldiers (A.C. XVL, Tappert, pp. 37.2 and 222.1); and

WHEREAS, The theological position of the Lutheran Church declares the individual's right to refuse participation in unjust wars (Commission on Theology and Church Relation's (CTCR) "Guidelines for Crucial Issues in Christian Citizenship"; "A Christian's Attitude Toward War," CTM, Feb., 1955; CTCR's "Civil Obedience and Disobedience"); and

WHEREAS, the present military draft law exempts only those objectors who on the basis of conscience oppose war in every form and allows them a 1-A-O status (military noncombatant) and a 1-O status (non-military service) and does not recognize objection to a specific war where the individual conscience is convinced that the government is engaged in an unjust war; therefore be it

RESOLVED, That the Synod encourage its members to pledge themselves anew to loyalty and obedience to the government also in the matter of military service; and be it further

RESOLVED, That the Synod reaffirm its historic theological position whereby it recognizes that conscientious objection to a war which an individual considers to be unjust is a valid stance; and be it further

RESOLVED, That the members of the Synod respect an individual's decision not to engage in a war which his conscience, enlightened by the word of God, considers to be unjust; and be it further

RESOLVED, That the pastors and congregations of the Synod be urged to make use of the CTCR's documents "Guidelines for Crucial Issues in Christian Citizenship" and "Civil Obedience and Disobedience" in providing a counseling and supporting ministry to those who conscientiously object to military service as well as to those who in conscience choose to serve in the military; and be it further

RESOLVED, That the Synod petition the government to grant equal status under the law to the conscientious objector to a specific war as it does to a conscientious objector to all wars; and be it further

RESOLVED, That the Board of Social Ministry study the matter of amnesty for those who have refused to serve in the armed forces for reasons of conscience and report its findings to the President of the Synod as soon as possible; and be it finally

RESOLVED, That this present resolution replace Resolution 2-35 of the New York convention (Proceedings, 1967, p. 96).

(Adopted by the Lutheran Church—Missouri Synod at its Denver Convention, July 1969.)

The Lutheran Confessions operate with the concept of a just war (cf. The Augsburg Confession, Art. XVI, and the Apology, Art. IV, 191). Before a Lutheran can rightly become a conscientious objector, he will need to formulate answers to the following questions that have been developed in the course of the history of Christian theology as a way of determining whether a war is just or not:
  A. Is a war being fought under legitimate authority?
  B. Is it being conducted within the framework of international agreement?
  C. Is it being waged in the interest of vindicating some obvious right that has suffered outrage?
  D. Have all peaceful means of achieving a settlement been exhausted?
  E. Is the destruction incurred excessive in terms of the goals to be achieved?
  F. Is it being waged with good intentions, or has it been undertaken for purposes of aggression?
  G. Will the results achieved by engaging in hostilities provide greater opportunity for justice and freedom to prevail than if such a war had not been entered into?
(Excerpt from "The Christian and Conscience" in the Report of the Commission of Theology and Church Relations, **Guidelines for Crucial Issues in Christian Citizenship.***)*

... When a Christian disobeys a law which he considers to be in conflict with the higher law of God, he should:
  1. Be quite sure that all legal means of changing the law have been exhausted;
  2. consult with men of good conscience to test the validity of his judgment;
  3. carry out his act of disobedience in a nonviolent manner;
  4. direct his act of disobedience as precisely as possible against the specific law or practice which violates his conscience;
  5. exercise restraint in using this privilege because of the danger of lawlessness.

Although a Christian may need to join a protest action, he should guard against identifying himself with groups and individuals who may be protesting the same law from apparently wrong motives and who may be seeking to capture a movement for their own improper ends.
(Excerpt from the Report of the Commission on Theology and Church Relations **Civil Obedience and Disobedience.***)*

FOR FURTHER INFORMATION: Write to The Lutheran Church—Missouri Synod, 500 North Broadway, Saint Louis, MO 63102.

MEGIDDO MISSION CHURCH

As a church we are conscientious objectors to military services as being opposed to the law of God. We believe that taking life in war is condemned by the Bible.

We must be kind to our adversaries; when they revile, we are not to revile again. We must follow peace with all men (Heb. 12:14). "Recompense to no man evil for evil" (Rom. 12:17). If any smite us, we cannot smite back, either with tongue or fist, or in any way try to resist evil. "Because Christ also suffered for us, leaving us an example, that we should follow his steps; . . . who, when he was reviled, reviled not again; when he suffered, he threatened not; but committed himself to him that judgeth righteously" (Matt. 5:38, 39; I Pet. 2:21-23). We must submit to the laws of our country. If they demand anything of us that is contrary to the Word of God, we must submit to the penalty without resistance, even as did Jesus.

When the soldiers came to John the Baptist and said to him, "What shall we do?" he answered them, "DO VIOLENCE TO NO MAN" (Luke 3:14), and we must obey his divine injunction. As Peter raised his sword and cut off the ear of the servant of the high priest, Jesus said to him, "put up again thy sword into his place; for all they that take the sword, shall perish with the sword" (Matt. 26:51, 52), "ALL THEY THAT TAKE THE SWORD SHALL PERISH WITH THE SWORD."

Therefore we do not serve in any branch of the Armed Forces, but will serve under civilian direction in work of national importance, such as farming, forestry, hospitals, etc.

This position of our church is long established. Our founder, the Rev. L.T. Nichols, held this belief and acted on it during the Civil War over a century ago. And standing up for his convictions in the unfriendly atmosphere existing at the time nearly cost him his life. An overzealous sergeant took it upon himself to act as judge, jury and executor, and placed Mr. Nichols as a target for a firing squad; but a superior officer appeared just in time and stopped the proceedings.

During World War I a delegation from our church organization appealed to the Selective Service Headquarters at Washington, and we were given recognition as conscientious objectors, and our rights have been recognized at all times since.

FOR FURTHER INFORMATION: Write to Rev. Kenneth E. Flowerday, 481 Thurston Road, Rochester, NY 14619.

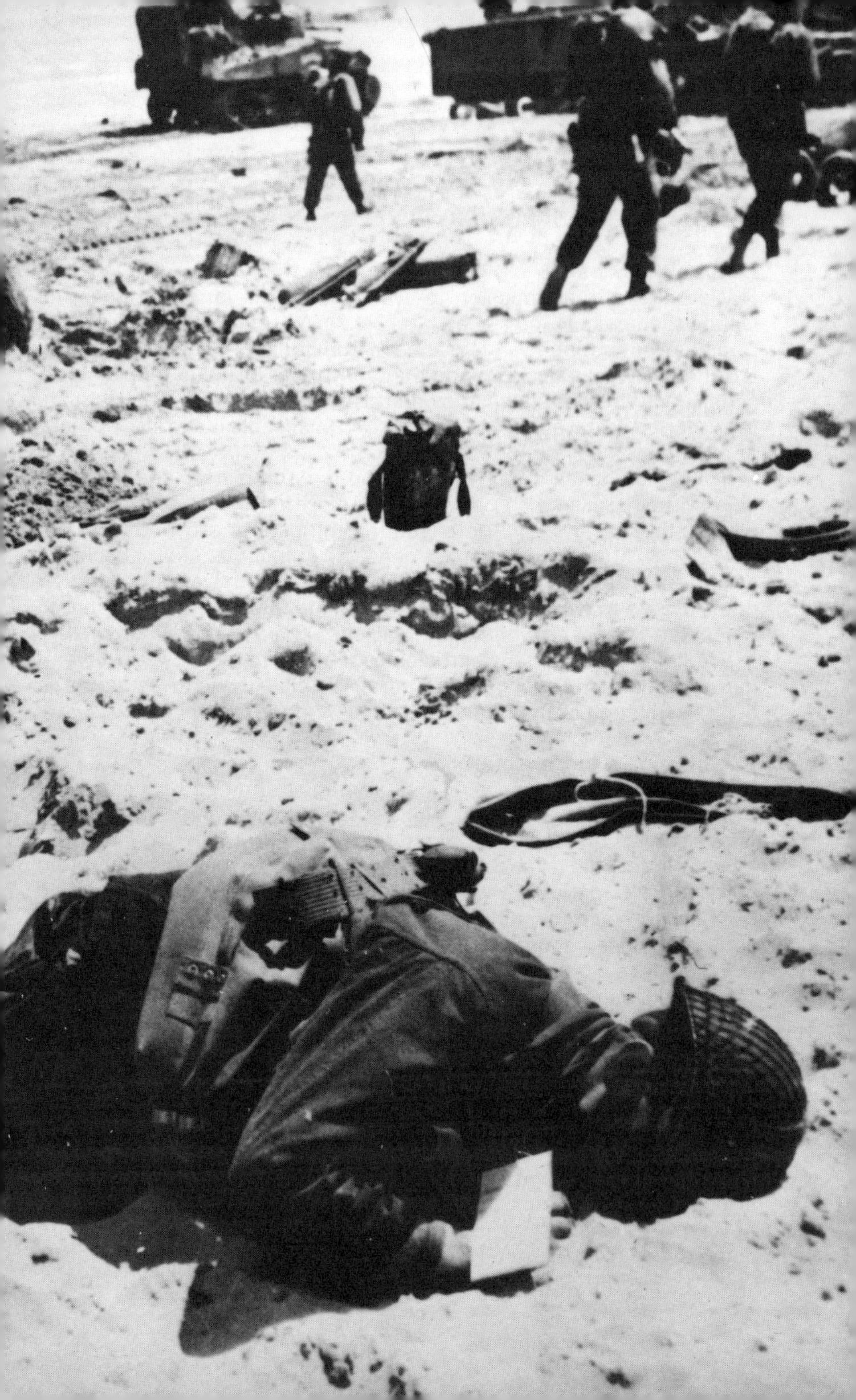

MENNONITE

BEACHY AMISH MENNONITE

Duty to the State

We believe in submission to every law of the land that does not violate the laws of God (1 Peter 2:13-17). We invoke the blessings of God upon our national leaders and are thankful that under their administration laws have been made that allow the Christian to exercise a conscience void of offense. We must pray "for kings, and for all that are in authority; that we may lead a quiet and peaceable life in all godliness and honesty" (1 Timothy 2:1,2).

We believe taxes are a legitimate option of the state and are to be paid without resistance. "Render therefore unto Caesar the things which are Caesar's; and unto God the things that are God's" (Matt. 22:17-21). "Wherefore ye must needs be subject, . . . for conscience sake . . . for they are God's ministers . . . Render therefore to all their dues; tribute to whom tribute is due; custom to whom custom; fear to whom fear; honor to whom honor" (Rom. 13:5-7).

We believe we cannot participate in any type of personal investments that directly support war efforts. We view these investments as being a violation of the Biblical principal of nonresistance.

Registration and Conscription

We look with disfavor upon military registration and conscription. Nevertheless, should these become mandatory, we can support alternative service under civilian or church administration.

If any individual takes the position of non-cooperation to registration and the draft, in keeping with the Scriptures the constituency would consider this action valid only if the person manifests a deeply-held conviction based upon solid Biblical evidences.

We believe conscription of women is a social and spiritual hazard. This would militate against women's Biblical role as "keepers at home" (Titus 2:5) and against the God-ordained distinction between men and women as revealed by the Scriptures (Deut. 22:5; 1 Cor. 11:3-16). Therefore, we earnestly pray that our government may continue to grant exemption to women.

Military Service

We believe war and armed force are contrary to New Testament principles for Christians. Jesus has forbidden His disciples to engage in any form of revenge or resistance by such means. Christians are commanded to return good for evil, "put up the sword into the sheath," or to "beat their swords into plowshares" (Matt. 5:39-44; Jn. 18:11; Rom. 12:14; 1 Pet. 3:9; Isa. 2:4; Micah 4:3). (See also Dortrecht Confession, Article XIV).

According to the Scriptures, therefore, it is inconsistent for Christians to participate in military service—whether combatant or noncombatant, whether in defense or offense.

In the event that our country becomes involved in war or violent conflict the Bible instructs us to maintain a spirit of Christian love and goodwill, avoid hatred and hysteria, and be obedient to all governmental laws and regulations that are not in conflict with Scriptural teachings. We are to turn the other cheek, rather than to retaliate (Matt. 5:39; Rom. 12:19). If necessary, the Scriptures require us to flee or suffer the spoiling of our goods (Matt. 10:23) rather than to inflict injury on any person, even on an enemy. "For the Son of man is not come to destroy men's lives, but to save them" (Luke 9:56).

(Statements excerpted from **Statement of Position on Peace, War, and Social Issues,** *1982.)*

FOR FURTHER INFORMATION: Write to Daniel King, Rt. 1, Box 110, Belleville, PA 17004.

MENNONITE CHURCHES

A DECLARATION OF CHRISTIAN FAITH AND COMMITMENT

I

At this mid-point of the 20th century, at a critical time in a generation marked by widespread and disastrous wars and shadowed by the threat of still more ruinous warfare, this conference of delegated representatives from the Mennonite and Brethren in Christ churches of the United States and Canada unites in a renewed declaration of faith in Jesus Christ, the Prince of Peace, in His Gospel, and in His power to redeem and transform in life and in human society all those who receive Him as Savior and Lord and are thus born anew by the Spirit of God. It also unites in a deeper commitment to follow Christ in full discipleship in a way of peace and love, the way of nonresistance and peacemaking. In this conference we have seen anew the high calling of the sons of God, having been confronted with the absolute claims which Christ makes upon us. We acknowledge these claims in full, and have sought to trace the meaning of His Lordship and the consequences of our commitment in earnest and informed conversation together and in urgent prayer to God for grace and light, seeking to know His will for us in this day.

In our common consideration we have come to certain united convictions expressed in the following declarations which we now humbly send as our message to all our churches both in America and throughout the world as well as to all others who own Christ as Lord. To our brethren we say, this is the day for us to take a clear and unwavering stand on the great essentials of the Gospel and Christian discipleship. It is a day in which to demonstrate and proclaim courageously and unflinchingly this redemptive Gospel and this life of love and service in its fullness and its glory. Let us do so in united purpose with one heart and voice, trusting in the power of God and the companionship of our Lord who has promised to be with us always.

II

1. It is our faith that one is our Master, even Christ, to whom alone supreme loyalty and obedience is due, who is our only Savior and Lord.

2. It is our faith that by the renewing grace of God alone thereby, we can through the power of the indwelling Spirit live the life of holy obedience and discipleship to which all the sons of God are called, for His grace does forgive and heal the penitent sinners and brings us to a new life of fellowship with Him and with one another.

3. It is our faith that redeeming love is at the heart of the Gospel, coming from God and into us to constrain us to love Him and our neighbor, and that such love must henceforth be at the center of every thought and act.

4. It is our faith that Christ has established in His church a universal community and brotherhood within which the fullness of Christ's reign must be practiced, into which the redeemed must be brought, and from which must go out into all human society the saving and healing ministry of the Gospel.

5. It is our faith that the life of love and peace is God's plan for the individual and the race, and that therefore discipleship means the abandonment of hatred, strife and violence in all human relations, both individual and social.

III

These declarations of faith give no blueprint for peace nor do they assume that human endeavor alone can bring about a warless world within history, for only when men come under the Lordship of Christ can they make peace and fulfill the prayers of our Lord, "Thy Kingdom come, Thy will be done on earth as in heaven." They do, however, require certain attitudes, duties and ministries of us, to which we do here by God's grace declare our adherence and our determination to undertake in His name.

1. Our love and ministry must go out to all men regardless of race or condition, within or without the brotherood, whether friend or foe, and must seek to bring the Gospel and all its benefits to every one. Race or class prejudice must never be found among us.

2. We do recognize fully that God has set the state in its place of power and ministry. But recognizing the relative and conditional validity of any particular form of government and of concrete legislative, executive, and judicial acts, we hold that we must judge all things in the light of God's Word and see that our responses to the relatives of the state and its workings are always conformed to the absolutes of Christian discipleship and love. We acknowledge our obligation to witness to the powers that be of the righteousness which God requires of all men, even in government, and beyond this to continue in earnest intercession to God on their behalf.

3. We do have the responsibility to bring to the total social order of which we are a part, and from which we receive so much, the utmost of which we are capable in Christian love and service. Seeking for all men first the kingdom of God and His righteousness, we must hold together in one united ministry the evangelism which brings men to Christ and the creative application of the Gospel to cultural, social and material needs; for we find that the true and ultimate goal of evangelism is the Christianization of the whole of life and the creation of the fully Christian community within the fellowship of faith. For this reason the social order, including our own segment of it, must be constantly brought under the judgment of Christ.

4. We cannot be satisfied to retain for ourselves and our communities alone, in any kind of self-centered and isolated enjoyment, the great spiritual and material goods which God has bestowed upon us, but are bound in loving outreach to all to bear witness and to serve, summoning men everywhere to the life of full discipleship and to pursuit of peace and love without limit. Separately and together we must use every feasible way and facility for this ministry; the spoken and written word; the demonstration of holiness and love in family, church, and community; relief work and social service; and all other ways. We must enlist many more of our people in such witness and service, both as a major purpose of their life and for specific projects and terms. Especially now must Christian love and redemptive action find expression in our ministry of service, when men are turning more and more to the use of force and war in futile attempts to solve the urgent problems of our world. In this service our youth can play a great part. They should give themselves to it in large numbers, both for shorter terms and in lifetime dedication.

5. Parallel with this we must practice an increasingly sharper Christian control of our economic, social, and cultural practices among ourselves and toward others, to make certain that love truly operates to work no ill to our neighbor, either short-range or long-range. Knowing how much the selfishness, pride and greed of individuals, groups, and nations, which economic systems often encourage, help to cause carnal strife and warfare, we must see to it that we do not contribute thereto, whether for the goals of direct military operations or to anything which destroys property or causes hurt or loss of human life.

6. While rejecting any social system of ideology such as atheistic communism, which opposes the Gospel and would destroy the true Christian faith and way of life, we cannot take any attitude or commit any act contrary to Christian love against those who hold or promote such views or practices, but must seek to overcome their evil and win them through the Gospel.

7. We cannot compromise with war in any form. In case of renewed compulsion by the state in any form of conscription of service or labor, money or goods, including industrial plants, we must find ways to serve our countries and the needs of men elsewhere, in ways which we give significant and necessary benefits, which will keep our Christian testimony uncompromised, particularly with respect to war, and which will make possible a faithful representation of Christ and His love. We cannot therefore participate in military service in any form. We cannot have any part in financing war operations or preparations through war bonds. We cannot knowingly participate in the manufacture of munitions, weapons, and instruments of war or destruction. We cannot take part in scientific, educational, or cultural programs designed to contribute to war, or in any propaganda or activity that tends to promote ill will or hatred among men or nations. We must rather foster good will, understanding, and mutual regard and help among all nations, races, and classes. And we cannot as churches lend ourselves to the direct administration of conscription or state compulsion, seeking rather to find voluntary patterns of service through which the demands of the state may be both satisfied and transcended, and going with our men in whatever civilian service they give.

8. If war does come with its possible serious devastation from bombings or other forms of destruction, such as atomic blasts, germ warfare, poison gas, etc., we will willingly render every help which conscience permits, sacrificially and without thought of personal safety, so long as we thereby help to preserve and restore life and not to destroy it.

While we are deeply grateful to God for the precious heritage of faith including the principle of love and nonresistance, which our Swiss, Dutch, and German Anabaptist-Mennonite forefathers purchased for us by their faith, obedience, and sacrifice, and which we believe is again expressed in the above declaration and commitments, we are convinced that this faith must be repossessed personally by each one out of his own reading and obeying of God's Word, and must ever be spelled out in life practice anew. Hence, we summon our brotherhood to a deeper mastery of the Scriptures as the infallible revelation of God's will for us, and to a finding afresh under Holy Spirit guidance of its total message regarding Christ's way and its application in our present world.

We humbly confess our inadequacies and failures for both in understanding and in following this way, knowing well that we have come short both in demonstration and proclamation of Christian love. As we renew our commitment of discipleship and ambassadorship for Christ, we know how much we need God's grace and each other's help in the fellowship of His body in learning and obeying. Let us therefore stand together and go on together in His Name and for His cause.

(Statement of Winona Lake Conference of Mennonites and Brethren in Christ Churches, 1950.)

Since 1950 Mennonite and Brethren in Christ Churches have spoken frequently as individual bodies and collectively through the Mennonite Central Committee Peace Section on issues of war, militarism and conscientious objection. These statements reaffirm the Winona Lake Statement; oppose war and militarism; advocate conscientious objection to war and in some cases recognize the validity of conscientious objection to conscription itself. The MCC Peace Section urges exemption from military service to all conscientious objectors. Mennonite and Brethren in Christ agencies stand ready to assist objectors who call on them for assistance.

FOR FURTHER INFORMATION: Write to Mennonite Central Committee, 21 South 12th Street, Akron, PA 17501. Information on the statements and beliefs of the dozen or more Mennonite groups affiliated with the Mennonite Central Committee is available.

METHODIST
FREE METHODIST CHURCH

1. We recognize the sovereign authority of government and the duty of every Christian to reverence the power, to obey the law, and to participate righteously in the administration of lawful order in the nation under whose protection he resides (Matthew 22:21; Romans 13:1-7). Members of our church should bear the responsibilities of good citizenship, and they have the right to act in the enforcement of law and the defense of the peace in accord with the conscience of each person.

2. We believe, however, that military aggression is indefensible as an instrument of national policy and strategy (Isaiah 2:3-4). The destruction of life and property and the deceit and violence necessary to warfare are contrary to the spirit and mind of Jesus Christ (Isaiah 9:6-7; Matthew 5:44-45). It is therefore the duty of every Christian to promote peace and goodwill, to foster the spirit of understanding and mutual trust among all people, and to work with patience for the renunciation of war as a means to the settlement of international disputes (Romans 12:18; 14-19).

3. It is our firm conviction that none of our people should be required to enter military training or to bear arms except in time of national peril and that the consciences of our individual members should be respected (Acts 4:19-20; 5:29). Therefore, we claim exemption from all military service for those who register officially with the church as conscientious objectors to war.

(From **Free Methodist Discipline***, 1979)*

FOR FURTHER INFORMATION: Write to General Conference Secretary, Free Methodist Church of North America, 901 College Avenue, Winona Lake, IN 46590.

UNITED METHODIST CHURCH

War and Peace

We believe war is incompatible with the teachings and example of Christ. We therefore reject war as an instrument of national foreign policy and insist that the first moral duty of all nations is to resolve by peaceful means every dispute that arises between or among them; that human values must outweigh military claims as governments determine their priorities; that the militarization of society must be challenged and stopped; and that the manufacture, sale and deployment of armaments must be reduced and controlled.

The United Methodist Church and Conscription

The United Methodist Church since its inception in 1968 has consistently opposed peacetime conscription. In doing so, it has heeded its Lord's injunction to know and to seek the things that make for peace. The vision of peace portrayed so graphically in Isaiah and Micah concludes with the expectation that the day will arrive when men and women shall no longer learn the ways of war.

Despite the fears of some, we do not believe that military conscription is essential to the security of nations in times of peace. In fact, evidence indicates that conscripted armed forces can be used to conduct unpopular unauthorized wars for which volunteers would be unavailable.

Some countries require that all young people perform national service, military or civilian, and other countries are proposing to do the same. The cost and bureaucracy of such massive undertakings are enormous; the opportunities for indoctrination pose a constant threat to peace and freedom; the invasion of personal liberty and privacy is alarming; and the value of such involuntary service is dubious.

We urge all United Methodists (1) to oppose induction of persons into any system of military or civilian conscription except in times of war or national emergency, and (2) to work toward the elimination of existing conscription systems in times other than those of war or national emergency. Further, we declare that registration of persons should not be undertaken for psychological reasons nor designed to affect only a limited age group.

(1980 Resolution)

Military Conscription, Training and Service

Conscription. We affirm our historic opposition to compulsory military training and service. We urge that military conscription laws still in effect be repealed; we also warn that elements of compulsion in any national service program which may be in effect or under consideration will jeopardize seriously the service motive and introduce new forms of coercion into national life. We advocate and will continue to work for the inclusion of the abolition of military conscription in disarmament agreements.

Conscientious objection. Each person must face conscientiously the dilemmas of conscription, military training, and service and decide his or her own responsible course of action. We affirm the historic statement; "What the Christian citizen may not do is to obey persons rather than God, or overlook the degree of compromise in even our best acts, or gloss over the sinfulness of war. The church must hold within its fellowship persons who sincerely differ at this point of critical decision, call all to repentance, mediate to all God's mercy, minister to all in Christ's name" (The United Methodist Church and Peace, 1968 General Conference).

Christian teaching supports conscientious objection to all war as an ethically valid position. It also asserts that ethical decisions on political matters must be made in the context of the competing claims of biblical revelations, church doctrine, civil law, and one's own understanding of what God calls him or her to do.

We therefore support all those who conscientiously object: to preparation for or participation in any specific war or all wars; to cooperation with military conscription; or to the payment of taxes for military purposes; and we ask that they be granted legal recognition.

Amnesty and reconciliation. We urge understanding of and full amnesty or pardon where necessary for those persons who refuse to participate in war, such as Vietnam.

(Section VI of The **United Methodist Church and Peace**, *adopted by the 1980 General Conference).*

Civil Obedience and Civil Disobedience

Governments and laws should be servants of God and of human beings. Citizens have a duty to abide by laws duly adopted by orderly and just process of government. But governments, no less than individuals, are subject to the judgment of God. Therefore, we recognize the right of individuals to dissent when acting under the constraint of conscience and after exhausting all legal recourse, to disobey laws deemed to be unjust. Even then respect for law should be shown by refraining from violence and by accepting the costs of disobedience. We offer our prayers for those in rightful authority who serve the public and we support their efforts to afford justice and equal opportunity for all people. We assert the duty of churches to support everyone who suffers for the cause of conscience, and urge governments seriously to consider restoration of rights to such persons while also maintaining respect for those who obey.

(From **Social Principles of the United Methodist Church**, *adopted by the 1980 General Conference.)*

FOR FURTHER INFORMATION: Write to Dept. of Peace and World Order, General Board of Church and Society, The United Methodist Church, 100 Maryland Ave. N.E., Washington, D.C. 20002.

THE WESLEYAN CHURCH

The Wesleyan Church teaches respect for properly constituted civil authority and the proper loaylty to one's country. It recognizes the responsibility of the individual to answer the call of his government and to enter into military service. However, there are those within the fellowship of the Wesleyan Church who believe that military service is contrary to the teaching of the New Testament and that their consciences are violated by being compelled to take part in such. The Wesleyan Church will therefore lend moral support to any member who asks and claims exemption by legal processes from military service as a sincere conscientious objector and who asks to serve his country as a noncombatant.

FOR FURTHER INFORMATION: Write to The General Superintendent, The Wesleyan Church, Box 2000, Marion, IN 46952.

THE MISSIONARY CHURCH

We believe that civil government is ordained of God for the welfare of society to promote and protect the good and to restrain and punish evil. Therefore we consider it the duty of Christians to pray for rulers and for those that are in authority over them and to give due loyalty, respect, and obedience to them. Where the demands of civil law would militate against the supreme law and the will of God, Christians should obey God rather than man (Dan. 4:17; Rom. 13:1-4; Pet. 2:13,14; I Tim. 2:14; Titus 3:1; Matt. 22:17-21; Acts 4:19, 5:29).

We believe that the teaching of the Scripture enjoins believers to love their enemies, to do good to them that hate them, to overcome evil with good, and inasmuch as possible, live peaceably with all men. Therefore, we conclude that it is not fitting for the Christian to promote strife between nations, classes, groups, or individuals.

We recognize that sincere Christians have conscientious differences as to their understanding of the teaching of the Word of God with reference to their responsibility as Christian citizens to human government both in times of war and times of peace. We therefore exercise tolerence and understanding and respect the individual conscience with regard to participation in war.

We further urge upon all the responsibility of searching the Scriptures with open heart and mind that their position may truly be one of Christian conviction and not of expedience.

Pastors are advised to instruct their churches and particularly their youth, on the teaching of the Scriptures regarding war and its evils, and to seek to give guidance in the Word to those subject to call in the service of their country (Matt. 5:43, 44; Rom. 12:20,21; Rom. 12:18; Rom. 13).
(From the Constitution of The Missionary Church.)

FOR FURTHER INFORMATION: Write to The Missionary Church, 3901 South Wayne Avenue, Fort Wayne, IN 46807.

MORAVIAN CHURCH (NORTHERN PROVINCE)

Resolved, That this Synod records its conviction that Jesus Christ came to be the Savior and Lord both of every man and of every relation and activity of men. Therefore, in obedience to the Lordship of Jesus Christ, be it

Resolved, That this Synod declare its conviction of the right of conscience on the part of the individual to refuse to bear arms, or to submit to military training.

Resolved, that the Provincial Board of Christian Education devise ways and means of preserving a record of the members of our congregations concerning warfare.

Resolved, That members of our Church applying for such enrollment with the Provincial Board of Christian Education shall have been members in good standing for at least one year previous to such application.
(Resolution of Moravian Synod, 1936.)

Whereas, War, the enmities it foments, the wanton distortion of truth it engenders, and the defiance of the righteousness of God it demonstrates are manifestly abhorrent to the Gospel and the Spirit of Christ; and

Whereas, "There is wide agreement with regard to the rights of the conscientious objector"; and

Whereas, The Moravian Church has within its membership some in good standing who are conscientiously opposed to participation in war, on the ground that it is incompatible with the mind of Christ; and

Whereas, in any conflict of loyalties Christians must unhesitatingly follow the Christ; therefore, be it

. . . Resolved: that this Synod reaffirms the position taken by the Provincial Synod of 1936, namely, "That Synod records its conviction that Jesus Christ came to be the Savior and Lord both of every man and of every relation and activity of men."

... Resolved, that this Synod declares its conviction of the right of those who in honest obedience to conscience refuse sto bear arms or to submit to military training;

... Resolved: That opportunity be continued for such conscientious objectors within the membership of the Moravian Church to file their declarations with the Christian Education Board, in accordance with the provisions determined upon by the Provincial Synod of 1936 in order that as occasion may warrant, their cases may be laid before the respresentative of Government with a view to determining their status. *(Resolution of Moravian Synod, 1941.)*

FOR FURTHER INFORMATION: Write to Dept. of Educational Ministries, Moravian Northern Province, S. W. Market St., Bethlehem, PA 18018.

NATIONAL COUNCIL OF CHURCHES OF CHRIST IN THE U.S.A.

Today many young people find that compulsory military service conflicts with their consciences. Christians should be especially sensitive to their dilemma. Experiences of a shrinking world, the development and use of new weaponry of awesome destructive potential, and new complications in international relationships combine to impress upon these young people the moral implications of their personal decision.

Every encouragement should be given to this moral seriousness among young people, especially when they confront this crucial choice—whether to participate in military action against other people at the nation's command. Although society has the power to press all its members into military duty, our nation has made room in its conscription laws for the operation of conscience by exempting certain classes of conscientious objectors from military service.

The General Board of the National Council of Churches considers this provision to be wise public policy, not only because intensely objecting men do not make the best soldiers, but because society should encourage men to live by conscience rather than compel them to violate it. The war-crimes trials at the conclusion of the Second World War asserted the inescapable responsibility which every human being bears for his own acts, even in obedience to military orders in time of war.

This social judgment accords with our Christian belief that conscience is the light given by God to every man to seek good and reject evil. In instances of conflict with human authorities, Christians have insisted, "We must obey God rather than man" (Acts 5:29). The Church, when it has been true to this insight, has nurtured and defended the right and duty of all men to obey God as each perceived His will in the leading of conscience.

However, "conscience" is not a monopoly of Christians or of the religious traditions. Neither is there one kind of conscience that is "religious" and another that is "nonreligious", but only the human conscience, which Christians see as God's gift, whether or not every individual so understands it (Cf. Romans 2:12-15).

The highest interests of a free society are served by giving to conscience the greatest freedom consonant with justice, public order and safety. Although we may have greater confidence in a conscience that is rooted in a religious tradition, we believe that ways and means should be provided so that the validity or sincerity of another's conscience may be recognized. Even though the majority may consider decisions based on such a conscience to be mistaken in a particular instance, or may be uncertain of its sincerity in another, our nation should protect the right of conscience in such cases for the sake of a greater good. Coercion of conscience can recruit no more than an unwilling body, while mind and spirit and a willing body are likely to serve society more fully in alternate tasks not repugnant to conscience. Therefore we urge the greatest possible protection for its free exercise.

In respect to the provisions for conscience in the selective service laws, we recommend the following:

(1) The retention of the provision of noncombatant military service for those conscientiously opposed to full military service and the retention of the provision for alternate civilian service for those who are conscientiously opposed to participation in war in any form.

(2) The extension of precisely the same provisions for those who are conscientiously opposed to a particular war, declared or undeclared, that is, to the one which a young person confronts at the time of induction.

(3) The elimination of the statutory requirement of a showing of "religious training and belief"—a requirement unnecessary to validate the operation of human conscience and placing "religious" conscience in a preferential position over "non-religious" conscience.

(4) Provision in the statute for the person in armed service who becomes a conscientious objector to obtain noncombatant service or to be honorably discharged through an orderly and expeditious process subject to administrative review.

(5) Adoption of a new disciplinary provision for the person in armed service who cannot in conscience take part in the use of certain wea-

pons or forms of warfare, or who cannot in conscience obey what is for him an unlawful or morally unacceptable order. We recognize that any military organization requires discipline, and that refusal to carry out an order for any reason is a disciplinary breach. When such refusal is motivated by conscience, however, this motivation should be considered as a factor with all other circumstances of the particular case in determining the nature of the disciplinary action to be taken.

(Adopted by the General Board February 23, 1967.)

In the Western tradition which shaped the American political system, it is generally agreed that the function of government is to secure justice, peace and freedom for its citizens, and to maintain order, not as an end in itself, but as a condition necessary for the existence of justice, peace and freedom. Christians find this tradition generally compatible with their understanding of the divinely-ordained function of the state.

When, however, a particular government fails to provide justice, peace or freedom, it is not maintaining the true order, and Christians should remain faithful to their understanding of what order ought to be, even at the cost of disobeying that government. In such circumstances, it is the government which has become insubordinate to God's order, and not those who disobey that government. Rather, they show their genuine respect for rightful "governing authority" by criticizing, resisting or opposing the current misusers of that authority.

Although Christians recognize the importance of order for human society, in every period of history there has been a Christian witness against giving absolute or unquestioning obedience to any civil authority. The first allegiance of Christians is to God, and when earthly rulers command what is contrary to the will of God, Christians reply as did Peter and John, "We must obey God rather than men." (Acts 5:29). Whatever the penalty for disobedience to human law, it has not deterred some Christian martyrs in every age from pointing by their death beyond man's order to God's order.

(From "Religious Obedience and Civil Disobedience", adopted by the General Board June 7, 1968.)

Resolution on Registration for Selective Service

WHEREAS the National council of the Churches of Christ in its policy statements affirms that national security rests on the development of international economic and political cooperation, the peaceful settlement of disputes, and the determination to abolish war; and

WHEREAS the National Council of the Churches of Christ in its policy statements opposes permanent universal military training as inimical to our heritage as a free nation under God and a step in the direction of a garrison state; and

WHEREAS registration for Selective Service is the initial essential step to a military draft, and represents one aspect of the growing militarization of the general population, and of young people in particular; and

WHEREAS the significant unresolved societal issues of racism, sexim and economic discrimination are exacerbated in and by the military, as evidenced by many veterans and others who are still victimized by the legacy of the Vietnam War, and are not allevaiated by a shift from an all volunteer military to registration and the draft; and

WHEREAS the proposal of the President of the United States to the Congress to institute registration for Selective Service is evidence of recurring and increasing reliance on military responses to world problems;

BE IT THEREFORE RESOLVED:
1. That the NCCC calls upon the Congress of the US to reject the President's request for appropriations and legislation to institute registration for the Selective Service.
2. That the NCCC calls upon both the President and the Congress to seek and pursue economic development and political cooperation as non-military methods to secure justice, peace and reconciliation among the nations of the world.
3. That the NCCC calls upon its member communions to:
a. oppose appropriations and legislation to implement registration for Selective Service;
b. establish, support and encourage educational and counseling programs, so that all men and women may make informed decisions regarding registration for the draft, with particular concern for those forced to consider military service by pressures of economic and racial discrimination;
c. increase efforts to achieve international security through respect for the integrity of other countries and their populations, through efforts at arms control and progressive disarmament, and through support of the United Nations' peacekeeping efforts.

(Resolution passed by NCCC Executive Committee, February 1980.)

FOR FURTHER INFORMATION: Write to National Council of Churches, 475 Riverside Drive, New York, NY 10027.

PRESBYTERIAN
PRESBYTERIAN CHURCH IN THE U.S.

Whereas, the General Assembly of the Presbyterian Church in the United States affirmed in 1949: 'Our church has consistently upheld the right of citizens to refuse to bear arms in conflict with their conscience or the tenets of their religious beliefs:' (General Assembly *Minutes,* 1949, pp. 100-110); and

Whereas, the church, having consistently upheld this right, dares not abandon those who exercise it; and

Whereas, the Universal Military Training and Service Act provides alternative service for any person who 'is conscientiously opposed to participation in war in any form' but fails to make alternative service possible for a person who conscientiously objects to service that would require him or her to be a combatant in particular conflicts without conscientiously objecting to participation in war in any form; and

Whereas, the failure of the Selective Service System to provide for conscientious objection to participation in a particular conflict is discriminatory in that it respects conscientious objection of one sort but not of another, and unjust in that it deprives an individual of his or her right to make a conscientious decision in a particular situation; and

Whereas, the consequences of this failure are disruptive to the health of the nation and harmful to the body politic in that loyal and patriotic citizens are punished as criminals because they dare to be faithful to the dictates of their consciences in objecting to combatant rather than alternative service in a particular conflict;

Therefore, be it resolved that the 109th General Assembly of the Presbyterian Church in the United States:

(1) Recognizes the right of citizens to object conscientiously to combative participation in a **particular** conflict as well as the right to object conscientiously to combative participation in **all** wars; and

(2) Urges the Congress of the United States to move with all dispatch in amending the Universal Military Training and Service Act to provide for suitable alternatives or military or civilian service for those who conscientiously object to combative participation in a particular conflict; and

(3) Commends with all urgency a full and immediate review of the entire Universal Military Training and Service Act, and immediate legislation, to remove the inequities that now exist in this archaic law; and

(4) Directs the Stated Clerk to send copies of this resolution to the President, the Secretary of Defense, the President of the Senate, and the Speaker of the House of Representatives of the Congress of the United States.
(109th General Assembly, 1969.)

FOR FURTHER INFORMATION: Write to James E. Andrews, Presbyterian Church in the U.S., 341 Ponce de Leon Ave., N.E., Atlanta, GA 30308.

REFORMED PRESBYTERIAN CHURCH, EVANGELICAL SYNOD

(The Reformed Presbyterian Church, Evangelical Synod, came into being in 1965 by the union of the Evangelical Presbyterian Church and the Reformed Presbyterian Church in North America, General Synod.)

"It was voted that whereas the United States is now at war and has a law giving privileges to conscientious objectors whose churches recognize such, the General Synod of the Reformed Presbyterian Church in North America recognizes the right of conscientious objectors within the church, and thereby gives any conscientious objector in the church the privileges extended by the United States Government, but in no case will the General Synod be responsible for their maintenance."

(Minutes of the Reformed Presbyterian Church in North America, General Synod, 1942.)

"A fundamental principle of this church as expressed in the Westminster Confession of Faith, is that God alone is Lord of the conscience. Therefore, the matter of conscientious objection is left up to the individual."

(This statement was suggested in a letter from the Stated Clerk, September 1968.)

FOR FURTHER INFORMATION: Write to the Rev. Paul R. Gilchrist, Ph.D., Stated Clerk, Reformed Presbyterian Church, Evangelical Synod, 107 Hardy Rd., Lookout Mountain, TN 37350.

UNITED PRESBYTERIAN CHURCH IN THE U.S.A., THE

The United Presbyterian Church does not teach a single response to war which all members must accept, for God alone is Lord of the conscience of those who, in good faith and sensitive spirit, conclude that military power must sometimes be employed to establish the preconditions for justice, order and freedom. God is also Lord of the conscience of those who conclude that they cannot support military action because they judge either it is antithetical to order and justice or against the teaching of the Gospel. . . .

Both of these—the agonized participant in war and the pacifist who objects to war—can draw equally upon the church's teaching in support of their position. And it is also clear that a third group—individuals who object to particular wars which they judge to be unjust or unconscionable—is entitled to appeal to the teaching of the Church as the foundation of their moral stand. God is the Lord of conscience, not only of a participant in war for moral reasons, or of the objector to all war on pacifist grounds, but also of those who conclude that a particular conflict is morally unconscionable and indefensible. . . .

. . .it is now evident that consideration must also be given to providing legal relief for the moral position of the selective conscientious objector. Objection to a particular war judged by the individual conscience to be wrong is a moral obligation which may stem from Christian just war teaching.

Despite the difficulties involved, a free society determined to respect conscience must seek ways to provide legal acceptability for this moral imperative. To do so is to serve the public interest by providing the dissenting conscience an alternative to disobedience, rebellion, or exile.

. . .To institute the right of selective conscientious objection will require considered thought and careful administration. It will require an examination of all claimants to conscientious objector status as to their sincerity, rationale, consistency, and depth of moral conviction. Such an examination should be provided according to nationally established criteria and uniform procedures and should be administered by area tribunals of specially qualified persons. Anything less than such a procedure could not hope to penetrate the ambivalence and complexity of human motivation or to avoid the injustices of impromptu decisions.

In addition to the three responses to war recognized above, there are many young men who, in good conscience, choose not to cooperate with the Selective Service System in any way. For them, any form of conscription in a democratic society is unconscionable, and they feel compelled either to ignore it, to oppose it, or to exile themselves, taking the consequences of the penalties the law provides for such choices, in the same manner as those selective conscientious objectors who are without relief under the present law. With such men, the church affirms that God is Lord of their conscience also, and hence along with those who make the other response to war the church offers them her ministries of compassion and pastoral care without necessarily approving or encouraging such responses...

Faced with the agonizing choices of war, each Christian must satisfy his own conscience under God and with his fellowmen, that any war is "just and necessary". We call upon each church member, facing these choices, to inform and enliven his conscience, using as resources the fellowship of the church, the counsel of the clergy, the Bible, sacraments, and prayer as a means of grace, the Confessions, statements, and traditions of the church, together with adequate information on the facts of a particular war. Without these resources, decisions may be ill-formed, ill-advised, and contrary both to the will of God and the best interests of mankind.

Further, the United Presbyterian Church calls for the implementation of the above statement by recommending:

That sessions and other judicatories take steps to initiate and/or support responsible draft information and counseling centers in and through which all young men of a community may receive expert guidance and help as they face (a) the legal options and demands of the Selective Service System, and (b) the problem of conscience involved in their response to it.

That pastors and selected laymen participate in educational events which will provide sensitivity to and information on the draft, voluntary enlistment, issues of conscience concerning war, peace, and alternatives to violence, and related subjects in order that the preaching, teaching, and pastoral ministries of the church may be more adequate to these crucial concerns.

That pastors and sessions interview, and counsel with, each young man in their congregation at age 17 regarding his own conscientious response to war and the draft...

That these ministries of pastoral care shall include those who take unpopular stands based on sincere religious grounds, including draft non-cooperation. Care and oversight may in these instances include full moral and functional support for young men who refuse induction, or stand trial, or go to prison. Such care may also include affirmative demonstration of support in several forms, such as undertaking ways to provide legal assistance, public statements of support, and other personal involvements of time, effort, influence and money. Visits to those in prison and concern for them following the completion of their prison terms are also appropriate. The families of these young men are

also commended to pastors and sessions. Such care may include direct moral and financial support to the men and their families to defray the sometimes burdensome cost resulting from the stand of conscience...
That sessions, or other judicatories, and the various boards and agencies of the church seek to provide employment, acceptable to the government, for conscientious objectors as a form of alternative service in the I-O category of the Selective Service System."
(Excerpts from Statement of the 181st General Assembly [1969] on War, Peace, and Conscience.)

The 193rd General Assembly of the United Presbyterian Church in the United States of America enacted the following:
a) "Publicly reaffirms its obligation to provide spiritual and pastoral support for those individuals affected by the reactivation of registration and conscription;
b) Encourages local churches and judicatories to provide impartial and objective counseling, information, and support to all registration-age youth;
c) Encourages judicatories to develop, and local congregations to offer, through departments of Christian education, classes to help youth examine their consciences and be ready to choose their appropriate responses to draft notification;
d) Encourages all young people who are or who have been required by law to register with the Selective Service to seek preliminary counseling in order that they may carefully evaluate all available options and their moral consequences before choosing a course of action; and
e) Encourages all United Presbyterian young people who may be opposed to participation in war to file a statement of their beliefs on war and conscription with the Stated Clerk of the United Presbyterian Church in the United States of America, together with the attestation of their membership in a United Presbyterian congregation."

(Excerpted from 193rd General Assembly Minutes, p. 89, 1981.)

FOR FURTHER INFORMATION: Write to the Youth and Young Adult Program Office, The United Presbyterian Church in the U.S.A., Rm. 1164, 475 Riverside Dr., New York, NY 10115.

REFORMED CHURCH IN AMERICA

The Right of Dissent and Conscientious Objection

The Reformed Church in America affirms the right of all Christians to engage in such debate and dissent as their conscience may compel them. Indeed, we believe that both laymen and clergy stand under the obligation to speak in terms of moral concerns which are likely to be lost in the heat of war. Churches are reminded that their ministers have a prophetic function to fulfill, which can be done only as the freedom of the pulpit is maintained. When hate and violence fill the air, it is the Church alone which can keep alive the voice of love and mercy and compassion.

The Reformed Church in America recognizes that while some may be led to support war by participation in the armed forces, there are others, who, for conscience's sake, cannot do so. We, therefore, reaffirm the position of past General Synods supporting the right of men to choose the path of conscientious objection, and we ask the churches to report such decisions and to support them in their ministry. For the sake of the record, we hereby include actions of past Synods:

1938 — "We should maintain our Christian fellowship both with those whose conscience leads them to participate in war and with those whose conscience forbids them to participate in war. Christians, as citizens, must resolutely resist the increasingly prevalent reliance upon militarism as expressed by militarizing our youth by compulsory military training in schools and colleges."

1939 — "We recognize, in the event of war, the right of any minister or communicant member to follow the leading of his conscience before God concerning the support and participation in any armed conflict."

1940 — "Remembering the words of our Lord—'They that take the sword shall perish by the sword'—and anticipating the powerful influence America may exert when fighting has ceased, we reaffirm our purpose to do all in our power to keep America out of present wars."

1941 — "We commend the government for its wisdom in recognizing the legitimacy of the conscientious objector's interpretation of Christ's commands."

1942 — "The General Synod approved a recommendation that: 'The Church acknowledge the right of individual conscience, and maintain the unity of Christian fellowship among (a) men in our armed forces; (b) religious objectors to war; and that the freedom of the pulpit be upheld."
(Endorsed by the General Synod of 1967.)

The 1968 General Synod:
Requests all churches and pastors to provide counsel to young men who are torn by the dilemma of conscience regarding war, making known to them the alternatives provided within the Selective Service Act both for service within the armed forces and for the provision of choosing conscientious objector status.

Asks the churches to give supportive help to young men who have chosen the unpopular position of conscientious objector, and help in interpreting this decision of conscience to the people in the church and in the community.

The 1971 General Synod:
Resolves to continue to urge local consistories and churches to support those young men among their constituents who have chosen the conscientious objector's position and [that] the recommendations [supporting positions of individual conscientious objectors] accordingly be made to the proper officials (local draft boards) and that they give support and assistance to competent draft counselling groups in their communities where possible, and, also, that the consistory assist the conscientious objectors in finding the type of employment which may satisfy the requirements of the law in lieu of military service.

The 1980 General Synod voted:
To remind pastors, youth leaders and consistories of their responsibility to counsel young people and congregations about Christian perspectives toward war and options relating to participation in the military service.

FOR FURTHER INFORMATION: Write to Office of the General Synod, 18th Floor, 475 Riverside Drive, New York, NY 10027.

REORGANIZED CHURCH OF JESUS CHRIST OF LATTER DAY SAINTS

The Church of Jesus Christ believes in the exercise of individual conscience and the preservation of agency. When a person freely chooses to become a Christian, he attempts to live in ways consistent with the Christian ethic. The present dilemma is whether or not the cruelties of war can ever be justified within the Christian ethic. It is recognized that not all members will hold the same view. Some will feel conscientiously obligated to render full military service. Since the church desires to maintain fellowship with all who sincerely follow the guidance of conscience, it will respect such sincere decisions.

"We, as a church, promote peace. People motivated by Christian love promote peace through constructive and peaceful activities . . .

"(We believe in) upholding law which supports individual and group dignity and freedom, and by opposing oppression and tyranny. It is a Christian duty to participate responsibly in governmental processes and to support good and wise persons in positons of governmental leadership . . .

"While acts of terrorism, unprovoked war, and wanton mental and physical abuse cannot be supported under any circumstances, we understand there are instances where reasonable avenues to reconcile differences appear to have been exhausted and resorting to force is deemed unavoidable . . .

"The contents of this resolution in no way condemn those who choose to work from within the military establishment to bring the love of God to bear in such a way that the cause of World Peace is promoted."

(Selected quotes from Resolution 1177 adopted by the 1982 World Conference.)

FOR FURTHER INFORMATION: Write to the Committee on Ministry to Armed Forces Personnel, The Auditorium, Independence, MO 64051.

ROMAN CATHOLIC

POPE JOHN PAUL II ON VIOLENCE AND LAW

... How is the very noble "principle of non-violence" to be evaluated, in the framework of law in general and canon law in particular? It should be pointed out in the first place that this principle, already not alien to the Old Testament, was taught and practiced to the utmost by the Redeemer himself, whom both the prophecies and the Gospels present to us as "a lamb led unjustly to be butchered, without any rebellion or lament on his side." With regard to acts of violence he even says: "To him who strikes you on the cheek, offer the other also" (Lk 6:29). But in the system of Christian thought the principle of non-violence has not only a negative aspect (not to meet violence with violence), but also a positive one, which is far superior. It can be said, in fact, that the most Christian of the maxims inculcated by the Redeemer by example and by an explicit precept, is the following: "Do not be overcome by evil, but overcome evil with good" (Rom. 12:21), that is, with a good that is even greater (which in contrast turns out to be love).

... Just as man is not destined only to live with others, but also *for* others, finding in that the highest perfection of his own personality, so each people cannot think exclusively of its own prosperity, but must also contribute to that of other peoples, verifying in this way the real humanity of its own particular civilization. The duty of solidarity, and therefore of love, cannot be alien to law since, being inscribed in the very existential reality of man, it is the first precept of the natural law, after that of love for God.

... In conclusion: just as it is impossible to construct a society with the negative principle of non-violence alone, so it is impossible to construct a "society without law and without a State," as certain modern utopias promise. But it is certainly possible to construct society based on love; we certainly can and must aim at a universal civilization of love. Here violence will be excluded because it is contrary to the law which is charity: *plentitudo legis dilectio* (the whole law is summed up in love - Rom. 13:10).

(Excerpted from an address to the Union of Italian Catholic Jurists, December 6, 1980 as published in the weekly English Edition of **L'osservatore Romano,** *January 26, 1981.)*

UNITED STATES CATHOLIC CONFERENCE

For many of our Catholic people, especially the young, the question of participation in military service has become a serious moral problem. They properly look to their spiritual leaders for guidance in this area of moral decision and for support when they judge their sentiments to be in keeping with Catholic Christian tradition. For this reason, we wish to express ourselves on the following principles.

The traditional teaching of the Church regarding the importance of individual conscience is crucial in this issue of conscientious objection and selective conscientious objection. The obligation to seek the truth in order to form right and true judgments of conscience and the obligation to follow conscience was put in positive terms by Pope Paul VI and the Fathers at the Second Vatican Council:

"Further light is shed on the subject if one considers that the highest norm of human life is the divine law—eternal, objective, and universal—whereby God orders, directs, and governs the entire universe and all the ways of the human community, by a plan conceived in wisdom and love. Man has been made by God to participate in this law, with the result that, under the gentle disposition of divine Providence, he can come to perceive ever increasingly the unchanging truth. Hence every man has the duty, and therefore the right, to seek the truth in matters religious, in order that he may with prudence form for himself right and true judgments of conscience, with the use of all suitable means.

"Truth, however, is to be sought after in a manner proper to the dignity of the human person and his social nature. The inquiry is to be free, carried on with the aid of teaching or instruction, communication, and dialogue. In the course of these, men explain to one another the truth they have discovered, or think they have discovered, in order thus to assist one another in the quest for truth. Moreover, as the truth is discovered, it is by a personal assent that men are to adhere to it.

"On his part, man perceives and acknowledges the imperatives of the divine law through the mediation of conscience. In all his activity a man is bound to follow his conscience faithfully, in order that he may come to God, for whom he was created." ("Declaration on Religious Freedom," n. 3)

Addressing the question in the "Pastoral Constitution on the Church in the Modern World," Our Holy Father and the Bishops at the Second Vatican Council wrote:

"In the depths of his conscience, man detects a law which he does not impose upon himself, but which holds him to obedience. Always summoning him to love good and avoid evil, the voice of conscience can when necessary speak to his heart more specifically: do this, shun that. For man has in his heart a law written by God. To obey it is the very dignity of man; according to it he will be judged.

"Conscience is the most secret core and sanctuary of a man. There he is alone with God, whose voice echoes in his depths. In a wonderful way conscience reveals that law which is fulfilled by love of God and neighbor. In fidelity to conscience, Christians are joined with the rest of men in the search for truth, and for the genuine solution to the numerous problems which arise in the life of individuals and from social relationships.

"Hence the more that a correct conscience holds sway, the more persons and groups turn aside from blind choice and strive to be guided by objective norms of morality." ("The Church in the Modern World," n.16)

In addition, the Church has always affirmed the obligation of individuals to contribute to the common good and the general welfare of the larger community. This is the basis for the participation of Christians in the legitimate defense of their nation.

The Council Fathers, recognizing the absence of adequate authority at the international level to resolve all disputes among nations, acknowledged that "governments cannot be denied the right to legitimate defense once every means of peaceful settlement has been exhausted." ("The Church in the Modern World," n.79)

When survival of the wider community has been threatened by external force, the Church has traditionally upheld the obligation of Christians to serve in the military defensive forces. Such community-oriented service, that is, soldiers devoted to the authentic purposes of securing peace and justice, has merited the Church's commendation.

The Catholic Bishops of the United States are gratefully conscious of the sacrifices and valor of those men who are serving and who have served in the armed forces and especially those who have given their lives in service to their country. Their courage in the defense of the common good must not be underestimated or forgotten. In the words of the Second Vatican Council, "As long as they (members of the armed forces) fulfill this role properly, they are making a genuine contribution to the establishment of peace." ("The Church in the Modern World," n.79)

It was also recognized by the Second Vatican Council that the common good is also served by the conscientious choice of those who renounce violence and war, choosing the means of nonviolence instead:

"...we cannot fail to praise those who renounce the use of violence in the vindication of their rights and who resort to methods of defense which are otherwise available to weaker parties too, provided that this can be done without injury to the rights and duties of others or of the community itself.' ("The Church in the Modern World," n.78)

Furthermore, the Council Fathers, addressing themselves more specifically to the rights of the conscientious objector to war, stated:

". . .it seems right that laws make human provisions for those who for reasons of conscience refuse to bear arms, provided however, that they accept some other form of service to the human community." ("The Church in the Modern World," n.79)

Although a Catholic may take advantage of the law providing exemption from military service because of conscientious opposition to all war, there often arises a practical problem at the local level when those who exercise civil authority are of the opinion that a Catholic cannot under any circumstances be a conscientious objector unless the individual is a member of one of the traditional pacifist churches (for example, a Quaker).

In the light of the Gospel and from an analysis of the Church's teaching on conscience, it is clear that a Catholic can be a conscientious objector to war in general or to a particular war "because of religious training and belief." It is not enough, however, simply to declare that a Catholic can be a conscientious objector or a selective conscientious objector. Efforts must be made to help Catholics form a correct conscience in the matter, to discuss with them the duties of citizenship, and to provide them with adequate draft counseling and information services in order to give them the full advantage of the law protecting their rights. Catholic organizations which could qualify as alternative service agencies should be encouraged to support and provide meaningful employment for the conscientious objector. As we hold individuals in high esteem who conscientiously serve in the armed forces, so also we should regard conscientious objection and selective conscientious objection as positive indicators within the Church of a sound moral awareness and respect for human life.

The status of the selective conscientious objector is complicated by the fact that the present law does not provide an exemption for this type of conscientious objection. We recognize the very complex procedural problems which selective conscientious objection poses for the civil community; we call upon moralists, lawyers and civil servants to work cooperatively toward a policy which can reconcile the demands of the moral and civic order concerning this issue. We reaffirm the recommendation on this subject contained in our November 1968 pastoral letter, "Human Life in Our Day":

1) a modification of the Selective Service Act making it possible for selective conscientious objectors to refuse to serve in wars they consider unjust, without fear of imprisonment or loss of citizenship, provided they perform some other service to the human community; and

2) an end to peacetime conscription.

In restating these recommendations, we are aware that a number of young men have left the country or have been imprisoned because of their opposition to compulsory military conscription. It is possible that in some cases this was done for unworthy motives, but in general we must presume sincere objections of conscience, especially on the part of those ready to suffer for their convictions. Since we have a pastoral concern for their welfare, we urge civil officials in revising the law to consider granting amnesty to those who have been imprisoned as selective conscientious objectors, and giving those who have emigrated an opportunity to return to the country to show responsibility for their conduct and to be ready to serve in other ways to show that they are sincere objectors.

(The American Catholic Bishops' "Declaration on Conscientious Objection and Selective Conscientious Objection" October 21, 1971. Reaffirmed by "Statement on Registration and Conscription for Military Service" by USCC Administrative Board, February 1980.)

FOR FURTHER INFORMATION: Write to the Office of International Justice and Peace, United States Catholic Conference, 1313 Massachusetts Ave. N.W., Washington, D.C. 20005.

CATHOLIC PEACE FELLOWSHIP:

If there was ever any question as to the right of a Roman Catholic to claim the conscientious objector position with regard to war in general or to a specific war, that question has been answered by the bishops of the Church assembled in the Second Vatican Council.

Addressing the problem in the pastoral Constitution on the Church in the Modern World, the Council Fathers wrote: "It seems right that laws make humane provisions for those who for reasons of conscience refuse to bear arms, provided, however, that they agree to serve the human community in some other way." (Sec. 79)

Those who renounce violence altogether, choosing to live lives of nonviolence, are praised in the Council text: "...we cannot fail to praise those who renounce the use of violence in the vindication of their rights and who resort to methods of defense which are otherwise available to weaker parties, too, provided this can be done without injury to the rights and duties of others or of the community itself." (Sec. 78)

Roman Catholics share with other Christians the support that Holy Scripture lends to the pacifist. Similarly they share in an historic witness ranging from the early Christians through the present.

The voices of the Popes of our own times have repeatedly called us from the way of war to the task of Christian peacemaking, most notably Pope John XXIII in his encyclical letter Pacem in Terris, and Pope Paul VI in his address to the United Nations: "No more war; war never again." Pius XII in his Christmas message of 1944 bade us "declare war upon war."

In our own generation these urgings are taking root in the unprecedented number of young Catholics who claim the conscientious objector position, either from the judgment that modern war cannot fulfill the requirements of the traditional "just war" theory or from a realization of the bankruptcy of violence as it has been shown by current history in light of the Gospel of Christ. Christian nonviolence offers many of these young men a way of life in which they feel not only more Christian but more relevant to the world in which they live. If nothing else could answer the question of whether a Roman Catholic can be a conscientious objector, the rising chorus of young Catholics should shout an unequivocal and undeniable **yes**.

Catholic young men (and their counselors) are urged to order the booklet "Catholics and Conscientious Objection", by James H. Forest, published by the Catholic Peace Fellowship, 339 Lafayette Street, New York, NY 10012, (25 cents plus postage) which bears the **imprimatur** of the archdiocese of New York. The Catholic Peace Fellowship also offers draft counseling to those interested.

FOR FURTHER INFORMATION: Write to the Catholic Peace Fellowship, 339 Lafayette Street, New York, NY 10012.

NATIONAL FEDERATION OF PRIESTS' COUNCILS

Resolution on Education and Counseling on the Draft

WHEREAS on February 15, 1980, the Administrative Board of the United States Catholic Conference issued a statement on the draft, which among other things, called attention to the need for education, consciousness-raising and counseling about this pressing item;

WHEREAS the questions of registration, conscription, and military service involve moral questions of great importance and also bear directly on the moral decision-making of our high school and college-age people;

WHEREAS the conscientious objection position is as valid a moral decision in Catholic teaching as is the decision to enter military service, yet such a choice does not as yet have a secure position in our legal and legislative process;

WHEREAS it is of value to have a place outside one's own person to state one's confirmed belief in the matter of conscientious objection;

BE IT RESOLVED, that the NFPC urge its member councils to ask their dioceses to provide draft counseling for high school and college-age people to help them to understand the moral and ethical questions related to the draft;

BE IT FURTHER RESOLVED, that NFPC urge its member councils to ask the Chancery of their respective dioceses to be official repositories for statements made by those who choose a conscientious objector's status.

(Resolution of the 1980 NFPC House of Delegates.)

FOR FURTHER INFORMATION: Write to National Federation of Priests's Councils, 1307 South Wabash Avenue, Chicago, IL 60605.

PAX CHRISTI—USA

Conscription serves the purpose of war in a time when war itself is seen as the most threatening enemy of mankind. At a time when Church teaching has focused more and more clearly on the immorality of modern war and of preparation for war, Pax Christi-USA's National Executive Council expresses its opposition to any plan of this nation to restore military conscription. Such a policy intrudes upon the privacy and freedom of the individual. Conscription violates and denies the fundamental principle that conscience must not be coerced.

(Approved by Pax Christi—USA Executive Council, March 1979.)

"Although we neither advise nor encourage such action, Pax Christi-USA recognizes non-registration for the draft based on conscientious objection to conscription and opposition to the growing militarization of this nation as a valid Christian witness deserving the respect and support of the entire Christian community."

(Resolution of National Council, October 1982.)

FOR FURTHER INFORMATION: Write to Paul Mazur, Pax Christi-USA, 6337 W. Cornelia, Chicago, IL 60634.

PAX CHRISTI—USA CENTER ON CONSCIENCE AND WAR

... What choices are there?

Conscientious participation—You may believe that it's right to register now and even decide later to enlist in the military or to accept induction if the draft returns. If you do eventually enter the military, the need to make hard decisions of conscience doesn't end. Catholic teaching holds that certain acts of war, such as direct attack on civilians, are wrong and that orders to commit them must be refused.

Conscientious objection (and other deferments)—You may register even though you believe it's wrong to participate in war, which means you're a "conscientious objector" (CO) . . . You can't apply for CO or other deferments now, but you should begin to learn more about them even if you're not sure you qualify.

Conscientious refusal—You may believe that you cannot, in conscience, register for the draft at all. Many Catholics chose not to register during Vietnam, and a few in previous wars, for a variety of reasons . . . If you do decide not to register, Pax Christi will support you in this, as in any conscientous choice, in whatever way we can.

Can Catholics be conscientious objectors? YES! For the first two centuries the Church was almost universally opposed to Christian participation in war. Many Catholics in later centuries, including such saints as Francis of Assisi and Martin of Tours, rejected military service. In our own century, a growing number of American Catholics have been recognized as CO's . . . The Catholic Church teaches two forms of conscientious objection: general, opposition to all wars, and selective, refusal to serve in a particular war which you consider to be unjust . . .

(Excerpted from "Catholic Conscience and Registration for the Draft"

FOR FURTHER INFORMATION: Write to Pax Christi—USA Ctr. on Conscience and War, Box 726-S Bigelow St., Cambridge, MA 02139.

THE SALVATION ARMY

Many young Salvationists have served, and are serving, with distinction in the Armed Forces (some as Chaplains), and The Salvation Army has always sought to bring them a ministry of help and guidance. We owe an equal ministry to others who, by reason of conscience, are opposed to military service. We respect the right of every individual to arrive at his own decision in this matter, based on his Christian conscience.

We teach respect for properly constituted civil authority and loyalty to our "nation under God." Therefore, we counsel those of our constituents who object to military service to take advantage of the legal means provided for alternate service.

We join with fellow Christians around the world in praying that all men may learn to live together in the love and power of the Lord Jesus Christ, which takes away the occasion for war and strife.

(Approved by the Commissioners' Conference, April 1971.)

FOR FURTHER INFORMATION: Write to The Salvation Army, 769 Bloomfield Ave., Verona, NJ 07044.

SEVENTH-DAY ADVENTISTS

The Adventist Church's major statement on military obligations for its members throughout the world is probably best presented in an action of the 1954 Annual Council of the General Conference Committee. It reads:

> Genuine Christianity manifests itself in good citizenship and loyalty to civil government. The breaking out of war among men in no way alters the Christian's supreme allegiance and responsibility to God or modifies his obligation to practice his beliefs and put God first.
>
> This partnership with God through Jesus Christ, who came into this world not to destroy men's lives but to save them, causes Seventh-day Adventists to take a noncombatant position, following their divine Master in not taking human life, but rendering all possible service to save it. In their accepting the obligations of citizenship, as well as its benefits, their loyalty to government requires them to serve the state in any noncombatant capacity, civil or military, in war or peace, in uniform or out of it, which will contribute to saving life, asking only that they may serve in those capacities which do not violate their conscientious convictions.

This statement is not a rigid position binding church members, but rather, a recital of principles which cause Seventh-day Adventists to act as they do. This gives guidance but leaves the individual member free to assess the situation for himself. The laws of military obligation differ from country to country and even change from time to time within a country.

(From **Seventh-day Adventist Teachings on Governmental Relationships and Noncombatancy,** *1982.)*

"WHEREAS, Under the present Selective Service Law the personal religious belief of the registrant is the vital point, and

"WHEREAS, The church while teaching noncombatancy has recognized that its members must make a personal decision in connection with their period of obligated service to the country, therefore

"WE RECOMMEND,

1. That those young men of the church making a decision concerning their obligated term of service to the country first consider the historic teaching of the church on noncombatancy, which could lead them to choose the I-A-O classification.

2. That for those then choosing the I-O classification, pastoral support, guidance, and counsel be provided when it is established that such a request is based on a consistent religious experience.

3. That such support be given by pastors, teachers, or other workers writing statements of their personal knowledge of the man's

   a. Church membership

   b. Attendance and participation in services of the church

   c. Personal standards of conduct

   d. Previous expressions of belief supporting his request for I-O classification

4. That those writing such statements request the draft board to respect and honor the man's personal convictions."

(From Actions on the Autumn Council of the General Conference, October 12, 1969.)

FOR FURTHER INFORMATION: Write to the Seventh-day Adventists National Service Organization, 6840 Eastern Avenue, N.W., Washington, D.C. 20012.

SOJOURNERS FELLOWSHIP

But I say to you that hear, love your enemies, do good to those who hate you, bless those who curse you, pray for those who abuse you. (Luke 6:27-28)

With these words, Jesus placed an eternal obstacle in the way of war. This obstacle has been repeatedly pushed aside by the nations as they have found endless justifications for hating and making war with one another.

All the wars to end war have failed to keep their promise. They have not brought peace but have instead only entrenched war itself as the characteristic way nations deal with their deepest conflicts...

Reviving our capacity to love has become an urgent political necessity as the superpowers come to regard millions of their neighbors as nothing more than expendable enemy populations in a nuclear exchange. We face unimaginable destruction unless our hearts are enlarged to recognize a neighbor in the face of our enemy. The possibility of nuclear annihilation shows Jesus' simple but long-ignored exhortation to love our enemies to be a politically relevant and necessary position.

. . .Refusing the call to arms is based on the fundamental moral reality that there is no longer any threat greater than war itself. . .

. . .The members of Sojourners Fellowship have determined to refuse the call to arms at every point, including registration for the draft. Further, we advocate that others likewise refuse. Specifically, we encourage young men and women to refuse to register for the draft and support them in that position. We regard this as our pastoral responsibility, and would invite others who have specific pastoral care for young people to consider it their responsibility as well. For those above draft age, the present situation should occasion a fresh look at the contradiction of paying for war with our tax dollars and at the risks we are taking for peace.

In the past, the church has told its pacifists that their position was important but politically irrelevant. Now the very real prospect of nuclear war shows Jesus' words to be supremely relevant. All complicated arguments and theological distinctions between "just" and "unjust" war must give way to the reality of nuclear war.

In ignoring Jesus' words, we in the church have sacrificed our vocation of being an obstacle to war. We must reclaim that vocation now.

(Excerpted from the article "Refusing The Call to Arms" written by Jim Wallis, March 1980.)

FOR FURTHER INFORMATION: Write to Sojourners Peace Ministry, 1321 Otis St., N.E., Washington, D.C. 20017.

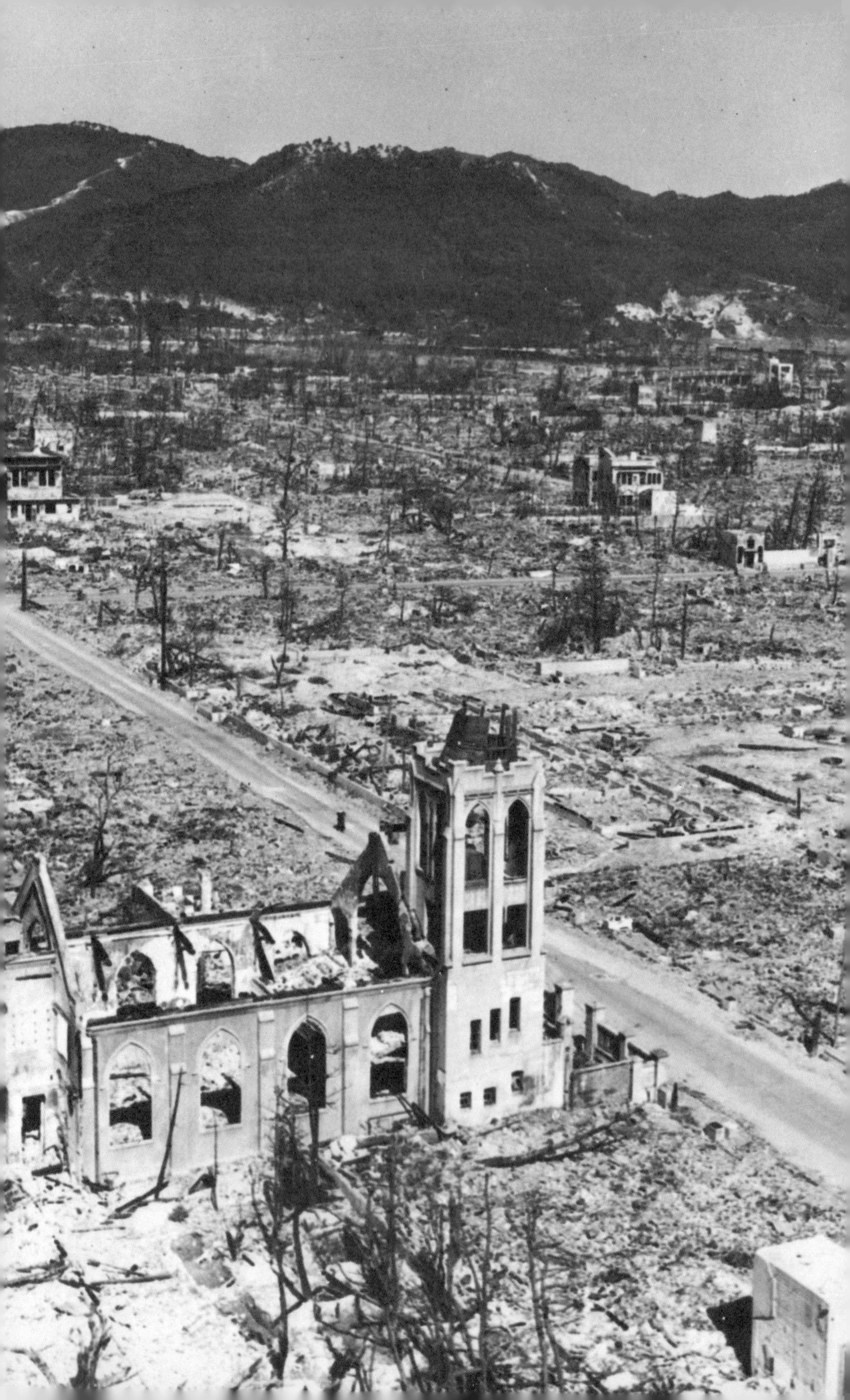

UNITARIAN UNIVERSALIST ASSOCIATION

Central to the democratic tradition of the United States is the inalienable right and unalterable duty of each citizen to obey the voice of conscience.

Liberal religion traditionally has recognized the right of its members to liberty of individual thought and conscience in all matters.

There have been in our Unitarian Universalist denomination, and its predecessors, individuals compelled by conscience to abstain from participation in war and its preparation.

The American Unitarian Association and the Universalist Church of America have repeatedly affirmed their support to those members who have taken the position of conscientious objection to military service.

The government of the United States for two decades has officially recognized the right of conscientious objectors not to participate in war and has provided several forms of alternative service.

Therefore the Board of Trustees of the Unitarian Universalist Association reaffirms its tradition and the position of its predecessor associations and recognizes the right of its members to refuse to bear arms.

The Association further supports the right of conscientious objectors to choose among several alternatives, and believes that individuals should be supported in the exercise of their moral choice publicly to refuse to register for Selective Service or publicly to refuse classifications which are contrary to their consciences.

The Association calls upon its ministers and other denominational leaders to give counsel and to aid persons considering conscientious objection.

The Association rejoices at the widening legal interpretations in the United States of "religious training and belief" and urges all young men committed to conscientious objection to apply for exemption, however liberal their theological convictions.

The Association calls upon all its members, especially those in local churches and fellowships, to maintain the bonds of love and fellowship with those who, because of conscience, refuse to participate in war.

The Association continues the Registry of Conscientious Objectors whereby any member, however young, may record with the Association nationally his membership in a local Unitarian Universalist church or fellowship and at the same time a statement of the reasons for his conscientious objection, such information to be made available on request to the proper governmental authorities.

The Association continues its responsibility for providing alternate service in lieu of induction for Class I-O registrants by assigning them

Hiroshima after the atomic bomb was dropped, August 6, 1945, killing 60,175 people.

to voluntary service programs of the Unitarian Universalist Service Committee, Inc., and by maintaining administrative responsibility and supervision of all Class I-O registrants so assigned under criteria established by the Association and within budgetary limitations established by the Board of Trustees.

(This statement was adopted by the Unitarian Universalist Association on October 11-12, 1965 and amended June 17-18, 1966.)

In view of possible reinstatement of military conscription and in light of expanding ROTC programs, the Assembly calls upon Unitarian Universalist members and societies to:
1. Oppose renewal of draft registration and induction.
2. Provide educational and counseling opportunities for draft-eligible youth in our communities.
3. Encourage peace registration of our conscientious objectors.
4. Encourage peace career programs to counterbalance recruitment into military-sponsored "career" preparation programs.
5. Urge action to eliminate ROTC programs in high schools and colleges.

(From Statement by the 18th Annual General Assembly, Unitarian Universalist Association, East Lansing, MI, June 25-30, 1979.)

BE IT RESOLVED: that the 1980 General Assembly of the Unitarian Universalist Association call upon its societies to establish, support, and encourage educational and counseling programs, so that all men and women may make informed decisions regarding registration for the draft and the option of conscientious objection or non-violent civil disobedience, with particular concern for those forced to consider military service by pressures of economic or racial discrimination.

(General Assembly, 1980.)

The Unitarian Universalist Association maintains a Registry of Conscientious Objectors. To be qualified for registration the applicant must provide the Unitarian Universalist Association with certification of his church membership and a written statement of his religious objection to participation in war. Such recorded statements shall be made available to the proper governmental authorities upon request.

FOR FURTHER INFORMATION: Write to the Unitarian Universalist Association, Registry for Conscientious Objectors, 25 Beacon Street, Boston, MA 02108.

UNITED CHURCH OF CHRIST

WHEREAS the United Church of Christ values the heritage of both the Congregational Christian Churches and the Evangelical and Reformed Church, particularly in their common testimony that every Christian has the right and the responsibility to make his daily decisions in the love of God and in the obedience to His living Word; and

WHEREAS there are within our fellowship members in good standing who are conscientiously opposed to participation in war or to military training and service, on the ground that war is incompatible with their Christian commitment; and

WHEREAS the United Church of Christ desires to hold within its fellowship in love all those whose consciences are bound to Christ—those who accept the call to military service as well as those who refuse to participate in it; and

WHEREAS both the General Council of Congregational Christian Churches and the General Synod of the Evangelical and Reformed Church have heretofore designated their appropriate instrumentalities to offer guidance and counsel to conscientious objectors in maintaining the integrity of conscience;

BE IT RESOLVED that the General Synod of the United Church of Christ affirm its recognition of the right of conscientious objection to participation in or support of war, extend moral and spiritual support to the members of its constituent congregations who for conscience' sake seek exemption from military service and elect the alternative of civilian national service provided in the law, call upon its pastors and congregations to hold closely within the fellowship of the church those who take this position, and charge the Board for Homeland Ministries to provide such information and assistance as may be desirable and necessary to aid such conscientious objectors in the enjoyment of their rights and in the fulfillment of their responsibilities.

(Statement of The General Synod of the United Church of Christ, Adopted July 7, 1961.)

WHEREAS the General Synod of the United Church of Christ, in keeping with the tradition of both the Evangelical and Reformed and the Congregational Christian Churches, has affirmed that "every Christian has the right and the responsibility to make his daily decisions in the love of God and in obedience to his living Word" and

WHEREAS the General Synod has by resolution previously taken action to "affirm its recognition of the right of conscientious objection to participation in or support of war," to "extend moral and spiritual support to the members of its constituent congregations who for conscience' sake seek exemption from military service and elect the alternative of civilian national service provided in the law," and to "call upon its pastors and congregations to hold closely within the fellowship of the church those who take this position"; and

WHEREAS there are, both within and without the fellowship of the United Church of Christ, persons who do not renounce the use of military force as in itself inconsistent with their understanding of their moral obligation but at the same time are persuaded on grounds of conscience that war under any given particular circumstances is wrong and that, therefore, they cannot under these conditions engage in military service; and

WHEREAS they are led to this conclusion by such factors as their belief that the nation has not adequately explored peaceful means of settling international disputes, that the aims of a particular war cannot be ethically justified, that the means used for the prosecution of the war violate the moral standards which should prevail among nations, or that the probable evil consequences would greatly outweigh the hoped-for good; and

WHEREAS such a decision, taking into account the many dimensions of the situation and of the individual's obligations, is a valid expression of a Christian's responsibility to make his daily decisions in the love of God and in obedience to his living Word; and

WHEREAS conscientious objectors are in any case required to substantiate their position before local draft boards, the burden of proof resting upon the individual taking this position;

THEREFORE BE IT RESOLVED that the General Synod of the United Church of Christ recognize the right of conscientious objection to participation in a particular war or in war waged under particular circumstances, as well as the right of conscientious objection to participation in war as such; and

BE IT FURTHER RESOLVED that the General Synod remind those who are disposed to take this position that they ought not to do so lightly but only after careful examination and weighing of their own motives, the moral issues at stake including their proper obligations to the nation as an instrument of justice and order, the social as well as personal consequences of their decision, and their readiness to accept military or civilian service of equivalent time, risk, and personal inconvenience if afforded them, or else such penalties as may be legally imposed; and

BE IT FURTHER RESOLVED that the General Synod call upon pastors, congregations, Conferences, officers, and instrumentalities of the Church, and specifically upon the Board for Homeland Ministries to provide information, assistance, and counsel for those who take this position in order that they may both maintain integrity of conscience and find suitable alternative means for discharging their obligation as citizens in a time of national emergency or danger; and

BE IT FURTHER RESOLVED that the General Synod urge the Congress of The United States to amend the Selective Service Act to provide suitable alternatives of military or civilian service for those who on grounds of conscience object to participation in a particular war.
(Statement adopted by the General Synod of the United Church of Christ, June 1967.)

WHEREAS, the Bible in such passages as Isaiah 2:4, "They shall beat their swords into plowshares" and Matthew 5:9, "Blessed are the Peacemakers" exhorts us to be peacemakers and peacekeepers, and

WHEREAS, the United Church of Christ, 3rd General Synod in 1961 adopted a resolution, affirmed and amended in 1971, which said in part:
". . . the United Church of Christ desires to hold within its fellowship in love all those whose consciences are bound to Christ—those who accept the call to military service as well as those who refuse to participate in it,"

THEREFORE BE IT RESOLVED that the Thirteenth General Synod reaffirms the ministry of the United Church of Christ pertaining to conscientious objectors; and

BE IT FURTHER RESOLVED that the 13th General Synod of the United Church of Christ calls upon all members and churches to support with prayers, love, and counsel, members and non-members who are conscientious objectors to war.

(Resolution of Support for the Conscientious Objector to War, 13th General Synod, 1981.)

FOR FURTHER INFORMATION: Write to Lee Moore, Board for Homeland Ministries, United Church of Christ, 132 W. 31st St., New York, NY 10001.

UNITED MOLOKAN CHRISTIAN ASSOCIATION

We the Russian Molokan Christian Spiritual Jumpers, a religious sect, in the United States, petition the government as follows:

From our forefathers, through the Holy Spirit, we have an inherent Spiritual Christian teaching which forbids military training, military service, and participation in war in any form.

For this faith, the founders of our religion were compelled to submit to severe suffering, tortures, and deadly bodily punishment. They were exiled to Siberia and to the wild regions of trans-Caucasia. Molokans were then given exemption from military service for fifty years, and upon the expiration of these fifty years, the Russian Tsarist Government inaugurated compulsory military service in Trans-Caucasia, and for a continuous period of about five years thereafter, our forefathers, without success, pleaded with that government for the exemption of our people from such service.

Therefore, following in the footsteps of their forefathers and fulfilling God's Holy Covenant, they were compelled to leave their native country and their material possessions.

In the early part of this century, our forefathers emigrated to the United States, where they, and now we, their descendants, have found peace, comfort, and liberty.

In the year of 1917, during the First World War, our people petitioned the President of the United States for exemption from military service, on a religious basis only. Their petition was acknowledged by the government, and they become recognized as religious objectors, although they were exempted as aliens. However, a number of our people elected not to register and they were imprisoned.

Again, in the year 1940, another petition was presented to the President by the Molokan elders on behalf of its community, asking for recognition as religious conscientious objectors. During World War II, this principle was adhered to by Molokan young men who worked in Civilian Work Camps in lieu of military service, and by some young Molokans who were imprisoned on the basis of their consciences.

During the years between the end of the Second World War and the present time, Molokans continued to maintain their position as religious conscientious objectors.

Today, the principle of religious objection to war remains prominent as a basic position in the over-all Molokan faith, as it did during its formation by its founding fathers and martyrs.

Wherefore, in view of what we have herein expressed, we once again re-affirm our position as religious objectors in that we cannot accept military training, military service, and participation in all wars. We pray that you grant complete exemption for our young men and women in accordance with our religious convictions.

We humbly rejoice in the blessings of the Lord for the freedom, peace, and prosperity afforded to us under the Constitution of the United States, and we continue to pray for the Lord's blessing upon this great country and its people.

We the presbyters, respectfully submit this petition with the consent of the membership of our brotherhood.

(Petition to the President, the White House, Congressmen and other U.S. officials signed by the presbyters March 1980.)

FOR FURTHER INFORMATION: Write to the Molokan Advisory Board, P.O. Box 447, Montebello, CA 90640.

UNITED PENTECOSTAL CHURCH, INTERNATIONAL

We recognize the institution of human government as being of divine ordination, and in so doing, affirm unswerving loyalty to our Government; however, we take a definite position regarding the bearing of arms or the taking of human life.

As followers of the Lord Jesus Christ, the Prince of Peace, we believe in implicit obedience to His commandments and precepts, which instruct us as follows; "...that we resist not evil..." (Matt. 5:39); "Follow peace with all men..." (Hebrews 12:14). (See also Matt. 26:52; Rom. 12:19; James 5:6; Revelation 13:10). These we believe and interpret to mean Christians should not shed blood nor take human life.

Therefore, we propose to fulfill all the obligations of loyal citizens, but are constrained to declare against participating in combatant service in war, armed insurrection, property destruction, aiding or abetting in or the actual destruction of human life.

Furthermore, we cannot conscientiously affiliate with any union, boycott, or organization which will force or bind any of its members to belong to any organization, perform any duties contrary to our conscience, or receive any mark, without our right to affirm or reject same.
(From Articles of Faith of the United Pentecostal Church, 1930.)

However, we regret the false impression created by some groups of so-called "conscientious objectors" that to obey the Bible is to have a contempt for law or magistrates, to be disloyal to our Government and in sympathy with our enemies, or to be unwilling to sacrifice for the preservation of our commonwealth. This attitude would be as contemptible to us as to any patriot. The Word of God commands us to do violence to no man. It also commands us that first of all we are to pray for rulers of our country. We therefore, exhort our members to freely and willingly respond to the call of our Government except in the matter of bearing arms. When we say service, we mean service—no matter how hard or dangerous. The true church has no more place for cowards than has the nation. First of all, however, let us earnestly pray that we will with honor be kept out of war.

We believe that we can be consistent in serving our government in certain noncombatant capacities, but not in the bearing of arms.
(From Articles of Faith of the United Pentecostal Church, 1940.)

FOR FURTHER INFORMATION: Write to United Pentecostal Church International, 8855 Dunn Rd., Hazelwood, MO 63042.

WORLDWIDE CHURCH OF GOD (FORMERLY RADIO CHURCH OF GOD)

It is the conviction and firm belief of this Church and its membership that Christian disciples of Christ are forbidden by Him and the commandments of God to kill, or in any manner directly or indirectly to take human life, by whatsoever means; we believe that bearing arms is directly contrary to this fundamental doctrine of our belief; we therefore conscientiously refuse to bear arms or to come under the military authority.
(Statement from the Consitution and By-Laws of the Worldwide Church of God, Article X, Section 2.)

FOR FURTHER INFORMATION: Write to Worldwide Church of God, 300 W. Green St., Pasadena, CA 91109.

WORLD COUNCIL OF CHURCHES

The Committee recommends:

1. Conscientious objection shall be recognized as objection to performing military training or service, and to performing combatant duties or activities in support of war, with the understanding that every conscientious objector has the duty to render equivalent service toward the safeguarding of the community.

2. In countries where legislation provides for the recognition of conscientious objection, conscientious objectors should make use of such provisions, including registration and other arrangements for an orderly witness to conscience.

3. In every country a conscientious objector shall be entitled to appeal to an impartially constituted civilian tribunal established to deal with cases of conscientious objection.

4. The proceedings of all civilian tribunals for conscientious objectors shall be open to the public.

5. In no country shall the death penalty be imposed in peace or war, upon any civilian for conscientious objection. The conscientious objector as such shall suffer no derogation of human rights.

6. A conscientious objector shall be entitled to exemption from the normal requirements of the laws of military training and service, it being understood that provisions shall be made for exemption in one of the following ways:
 (a) exemption without conditions;
 (b) exemption conditional upon the acceptance of work of a civilian nature under civilian control, such work to be specified by a civilian tribunal;
 (c) exemption conditional upon the performances of non-combatant duties only.

7. Every conscientious objector granted exemption shall receive a certificate of status and exemption for purposes of identification.

8. An applicant for registration as a conscientious objector who is aggrieved by any order of a civilian tribunal for conscientious objectors shall be entitled to appeal to a higher civilian tribunal.

9. A conscientious objector shall be entitled at any time to request a civilian tribunal to change the classification of his exemption.

10. With due recognition of the sacrifices demanded of all citizens in time of crisis, the conditions of alternative non-military service to which a conscientious objector is directed shall not be different from current conditions of similar non-military employment.

11. A conscientious objector performing alternate service of a non-military character shall be entitled to appeal to the tribunal if required to perform work which he deems to be of a military nature.

12. A conscientious objector shall be in the same position as a person in military service in respect to reinstatement in his previous occupation after this period of service.

13. The "noncombatant" conscientious objector shall be entitled to receive an official assurance that he will not be called upon at any time to bear arms.

NOTE: In every case these rights should be taken to apply equally to women as to men.

That member churches and National Commissions be invited to study the above provisions and to report their proposals for modification and amendment.

That, when the reports of member churches and National Commissions show sufficient agreement on specific provisions to ensure the right of conscientious objection, the Church Commission on International Affairs (CCIA) be requested to seek their incorporation in international agreements.

incorporation in international agreements.

That meanwhile the CCIA in its inter-governmental contacts be requested to continue its support of such general provisions to insure the right of conscientious objection as are known to be widely endorsed within its constituency.

(Adopted by Central Committee of the World Council of Churches, 1951.)

Protection of conscience demands that the churches should give spiritual care and support not only to those serving in armed forces but also those who, especially in the light of the nature of modern warfare, object to participation in particular wars they feel bound in conscience to oppose, or who find themselves unable to bear arms or to enter the military service of their nations for reasons of conscience. Such support should include pressure to have the law changed where this is required, and be extended to all in moral perplexity about scientific work on weapons of mass human destruction.

(From the report of Section IV: **Toward Justice and Peace In International Affairs**, *paragraph 21, to the Fourth Assembly of the World Council of Churches, 1968. The Assembly approved the substance of this report and commended it to the Churches for study and appropriate action.)*

FOR FURTHER INFORMATION: Write to the United States Conference for the World Council of Churches, 475 Riverside Dr., New York, NY 10027, or to the World Council of Churches, 150, route de Ferney, CH-1211 GENEVE 20, Switzerland.

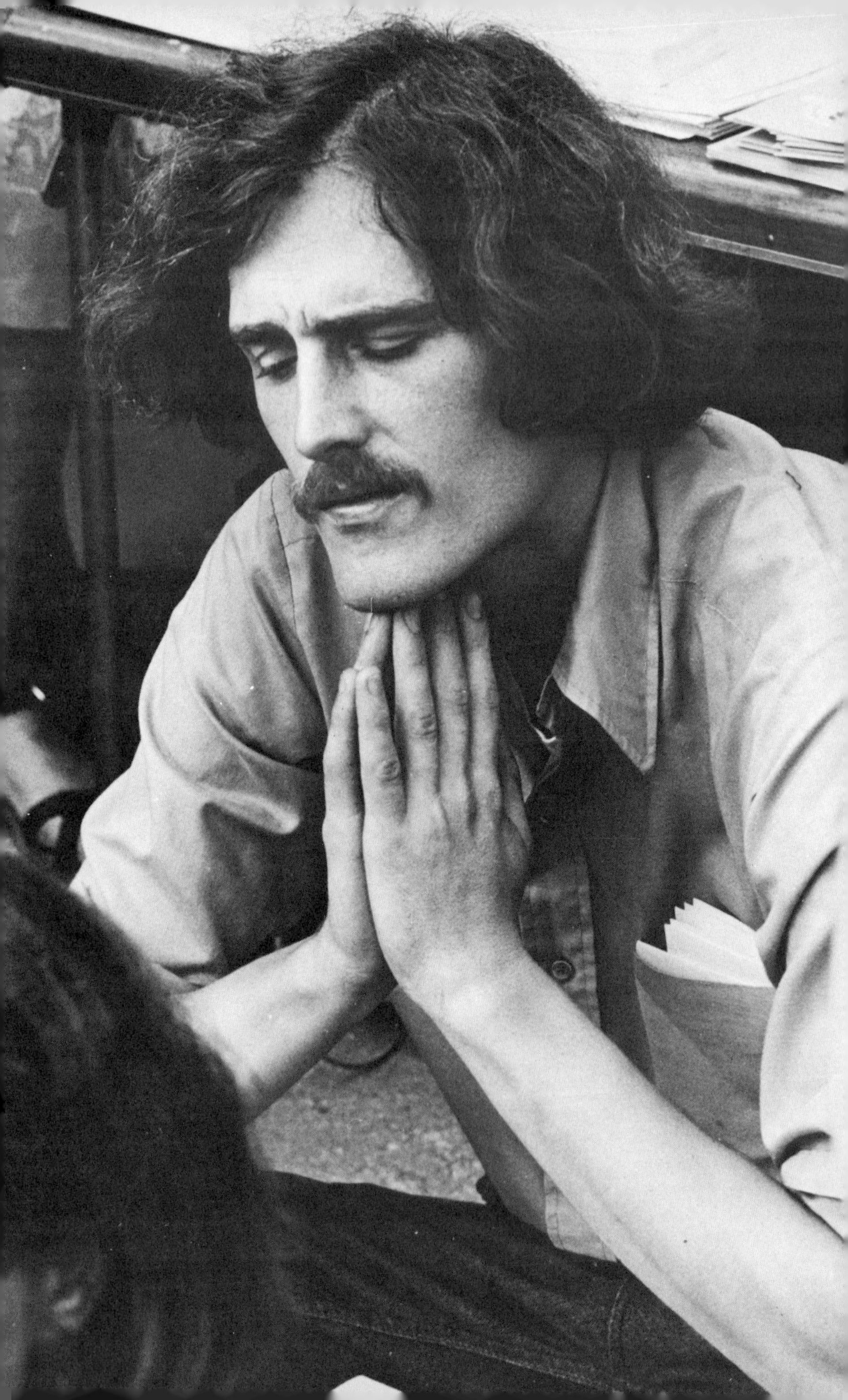

Words of Conscience:

"Unofficial" Statements of Religious Groups

Peace cannot be kept by force.
It can only be achieved
by understanding.

—Albert Einstein

AMERICAN INDIAN

(The following articles are the results of research done by American Indian GIs and their supporters.)

Many Indian men, members of their own natural religions, are drafted into the Armed Services every day. Some of them are natural pacifists, but because they are not pacifists by creed obtained by their membership in a legal religion, their religious freedom often is not respected by Selective Service Boards.

Perhaps the only natural and free religion left in the U.S. exists in the Medicine Lodges of the Plains Indian, the Kivas of the Pueblos, the Smoke Houses of the Northwest Coast Indian, the Long Houses of the Eastern Indians—for they have not seen any reason to write a bible or articles of faith . . . they have no charter issued to them by the legal world system and still remain a natural, spiritual religion undefiled by the tampering of man.

Because the legal religions do have a charter issued to them from the legal world they receive protection from their laws where freedom of religion is concerned. The natural religions of the Indians are not so protected. The Command Authority at Fort Lewis military base has stated to us over and over that our religion is not a recognized or authorized religion and therefore they are not required by their rules and regulations to respect the religious beliefs of the Indians.

Many of the Indian people do not recognize the forced citizenship act of 1924 and, consequently, do not consider themselves citizens of the United States, but look at themselves as citizens of the natural world and universe. As a result of that outlook, some Indian men do not feel that they should appease the legal world and its assumed authority over the people of the world and they simply refuse to recognize the draft or respond to its demands to serve as instruments of war.

—Janet McCloud, Tulalip

SOME BASIS FOR INDIAN BELIEFS

There is a legal world but there is no legal universe. There is a legal world controlled by man's law.

There is a universe and it is a natural universe which is controlled by the natural laws of the Great Spirit.

The Great Spirit is the creator of the natural universe so this gives him the sole authority to make its laws.

The perfection of this natural creation is so great that much of it is self operated by its own law—(these natural laws and spiritual laws operate themselves but it takes men to make man-laws and they are inert things which require men to operate them.) Because men have free will given them by The Great Spirit under the spiritual and natural laws—legal minded men have created their legal oriented world or culture controlled by their own laws, and they have put their man-made laws above the spiritual and natural laws of the natural universe and the Great Spirit.

On the other hand, these natural persons of the natural brotherhood and sisterhood are believers in The Great Spirit and their church is the house of natural world which is one of the many houses in the natural universe. In this house The Great Spirit is the Supreme Being.

1) If we say that the relationship between the worshipper of the Great Spirit and the Great Spirit is an individual relationship—then we can have no church in the usual sense of the word—as used in the legal world.
2) These believers are able to assemble together in association with each other, but no such group has anything to say and no control over this relationship between any such individual—he has no say over the relationship of any other individual with The Great Spirit.
3) The Great Spirit is the Supreme Being and the Supreme Authority because it is the creator of all. No person, no church, no nation and no world can without blasphemy and the penalties involved in blasphemy put themselves in place of ar above the Great Spirit. This includes the man-made laws and the legal world. If anyone tries to do this they are making The Great Spirit out of themselves and they are blasphemers and idolators and cannot do this without suffering perhaps death, because they are created beings, not the creators of beings.

DISCUSSION OF PROPOSED TERMINOLOGY TO BE USED IN C.O. APPLICATIONS

Terminology is to be restricted as much as possible to have a minimum of terms so that the natural religion will not fall into the trap that all civilized religions have fallen into—defined to the last detail and therefore limited by man-made laws.

The civilized religions proceeded by having a religious philosophy; these philosophies are attempts by men to limit, define and thus control religion and ultimately to god. They progress to laws and systems and rituals that become such a big barrier that is impossible for any man to get to god and spiritual benefits within that system. Therefore if we can restrict our use of terms to a minimum quantity we won't get into the law of man's legal system and we will remain in the Great Spirit's law.

The following definitions are suggested;

Between a person and the Great Spirit there is an individual relationship and no other man and no other country and no other religion or culture has a right to say what will be between that person and the Great Spirit—as the Great Spirit is the god of the universe and the Supreme Being above all things.

The natural religions of earth are made up of natural-minded members, who are a natural group of people living locally according to the laws of the Great Spirit, which are universal laws.

We have no right to make legal definitions under man laws to try and put The Great Spirit in the legal world. The legal world has been at war with the natural world throughout the history of the legal world AND THE NATURAL CHURCH DOES NOT WANT TO BE AT WAR WITH ANYONE. War and competition amongst mortals is not the way of The Great Spirit, natural people want to be at peace because no man has the authority to kill another man. So the legal world's war with the natural world has been a one-sided war. The legal world is the aggressor and the natural world still does not want to make war, either against human beings or the environment. The Church of the natural world is their way of life, the way they live in their connection with The Great Spirit and the natural universe. The laws they obey are the universal laws made by The Great Spirit.

(Excerpted from material gathered by HEW-KECAW-NA-YO (To Resist) P.O. Box H, Yelm, WA 98597 (1971) and published in newsletter of the Native American Free University.

Excerpts from the First Hopi Message to the President of the United States:

Hopi Indian Empire
Oraibi, Arizona
March 28, 1949

The President
The White House
Washington, D.C.

To the President:

We, the hereditary Hopi Chieftains of the Hopi pueblos of Hoteville, Shungopovy, and Mushongnovi humbly request a word with you.

Thoroughly acquainted with the wisdom and knowledge of our traditional form of government and our religious principles, sacredly authorized and entrusted to speak, act, and to execute our duties and obligations for all the common people throughout this land of the Hopi Empire in accordance with the fundamental principles of life which were laid down for us by our Great Spirit, Masau'u, and by our forefathers, we hereby assembled in the Hopi Pueblo in Shungopovy . . . make known to the government of the United States and others in this land that the Hopi Empire is still in existence, its traditional path unbroken and its religious order intact, and the Stone Tablets, upon which are written the boundaries of the Hopi Empire, are still in the hands of the Chiefs of Oraibi and Hoteville pueblos.

. . . We speak as the first people in this land you call America. And we speak to you, a white man, the last people who came to our shores seeking freedom of worship, speech, assembly and a right to life, liberty, and the pursuit of happiness. And we are speaking to all the American Indian people . . .

The Hopi form of government was established solely upon religious and traditional grounds. The divine plan of life in this land was laid out for us by our Great Spirit, Masau'u . . . We can not do otherwise but to follow this plan . . .

This land is a sacred home of the Hopi people and all the Indian Race in this land. It was given to the Hopi people the task to guard this land. Not by force of arms, not by killing, not by confiscating of properties of others, but by humble prayers, by obedience to our traditional and religious instructions and by being faithful to our Great Spirit, Masau'u. We are still a sovereign nation. Our flag still flies throughout our land (the flag of our ancient ruins). We have never abandoned our sovereignty to any foreign power or nation. We've been self-governing people long before any white man came to our shores. What Great Spirit made and planned no power on earth can change.

Now we have heard about the Atlantic security treaty. . .an alliance in which an attack against one would be considered an attack against all.

We the traditional leaders want you and the American people to know that we will stand firmly upon our own tradition and religious grounds. And that **we will not bind** ourselves to any foreign nation at this time. Neither will we go with you on a wild and reckless adventure which we know will lead us only to a total ruin. Our Hopi form of government is all set and ready for such eventuality. We have met all other rich and powerful nations who have come to our shores, from the early Spanish Conquistadores down to the present government of the United States, all of whom have used force in trying to wipe out our existence here in our own home. We want to come to our destiny in our own way. We have no enemy. We will neither show our bows and arrows to anyone at this time. This is our only way to everlasting life and happiness. Our traditional and religious training forbids us to harm, kill and molest anyone. We, therefore, objected to our boys being forced to be trained for war to become murderers and destroyers. It is you who should protect us. What nation who has taken up arms ever brought peace and happiness to his people?

All the laws under the Constitution of the United States were made without our consent, knowledge, and approval yet we are being forced to do everything that we know is contrary to our religious principles and those principles of the Constitution of the United States.

Now we ask you, American people, what has become of your religion and your tradition? Where do we stand today? The time has now come for all of us as leaders of our people to reexamine ourselves. The judgement day will soon be upon us. Let us set our house in order before it is too late.

BLACK MUSLIM

The Nation of Islam is based on a belief in Allah as the Supreme Being, and the Koran or Holy Qur'an is the chief source of its dogma. The religious doctrines and rituals of the members of the Nation, also known as Muslims or Black Muslims, are derived largely from classical Islam, but their beliefs on certain fundamental points have clearly been shaped by the experience of the black man in the United States.[3] Despite certain wide departures from the traditions of orthodox Islam, however, Elijah Muhammad, the Nation's spiritual leader, was welcomed to Mecca in 1960 by the powerful Hajj Committee, which is responsible for accepting or rejecting pilgrims journeying to the Holy City.[4]

Elijah Muhammad explained the meaning of Islam in his **Message to the Blackman in America** (1965) (Ex. D to Special Hearing, A. 41a) in this way:

"The author of Islam is Allah (God). We just cannot imagine God

---

[3] C. E. Lincoln, *The Black Muslims in America* 219 (1961). The Nation's formal organization can be traced to the early 1930s in Chicago, but its spiritual roots probably lie in the Moorish Science Temple movement of Noble Drew Ali and the United Negro Improvement Association of Marcus Garvey, both of which flourished after World War I. *Id.* at 50. Ever since the early years of the movement Elijah Muhammad, known as the "Prophet" and the "Messenger of Allah," has been its spiritual leader. Under his guidance, the membership of the Nation of Islam has increased to what was conservatively estimated at 100,000 in 1961, with more than fifty temples in major cities from coast to coast. *Id.* at 217.

[4] B. E. Garnett, "Invaders From the Black Nation: The Black Muslims in 1970," p. 12. Special Report, Race Relations Information Center, Nashville, Tenn. (1970)

being the author of any other religion but one of peace. Since peace is the very nature of Allah (God), and peace He seeks for his people and peace is the nature of the righteous, most surely Islam is the religion of peace (p. 68).

"The very dominant idea in Islam is the making of peace and not war; our refusing to go armed is our proof that we want peace" (p. 322). Muslims are, therefore, forbidden to carry weapons or to participate in any war and one of the central dogmas of their faith states:
"We believe that we who declared ourselves to be righteous Muslims should not participate in wars which take the lives of humans" (*Id.* at 164).

The only use of force that is consistent with the Muslim faith is self-defense, which Elijah Muhammad believes is justified by God and by Divine Law (*Id.* at 217). But even then, Muslims may not use weapons; if they are attacked by armed persons they must rely upon Allah to protect them (*Id.* at 319).[15]

Although Muslim doctrine condemns war among nations and men, an ultimate theocratic war has an important place in religion. This war is foreseen as one directed by Allah which will destroy the enemies of the black people. After this destruction, which is variously described as a series of natural disasters, the falling of bombs from a wheel shaped plane in the sky or an ultimate war among nations, black people will live in peace under the guidance of Allah (*Id.* at 270, 291-92).

"We believe that we who declare ourselves to be righteous Muslims, should not participate in wars which take the lives of humans. We do not believe this nation should force us to take part in such wars, for we have nothing to gain from it unless America agrees to give us the necessary territory wherein we may have something to fight for" (A. 120a).

(Excerpted from Brief for Petitioner in Clay (Muhammad Ali) v. United States, U.S. Supreme Court, October Term, 1970, pp. 15, 30-32.

---

[15] The Black Muslim doctrines concerning war can be clearly traced, moreover, to the Holy Qur'an, translated by Maulana Muhammad Ali which was submitted by petitioner as Exhibit C at the Special Hearing (A. 41a). This version of the Qur'an views war as an evil that can only be justified when it is necessary to defend Muslims against religious persecution. See Maulana Muhammad Ali, *Translation of the Holy Qur'an* 2:190, 2:191, 2:216, 2:17 and commentary at pp. 80-81, notes 238, 239, pp. 90-91, note 277 (5th ed. 1963).

HINDU

The caste personality determines one's social duties, including war which thus cannot become the duty of the citizens of all castes and all personality traits indiscriminately. This duty, based on natural disposition, and the sacred law binding an individual to do such duty is called *dharma*. There is no other law but the law of *dharma*. According to the epic scripture *Mahabharata*, "when all citizens (indiscriminately) take the weapons, they transgress their respective natural duties *(dharmas)* "— *Santi-parvan* 78.12 (Gita Press edition). "Better death in the discharge of one's own dharma; the *dharma* of another is frought with danger"—*Bhagavadgita* III. 35. This limits the war duty only to a segment of the citizenry, to a volunteer army and not to a conscript army, only to those who are predisposed towards such a life.

. . . a war tempered with restraints is more ethical than a war totally unrestrained. So that objection to selected wars is appropriate.

The principle of a limited war can be accepted only because
(a) not all people can be equally non-violent; they may use their rajasic tendencies in the service of the non-violent.
(b) the non-violent are often attacked by those who cannot curb their violence.

This would seem to echo exactly the arguments of the warmongers of all times who attempt to justify their wars as 'righteous'. However, the argument of the *Bhagavadgita* is very clear in the passages below:

"The supreme self is in harmony with him who is self-conquered and pacific; (such a one is alike) in heat and cold, pain and pleasure as well as in honour and dishonour. VI. 7.

"He who regards impartially lovers, friends and foes, strangers, neutrals, aliens and kinsmen, also the righteous and unrighteous, he excels. VI. 9.

"He from whom the people do not get perturbed (and draw away), and who does not draw away from the people, free from the anxieties of joy, anger and fear, he is dear to me. XII. 15.

The decision to engage in a battle must be taken after one has totally freed himself of all mental agitation. One must be freed of all anger and ill-will, with no selfish aims or ego, no mental fever. When one has reached such a state of equilibrium, a battle can be fought only as an act of devotion to a duty to protect and guard, and not to win and conquer others. The only true conquest is the conquest over oneself; he who has not conquered the self is not qualified to engage in a battle with others. In other words, *one may fight a battle within the macrocosmic self as one fights battles of good against evil within his own microcosmic self.* Such a war can be undertaken only after careful introspection, only after removing all ill-will, anger, personal ego and national pride, only as an act of service, otherwise it is an unrighteous war. A righteous war, then, would be extremely hard to embark upon, and only as a last resort; because of the purity and strength of character of the participants, such a war will never be lost.

It is obvious, then, that any war in which non-combatants, civilians, suffer is not a *dharma-yuddha* and any *ksatriya* whether a conscript or a volunteer, participating in such a war would be violating his religious and moral obligations; furthermore, under a constitution based on Hindu principles, he will lose his rights to sit in any council, especially if the specific war was disapproved of by the educators and the clergymen of the country. There is, of course, no question of anyone participating in war who is primarily devoted to pursuits of knowledge and intellect *(brahmana)*, trade, industry and agriculture *(vaisya)* or even mere physical labour *(sudra)*. In practice *only those may participate in a war who prove themselves to be personalities of the rajasic type.*

In a society where this principle is observed, the *conscientious warrior alone* will be recruited, after demonstrating his inclinations in psychological tests and social/educational situations . . . In a society accepting such a principle *everyone is a conscientious objector unless proved otherwise.*

In conclusion, to be applicable to modern western states, the principles we are discussing can be summed up as follows:

1) Total non-violence is the aim of any civilized society, and it is the state's duty to inculcate this principle in all its citizens.

2) Only those who have predominately rajasic tendencies may volunteer for army service.

3) There cannot be a conscript army.

4) All citizens and soldiers *must* refuse to co-operate in a war in which civilians are liable to get hurt. (A civilian is anyone unarmed; anyone armed and participating in the war is a soldier). Thus, there *can* be objection to specific wars even by soldiers in a volunteer army.

5) All citizens are conscientious non-participants in a war unless proved otherwise. The burden of proof rests on the state.

6) Those engaged in intellectual pursuits are in the same category as priests (the Hindus regard brahmins to be educators/priests). Also those in economically productive professions are free from army duty.

7) If the Hindu-Buddhist ideal is practiced, education should be the

fourth separate principle of power in a modern state along with the executive, legislative and the judiciary. Educators should hold the right to curb any infringements of such moral principles as non-violence.

8) The sum total of the pain and pleasure in the whole world should be the primary consideration of all civilized states. A war being waged to enhance the selfish aims of a given state is illegal.

9) Following (8) above, citizens have a duty towards the world community which surpasses duty to their own countries. A citizen may challenge a war if it harms the world community.

10) The citizens do not have uniform duties towards the state. Each citizen makes his contribution according to his own psychological make-up. This, of course, also applies to participation in a war.

11) There cannot be uniform laws enforceable on all citizens without consideration of their individual dispositions.

Finally, the question of conscientious objection cannot be resolved in isolation. It is interwoven with moral and political philosophies and constitutional structures of the modern states. The Hindu view regards only the meditative union of individual self with the Universal Self as the goal of all aspects of life; all that goes against this goal is invalid and unethical.

(Excerpted from a paper "Hinduism and Conscientious Objection to War" by Usharbudh Arya.) Published **East and West** *(Journal of the Italian Institute of the Middle and Far East), 1-2, vol. xxii 1972.*

ISLAM

The word Islam comes from the root, **silm,** which literally means peace; its translation by some western scholars as Mohammedanism (or the religion of Mohammed) is not only a semantic mistake but a basic and substantial mistake. Unlike Christianity, Buddhism, or Jainism, Islam is not named after its founder, but after its central purpose which is the promotion of peace and good fellowship in the world. In the words of the Koran: "There has been not a community to which God's messengers have not come and Muslims should make no distinctions between them." The Islamic concept of God is not the god of any particular race, nation, or community, but of the entire human race and a source of **rahlmat** (beneficience) for all. Its greeting for everyone is "Peace be upon you," whether one be Hindu, Muslim, Christian, Buddhist, Parsi, Jew—or atheist for that matter. In love, service, unwillingness to offend, settling of disputes by amicable discussion, and the promotion of peace lies the reality of life. They are the objectives of Islam.

Let a few extracts from Hadis speak for themselves: "All God's creatures are his family and He is most beloved of God who does real good to the members of God's family." This means that those who indulge in the game of killing and torture can claim no favored place in God's bosom.

This is an injunction that all individuals and nations today will do well to take to heart: "God fills the heart of him with faith and contentment who, having the power to avenge himself, exercises restraint and toleration."

...Islam tries to knock down one by one the psychological props on which the mentality of hatred and war is built up; it probes into the bigger causes which play their ugly part in the precipitation of modern wars—race, religion, color, and nationality. Islam rejects all these totally and unequivocally. The first person, appointed by the Prophet to the high and much prized office of **meuzzin,** the man who called the faithful to prayer five times a day, was a black named Balal. The white, high-born aristocratic members of the tribe of Quarish were displeased and complained to him. He replied that a righteous, God-fearing Negro was in his view, superior to the highest born member of the tribe of Quarish. This was a knock-out blow to the whole doctrine of race and color superiority, which today is one of the most potent causes of war. He went on to reject the claim of the nation or **patrie** to be the arbiter of right and wrong and refused to accept the support of wrong-doing by one's country as either proof of patriotism or an act of virtue.

The Koran says in uncompromising and unambiguous words:

> O, Ye who believe, be steadfast in the service of God's truth and bear witness for justice and let not hatred of a people seduce you so that you deal with them unjustly. Act justly for that is what piety demands.

Modern war is a technological, nuclear, poison gas, germ war which is calculated to torture and annihilate the human race, to poison the healthy sources of life, including food and water, to maim the unborn child in the mother's womb physically and psychologically, to abolish the frontiers between combatants and noncombatants, and to wipe out the gracious fruits of man's precious cultural heritage. It cannot, obviously, be carried on within the kind of conditions envisioned by Islam.

According to the faith of Islam only good can conquer evil, only love can conquer force. Evil and force can never do so because in their interaction, they set up a chain reaction of hatred and injustice which never ends.

(Excerpted from an essay by K. G. Saiyadain in **World Religion and World Peace***, edited by Homer Jack.*

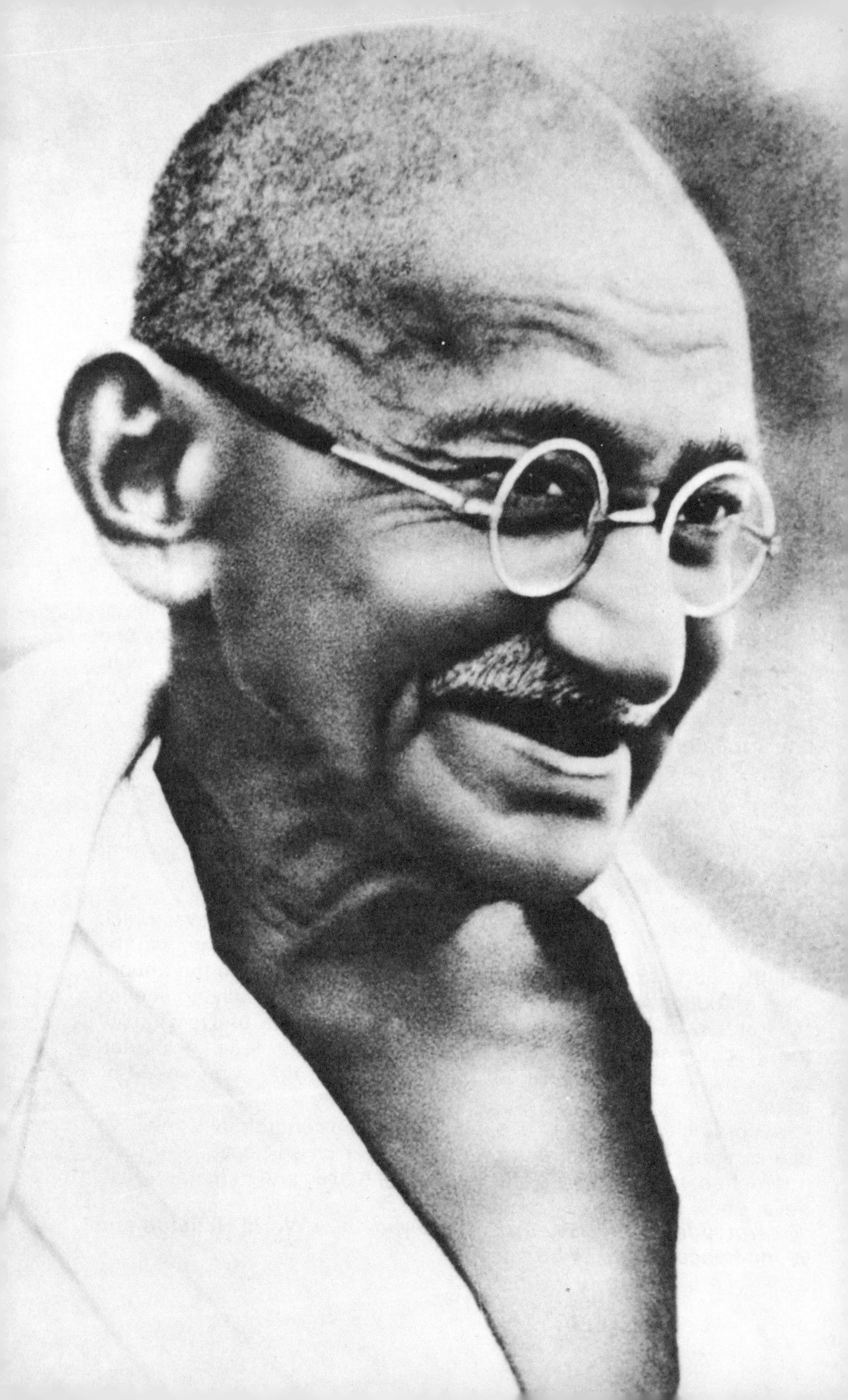

Words of Conscience: Individuals Speak

Conscientious Objector

I shall die, but that is all that I shall do for Death.
I hear him leading his horse out of the stall; I hear the clatter on
 the barn-floor.
He is in haste; he has business in Cuba, business in the Balkans,
 many calls to make this morning.
But I will not hold the bridle while he cinches the girth.
And he may mount by himself: I will not give him a leg up.
Though he flick my shoulders with his whip, I will not tell him
 which way the fox ran.
With his hoof on my breast, I will not tell him where the black
 boy hides in the swamp.
I shall die, but that is all that I shall do for Death; I am not on
 his pay-roll.
I will not tell him the whereabouts of my friends nor of my
 enemies either.
Though he promise me much, I will not map him the route to
 any man's door.
Am I a spy in the land of the living, that I should deliver men to
 Death?
Brother, the passwords and the plans of our city are safe with me;
 never through me
Shall you be overcome.

—Edna St. Vincent Millay

Albert Camus

What with the general fear of a war now being prepared by all nations and the specific fear of murderous ideologies, who can deny that we live in a state of terror? We live in terror because persuasion is no longer possible; because man has been wholly submerged in History; because he can no longer tap that part of his nature, as real as the historical part, which he recaptures in contemplating the beauty of nature and of human faces; because we live in a world of abstractions, of bureaus and machines, of absolute ideas and of crude messianism. We suffocate among people who think they are absolutely right, whether in their machines or in their ideas. And for all who can live only in an atmosphere of human dialogue and sociability, this silence is the end of the world.

To emerge from this terror, we must be able to reflect and to act accordingly. But an atmosphere of terror hardly encourages reflection. I believe, however, that instead of simply blaming everything on this fear, we should consider it as one of the basic factors in the situation, and try to do something about it. No task is more important. For it involves the fate of a considerable number of Europeans who, fed up with the lies and violence, deceived in their dearest hopes and repelled by the idea of killing their fellowmen in order to convince them, likewise repudiate the idea of themselves being convinced that way... And if an atmosphere of fear does not encourage accurate thinking, then they must first of all come to terms with fear.

To come to terms, one must understand what fear means: what it implies and what it rejects. It implies and rejects the same fact: a world where murder is legitimate, and where human life is considered trifling. This is the great political question of our times, and before dealing with other issues, one must take a position on it. Before anything can be done, two questions must be put: "Do you or do you not, directly or indirectly, want to be killed or assaulted? Do you or do you not, directly or indirectly, want to kill or assault?"

... What strikes me, in the midst of polemics, threats and outbursts of violence, is the fundamental good will of everyone. From Right to Left, everyone, with the exception of a few swindlers, believes that his particular truth is the one to make men happy. And yet the combination of all these good intentions has produced the present infernal world, where men are killed, threatened and deported, where war is prepared, where one cannot speak freely without being insulted or betrayed.

We know today that there are no more islands, that frontiers are just lines on a map. We know that in a steadily accelerating world, where the Atlantic is crossed in less than a day and Moscow speaks to

Washington in a few minutes, we are forced into fraternity—or complicity . . .

Many Americans would like to go on living closed off in their own society, which they find good. Many Russians perhaps would like to carry on their Statist experiment holding aloof from the capitalist world. They cannot do so, nor will they ever again be able to do so. Likewise, no economic problem, however minor it appears, can be solved outside the comity of nations. Europe's bread is in Buenos Aires, Siberian machine-tools are made in Detroit. Today, tragedy is collective.

. . . Little is to be expected from present-day government, since these live and act according to a murderous code. Hope remains only in the most difficult task of all: to reconsider everything from the ground up, so as to shape a living society inside a dying society. Men must therefore, as individuals, draw up among themselves, within frontiers and across them, a new social contract which will unite them according to more reasonable principles. . .

To save what can be saved so as to open up some kind of future—that is the prime mover, the passion and the sacrifice that is required. It demands only that we reflect and then decide, clearly, whether humanity's lot must be made still more miserable in order to achieve far-off and shadowy ends, whether we should accept a world bristling with arms where brother kills brother; or whether, on the contrary, we should avoid bloodshed and misery as much as possible so that we give a chance for survival to later generations better equipped than we are.

For my part, I am fairly sure that I have made the choice. And, having chosen, I think that I must speak out, that I must state that I will never again be one of those, whoever they be, who compromise with murder, and that I must take the consequences of such a decision.

We are asked to love or to hate such and such a country and such and such a people. But some of us feel too strongly our common humanity to make such a choice. Those who really love the Russian people, in gratitude for what they have never ceased to be—that world leaven which Tolstoy and Gorky speak of—do not wish for them success in power-politics, but rather want to spare them, after the ordeals of the past, a new and even more terrible bloodletting. So, too, with the American people, and with the peoples of unhappy Europe. This is the kind of elementary truth we are liable to forget amidst the furious passions of our time.

Yes, it is fear and silence and the spiritual isolation they cause that must be fought today. And it is sociability and the universal intercommunication of men that must be defended . . .

To conclude: all I ask is that, in the midst of a murderous world, we agree to reflect on murder and to make a choice. After that, we can distinguish those who accept the consequences of being murderers themselves or accomplices of murderers, and those who refuse to do so with all their force and being.

... But I have always held that, if he who bases his hopes on human nature is a fool, he who gives up in the face of circumstances is a coward. And henceforth, the only honorable course will be to stake everything on a formidable gamble: that words are more powerful than munitions.

(Excerpted from **"Neither Victims nor Executioners"***)*

Dorothy Day

Dorothy Day

We all know that there is a frightful persecution of religion in Spain. Churches have been destroyed and desecrated, priests and nuns have been tortured and murdered in great numbers.

In the light of this fact it is inconceivably difficult to write as we do. It is folly—it seems madness—to say as we do—"we are opposed to the use of force as a means of settling personal, national, or international disputes." As a newspaper trying to affect public opinion, we take this stand. We feel that if the press and the public throughout the world do not speak in terms of the counsels of perfection, who else will?

We pray those martyrs of Spain to help us, to pray for us, to guide us in the stand we take. We speak in their name. Their blood cries out against a spirit of hatred and savagery which aims toward a peace founded upon victory, at the price of resentment and hatred enduring for years to come. Do you suppose they died, saying grimly: "All right—we accept martyrdom—we will not lift the sword to defend ourselves but the lay troops will avenge us!" This would be martyrdom wasted. Blood spilled in vain. Or rather did they say with St. Stephen, "Father, forgive them," and pray with love for their conversion. And did they not rather pray, when the light of Christ burst upon them, that love would overcome hatred, that men *dying* for faith, rather than *killing* for their faith, would save the world?

Truly this is the folly of the cross! But when we say "Savior of the World, save Russia," we do not expect a glittering army to overcome the heresy.

As long as men trust to the use of force—only a superior, a more savage and brutal force will overcome the enemy. We use his own weapons, and we must make sure our own force is more savage, more bestial than his own. As long as we are trusting to force—we are praying for a victory by force.

We are neglecting the one means—prayer and the sacraments—by which whole armies can be overcome. "The King is not saved by a great army," David said. "Proceed as sheep and not wolves," St. John Chrysostom said.

St. Peter drew the sword and our Lord rebuked him. They asked our Lord to prove His Divinity and come down from the cross. But He suffered the "failure" of the cross. His apostles kept asking for a temporal Kingdom. Even with Christ Himself to guide and enlighten them they did not see the primacy of the spiritual. Only when the Holy Ghost descended on them did they see.

Today the whole world has turned to the use of force.

While we take this stand we are not condemning those who have seized arms and engaged in war.

Who of us as individuals if he were in Spain today, could tell what he would do? Or in China? From the human natural standpoint men are doing good to defend their faith, their country. But from the standpoint of the Supernatural—there is the "better way"—the way of the Saints—the way of love.

Who of those who are combating *The Catholic Worker* stand would despise the Christian way—the way of Christ? Not one.

Yet again and again it is said that Christianity is not possible—that it cannot be practiced.

Today the whole world is in the midst of a revolution. We are living through it now—all of us. History will record this time as a time of world revolution. And frankly, we are calling for Saints. The Holy Father in his call for Catholic Action, for the lay apostolate, is calling for Saints. We must prepare now for martyrdom—otherwise we will not be ready. Who of us if he were attacked now would not react quickly and humanly against such attack? Would we love our brother who strikes us? Of all at *The Catholic Worker* how many would not instinctively defend himself with any forceful means in his power? We must prepare. We must prepare now. There must be a disarmament of the heart.

Yes, wars will go on. We are living in a world where even "Nature itself travaileth and groaneth" due to the Fall. But we cannot sit back and say "human nature being what it is, you cannot get a man to overcome his adversary by love."

We are afraid of the word love and yet love is stronger than death, stronger than hatred.

If we do not, as the press, emphasize the law of love, we betray our trust, our vocation. We must stand opposed to the use of force.

St. Paul, burning with zeal, persecuted the church. But he was converted.

Again and again in the history of the church, the conquered overcome the conquerors.

We are not talking of passive resistance. Love and prayer are not passive, but a most active glowing force.

(From **Catholic Worker** *editorial "On the Use of Force." September 1938)*

Mahatma Gandhi

Merely to refuse military service is not enough... this is [to act] after all the time for combating evil is practically gone.

The true democrat is he who with purely non-violent means defends his liberty and therefore his country's and ultimately that of the whole of mankind. In the coming test pacifists have to prove their faith by resolutely refusing to do anything with war, whether of defense or offense. But the duty of resistance accrues only to those who believe in non-violence as a creed—not to those who will calculate and will examine the merits of each case and decide whether to approve or oppose a particular war. It follows that such resistance is a matter for each person to decide for himself and under the guidance of an inner voice, if he recognizes its existence.

It is open to a war resister to judge between the combatants and wish success to the one who has justice on his side. By so judging he is more likely to bring peace between the two than by remaining a mere spectator.

It is permissible for, it is even the duty of, a believer in **ahimsa** ["reverence for life", dynamic harmlessness"] to distinguish between the aggressor and the defender. Having done so, he will side with the defender in a non-violent manner, i.e., give his life in saving him.

To benefit by other's killing and delude oneself into the belief that one is being very religious and nonviolent is sheer self-deception.

So far as I can see, the atomic bomb has deadened the finest feeling that has sustained mankind for ages. There used to be the so-called laws of war which made it tolerable. Now we know the naked truth. War knows no law except that of might. The atom bomb brought an empty victory to the allied arms but it resulted for the time being in destroying the soul of Japan. What has happened to the soul of the destroying nation it is yet too early to see.

(From **NonViolence in Peace & War.***)*

A satyagrahi is nothing if not instinctively law-abiding, and it is his law-abiding nature which exacts from him implicit obedience to the highest law, that is, the voice of conscience which overrides all other laws.

I hate the ruthless exploitation of India even as I hate from the bottom of my heart the hideous system of untouchability for which millions of

Hindus have made themselves responsible. But I do not hate the domineering Englishmen as I refuse to hate the domineering Hindus. I seek to reform them in all the loving ways that are open to me. My noncooperation has its roots not in hatred, but in love.

The people of a village near Bettiah told me that they had run away whilst the police were looting their houses and molesting their womenfolk. When they said that they had run away because I had told them to be nonviolent, I hung my head in shame. I assured them that such was not the meaning of my nonviolence. I expected them to intercept the mightiest power that might be in the act of harming those who were under their protection, and draw without retaliation all harm upon their own heads even to the point of death, but never to run away from the storm center.

(From **Selections from Gandhi.***)*

Martin Luther King, Jr.

I've seen too much hate to want to hate, myself, and I've seen hate on the faces of too many sheriffs, too many white citizens' councils, and too many Klansmen of the South to want to hate, myself; and everytime I see it, I say to myself, hate is too great a burden to bear. Somehow we must be able to stand up before our most bitter opponents and say: "We shall match your capacity to inflict suffering by our capacity to endure suffering. We will meet your physical force with soul force ... We will not only win our freedom for ourselves; we will so appeal to your heart and conscience that we will win you in the process, and our victory will be a double victory.

In the guilt and confusion confronting our society, violence only adds to the chaos. It deepens the brutality of the oppressor and increases the bitterness of the oppressed. Violence is the antithesis of creativity and wholeness. It destroys community and makes brotherhood impossible.

The ultimate weakness of violence is that it is a descending spiral, begetting the very thing it seeks to destroy. Instead of diminishing evil, it multiplies it. Through violence you may murder the liar, but you cannot murder the lie, nor establish the truth. Through violence you may murder the hater, but you do not murder hate. In fact, violence merely increases hate. So it goes. Returning violence for violence multiplies violence, adding deeper darkness to a night already devoid of stars. Darkness cannot drive out darkness: only light can do that. Hate cannot drive out hate: only love can do that.

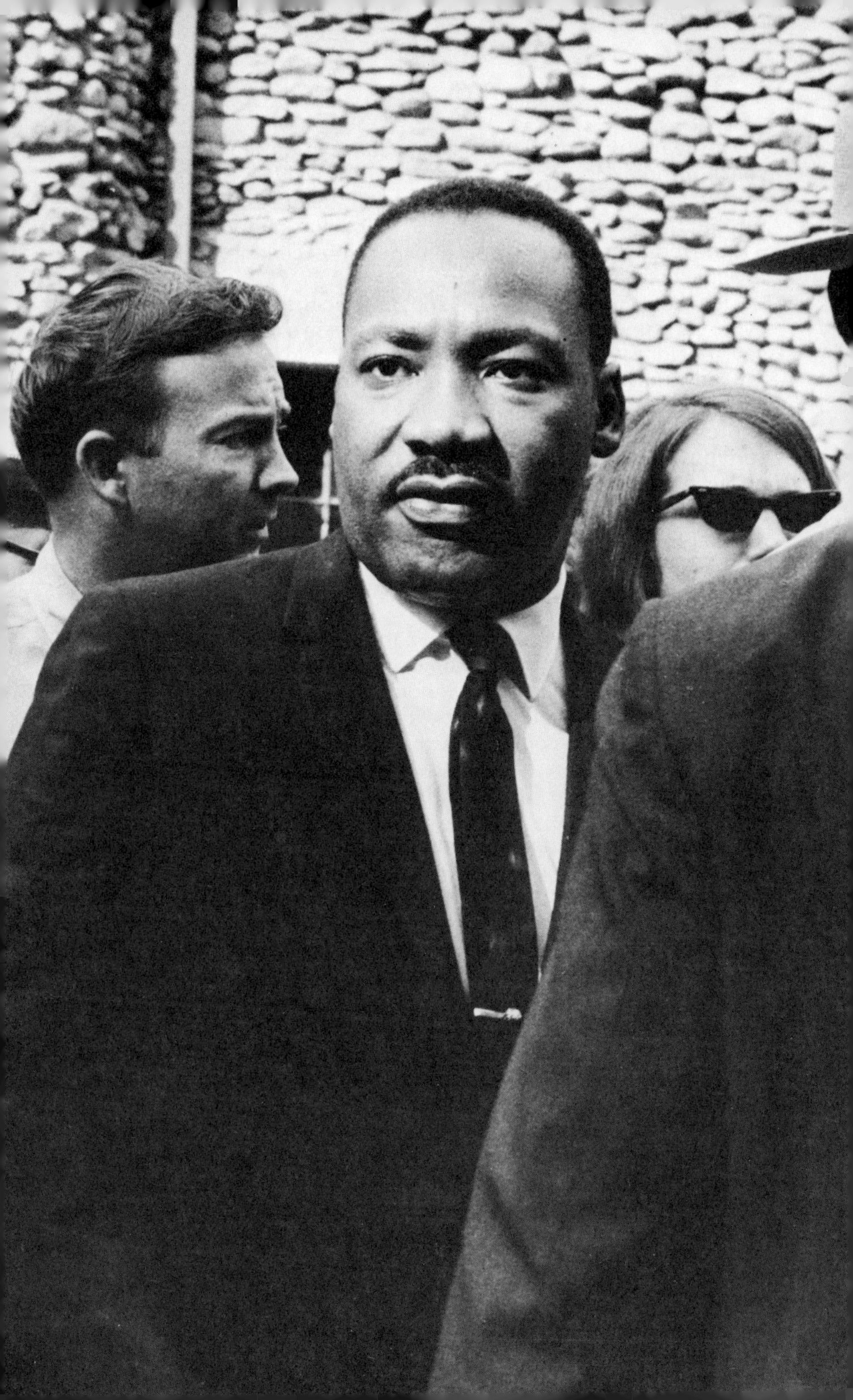

The beauty of nonviolence is that in its own way and in its own time it seeks to break the chain reaction of evil. With a majestic sense of spiritual power, it seeks to elevate truth, beauty and goodness to the throne. Therefore, I will continue to follow this method because I think it is the most practically sound and morally excellent way for the Negro to achieve freedom.

Of course you may say, this is not **practical**; life is a matter of getting even, of hitting back, of dog eat dog. Maybe in some distant utopia, you say, that idea will work, but not in the hard, cold world in which we live. My only answer is that mankind has followed the so-called practical way for a long time now, and it has led inexorably to deeper confusion and chaos. Time is cluttered with the wreckage of individuals and communities that surrendered to hatred and violence. For the salvation of our nation and the salvation of mankind, we must follow another way.

The agony of the poor impoverishes the rich; the betterment of the poor enriches the rich. We are inevitably our brother's keeper because we are our brother's brother. Whatever affects one directly affects all indirectly.

The question now is, do we have the morality and courage required to live together as brothers and not be afraid? (P. 181-2)

We still have a choice today: nonviolent coexistence or violent co-annihilation. This may well be mankind's last chance to choose between chaos and community. (p. 191)

(From **Where Do We Go From Here***, 1967.)*

. . . Advocating violence is imitating the worst, the most brutal and the most uncivilized value of American life.

And when we truly believe in the sacredness of human personality, we won't exploit people, we won't trample over people with iron feet or oppression, we won't kill anybody. (p. 72)

One thing we must be concerned about if we are to have peace on earth and goodwill toward men is the nonviolent affirmation of the sacredness of all human life. Every man is somebody because he is a child of God. And so when we say "Thou shalt not kill," we're really saying that human life is too sacred to be taken on the battlefields of the world. (p. 72)

(From **The Trumpet of Conscience***, 1967.)*

Peter Maurin

War and Peace

Some people say:
  "My country is always right."
Some people say:
  "My country is always wrong."
Some people say:
  "My country is sometimes right
  and sometimes wrong,
  but my country right or wrong."
To stick to one's country
  when one's country is wrong
  does not make the country right.
To stick to the right
  even when the world is wrong
  is the only way we know of
  to make everything right.
We call barbarians
  people living
  on the other side of the border.
We call civilized
  people living
  on this side of the border.
We civilized,
  living on this side of the border
  are not ashamed
  to arm ourselves to the teeth
  so as to protect ourselves
  against the barbarians.
  living on the other side.
And when the barbarians
  born on the other side of the border
  invade us,
  we do not hesitate
  to kill them
  before we have tried
  to civilize them.
So we civilized
  exterminate barbarians
  without civilizing them.
And we persist
  in calling ourselves civilized.

(From **Radical Christian Thought—Easy Essays** *by Peter Maurin.)*

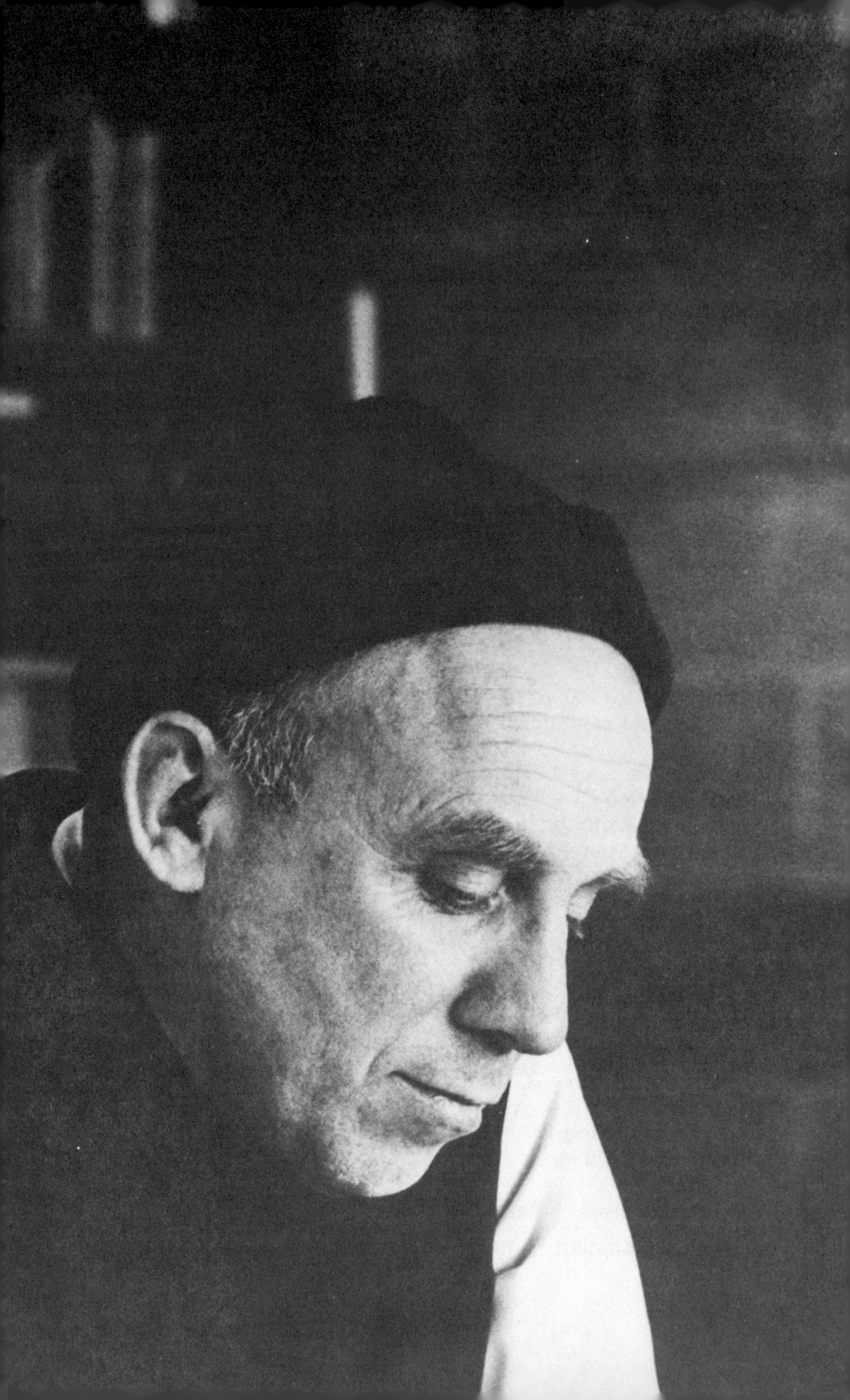

Thomas Merton

..."Pacifism" tends, as a cause, to take on the air of a quasi-religion, as though it were a kind of faith in its own right. A pacifist is then regarded as one who "believes in peace" so to speak as an article of faith, and hence puts himself in the position of being absolutely unable to countenance any form of war, since for him to accept any war in theory or in practice would be to deny his faith. A Christian pacifist then becomes one who compounds this ambiguity by insisting, or at least by implying, that pacifism is an integral part of Christianity, with the evident conclusions that Christians who are not pacifists have, by that fact, apostatized from Christianity.

This unfortunate emphasis gains support from the way conscientious objection is in fact treated by the selective service laws of the United States. An objector who is a religious "pacifist" is considered as one who for subjective and personal reasons of conscience and belief refuses to go to war, and whose "conscientious objection" is tolerated and even recognized by the government. There is of course something valuable and edifying in this recognition of the personal conscience, but there is also an implication that any minority stand against war on grounds of conscience is ipso facto a kind of deviant and morally eccentric position, to be tolerated only because there are always a few religious half-wits around in any case, and one has to humor them in order to preserve the nation's reputation for respecting individual liberty.

In other words, this sanctions the popular myth that all pacifism is based on religious emotion rather than on reason, and that it has no objective ethical validity, but is allowed to exist because of the possibility of harmless and mystical obsessions with peace on the part of a few enthusiasts. It also sanctions another myth, to which some forms of pacifism give support, that pacifists are people who simply prefer to yield to violence and evil rather than resist it in any way. They are fundamentally indifferent to reasonable, moral or patriotic ideals and prefer to sink into their religious apathy and let the enemy overrun the country unresisted.

To sum it all up in a word, this caricature of pacifism which reduces it to a purely eccentric individualism of conscience declares that the pacifist is willing to let everyone be destroyed merely because he himself does not have a taste for war. It is not hard to imagine what capital can be made out of this distortion by copy writers for, say *Time* magazine or the *New York Daily News*. It is also easy to see how the Catholic clergy might be profoundly suspicious of any kind of conscientious objection to war when myths like these have helped them to form their judgment.

Speaking in the name of Christ and of the Church to all mankind, Pope John [in the encyclical *Pacem in Terris*] was not issuing a pacifist document in this sense. He was not simply saying that if a few cranks did not like the bomb they were free to entertain their opinion. He was saying, on the contrary, that we had reached a point in history where it was clearly no longer reasonable to make use of war in the settlement of international disputes, and that the important thing was not merely protest against the latest war technology, but the construction of permanent world peace on a basis of truth, justice, love and liberty. This is not a matter for a few individual consciences, it urgently binds the conscience of every living man. It is not an individual refinement of spirituality, a luxury of the soul, but a collective obligation of the highest urgency, a universal and immediate need which can no longer be ignored.

He is not saying that a few Christians may and ought to be pacifists (i.e., to protest against war) but that all Christians and all reasonable men are bound by their very rationality to work to establish a real and lasting peace.

(From "The Christian in World Crisis", in **The Nonviolent Alternative.***)*

The expression "No man is an island," which is now almost proverbial in the English language, comes from the meditation of a seventeenth-century English Christian poet, John Donne. In the midst of the new optimistic individualism of the Renaissance he pointed out that it was an illusion for man to imagine himself perfectly and completely autonomous in himself, as if he were able to exist independently from his relation to other men and other living beings. This intuition was brought home to the poet by the fact of death. Hearing the bell toll for the funeral of a dead man, he reflected that there is one death for all and when the bell tolls "it tolls for thee."

Death is a silent yet eloquent teacher of truth. Death is a teacher that speaks openly and yet is easily heard. Death is very much present in our modern world: and yet it has become an enigma to that world. Instead of understanding death, it would seem that our world simply multiplies it. Death becomes a huge, inscrutable **quantity.** The mystery of death, more terrible and sometimes more cruel than ever, remains incomprehensible to men who, though they know they must die, retain a grim and total attachment to individual life as if they could be physically indestructible.

Perhaps it is this failure to understand and to face the fact of death that helps beget so many wars and so much violence. As if men, attached to individual bodily life, thought they could protect themselves against death by inflicting it on others.

Death cannot be understood without **compassion**. Compassion teaches me that when my brother dies, I too die. Compassion teaches me that my brother and I are one. That if I love my brother, then my love benefits my own life as well, and if I hate my brother and seek to destroy him, I destroy myself also. The desire to kill is like the desire to attack another with an ingot of red-hot iron: I have to pick up the incandescent metal and burn my own hand while burning the other. Hate itself is the seed of death in my own heart, while it seeks the death of the other. Love is the seed of life in my own heart when it seeks the good of the other...

It is true, political problems are not solved by love and mercy. But the world of politics is not the only world, and unless political decisions rest on a foundation of something better and higher than politics, they can never do any real good for men. When a country has to be rebuilt after war, the passions and energies of war are no longer enough. There must be a new force, the power of love, the power of understanding and human compassion, the strength of selflessness and cooperation, and the creative dynamism of **the will to live and to build, and the will to forgive. The will for reconciliation.**

...For centuries, man has slowly and with difficulty built a civilized world in the effort to make happiness possible, not merely by making life materially better, but by helping men **to understand and live their life more fruitfully.**

The key to this understanding is the truth that "no man is an island." A selfish life cannot be fruitful. It cannot be true. It contradicts the very nature of man. The dire effort of this contradiction cannot be avoided: where men live selfishly, in quest of brute power and lust and money, they destroy one another. The only way to change such a world is to change the thoughts and the desires of the men who live in it. The conditions of our world are simply an outward expression of our own thoughts and desires.

(From "Preface to Vietnamese Translation of No Man Is an Island", in **The Nonviolent Alternative.***)*

A. J. Muste

...It is not really possible to separate conscription and war...even if the question is the conscription of non-pacifist youth, it is a fundamental mistake for pacifists ever to relent in their opposition to this evil, ever to devote their energies primarily to securing provisions for COs in a draft law or to lapse into a feeling that conscription has somehow become more palatable if such provisions are made by the State. It is not our own children if we are pacifist parents, our fellow-pacifist Christians if we are churchmen, about whom we should be most deeply concerned. In the first place, that is a narrow and perhaps self-centered attitude. In the second place, pacifist youths have some inner resources for meeting the issue under discussion. The terrible thing which we should never lose sight of, to which we should never reconcile our spirits, is that the great mass of 18-year olds are drafted for war. They are given no choice. Few are at the stage of development where they are capable of making fully rational and responsible choices. Thus the fathers immolate the sons, the older generation immolates the younger, on the altar of Moloch. What God centuries ago forbade Abraham to do even to his own son—"Lay not thy hand upon the lad, neither do thou anything unto him"—this we do by decree to the entire youth of a nation.

Non-conformity, Holy Disobedience, becomes a virtue and indeed a necessary and indispensable measure of spiritual self-preservation, in a day when the impulse to conform, to acquiesce, to go along, is the instrument which is used to subject men to totalitarian rule and involve them in permanent war. To create the impression at least of outward unanimity, the impression that there is no "real" opposition, is something for which all dictators and military leaders strive assiduously. The more it seems that there is no opposition, the less worthwhile it seems to an ever larger number of people to cherish even the thought of opposition. Surely, in such a situation it is important not to place the pinch of incense before Caesar's image, not to make the gesture of conformity which is involved, let us say, in registering under a military conscription law. When the object is so plainly to create a situation where the individual no longer has a choice except total conformity or else the concentration camp or death; when reliable people tell us seriously that experiments are being conducted with drugs which will paralyze the wills of opponents within a nation or in an enemy country, it is surely neither right nor wise to wait until the "system" has driven us into a corner where we cannot retain a vestige of self-respect unless we say No. It does not seem wise or right to wait until this evil catches

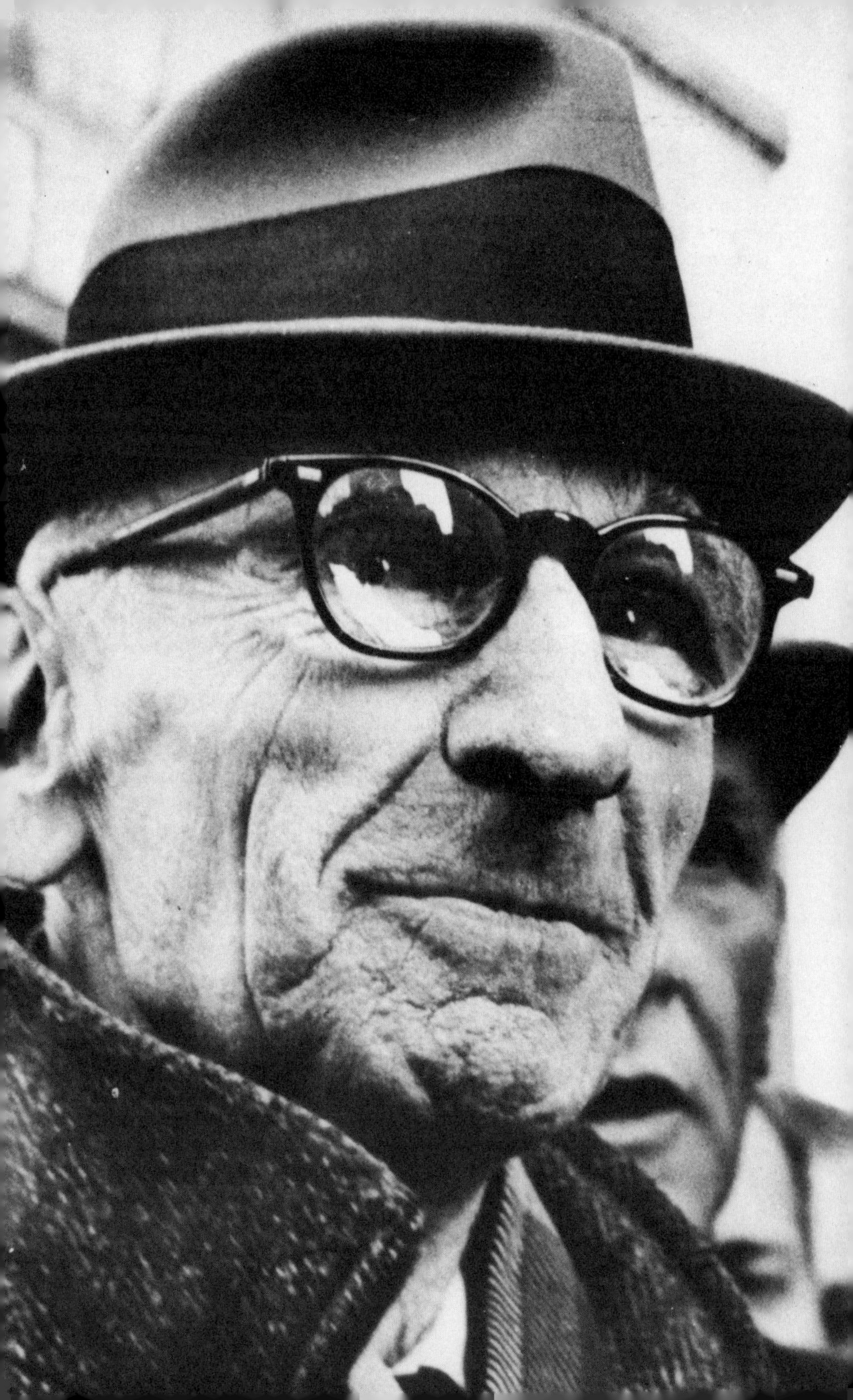

up with us, but rather to go out to meet it—to resist—before it has gone any further...

To me it seems that submitting to conscription even for civilian service is permitting oneself thus to be branded by the State. It makes the work of the State in preparing for war and in securing the desired impression of unanimity much easier. It seems, therefore, that pacifists should refuse to be thus branded.

...A decision by the pacifist movement in this country to break completely with conscription, to give up the idea that we can "exert more influence" if we conform in some measure, do not resist to the uttermost—this might awaken our countrymen to a realization of the precipice on the edge of which we stand. It might be the making of our movement.

Thus to embrace Holy Disobedience is not to substitute Resistance for Reconciliation. It is to practice both Reconciliation and Resistance. In so far as we help to build up or smooth the way for American militarism and the regimentation which accompanies it, we are certainly not practicing reconciliation toward the millions of people in the Communist bloc countries against whom American war preparations, including conscription, are directed. Nor are we practicing reconciliation toward the hundreds of millions in Asia and Africa whom we condemn to poverty and drive into the arms of Communism by our addiction to military "defense." Nor are we practicing love toward our own fellow-citizens, including also the multitude of youths in the armed services, if, against our deepest insight, we help to fasten the chains of conscription and war upon them.

...It will be when we have gotten off the back of what someone has called the wild elephant of militarism and conscription on to the solid ground of freedom, and only then, that we shall be able to live and work constructively. Like Abraham we shall have to depart from the City-which-is in order that we may help to build the City-which-is-to-be, whose true builder and maker is God.

It is, of course, possible, perhaps even likely, that if we set ourselves apart as those who will have no dealings whatever with conscription, will not place the pinch of incense before Caesar's image, our fellow-citizens will stone us, as Stephen was stoned when he reminded his people that it was they who had "received the law as it was ordained by angels and kept it not." So may we be stoned for reminding our people of a tradition of freedom and peace which was also, in a real sense, "ordained by angels" and which we no longer keep. But, it will thus become possible for them, as for Paul, even amidst the search for new victims to persecute, suddenly to see again the face of Christ and the vision of a new Jerusalem...

Finally, it is of crucial importance that we should understand that for the individual to pit himself in Holy Disobedience against the war-making and conscripting State, wherever it or he be located, is not an act of despair or defeatism. Rather, I think we may say that precisely this individual refusal to "go along" is now the beginning and the core of any realistic and practical movement against war and for a more peaceful and brotherly world. For it becomes daily clearer that political and military leaders pay virtually no attention to protests against current foreign policy and pleas for peace when they know perfectly well that when it comes to a showdown, all but a handful of the millions of protesters will "go along" with the war to which the policy leads. All but a handful will submit to conscription. Few of the protesters will so much as risk their jobs in the cause of "peace." The failure of the policy-makers to change their course does not, save perhaps in very rare instances, mean that they are evil men who want war. They feel, as indeed they so often declare in crucial moments, that the issues are so complicated, the forces arrayed against them so strong, that they "have no choice" but to add another score of billions to the military budget, and so on and on. Why should they think there is any reality, hope or salvation in "peace advocates" who when the moment of decision comes also act on the assumption that they "have no choice" but to conform?

Precisely in a day when the individual appears to be utterly helpless, to "have no choice," when the aim of the "system" is to convince him that he is helpless as an individual and that the only way to meet regimentation is by regimentation, there is absolutely no hope save in going back to the beginning. The human being, the child of God, must assert his humanity and his sonship again. He must exercise the choice which he no longer has as something accorded him by society, which he "naked, weaponless, armourless, without shield or spear, but only with naked hands and open eyes" must create again. He must understand that his naked human being is the one real thing in the face of the mechanics and the mechanized institutions of our age. He, by the grace of God, is the seed of all the human life there will be on earth in the future, though he may have to die to make that harvest possible. As *Life* magazine stated in its unexpectedly profound and stirring editorial of August 20, 1945, its first issue after the atom bombing of Hiroshima: "Our sole safeguard against the very real danger of a reversion to barbarism is the kind of morality which compels the individual conscience, be the group right or wrong. The individual conscience against the atomic bomb? Yes. There is no other way."

(Excerpts from **Of Holy Disobedience**.*)*

Henry David Thoreau

...Can there not be a government in which majorities do not virtually decide right and wrong, but conscience?—in which majorities decide only those questions to which the rule of expediency is applicable? Must the citizen ever for a moment, or in the least degree, resign his conscience, then? I think that we should be men first, and subjects afterward. It is not desirable to cultivate a respect for the law, so much as for the right. The only obligation which I have a right to assume, is to do at any time what I think right. It is truly enough said, that a corporation has no conscience; but a corporation of conscientious men is a corporation *with* a conscience. Law never made men a whit more just; and, by means of their respect for it, even the well-disposed are daily made the agents of injustice. A common and natural result of an undue respect for law is, that you may see a file of soldiers, colonel, captain, corporal, privates, powder-monkeys and all, marching in admirable order over hill and dale to the wars, against their wills, aye, against their common sense and consciences, which makes it very steep marching indeed, and produces a palpitation of the heart. They have no doubt that it is a damnable business in which they are concerned; they are all peaceably inclined. Now, what are they? Men at all? or small moveable forts and magazines, at the service of some unscrupulous man in power? Visit the Navy Yard, and behold a marine, such a man as an American government can make, or such as it can make a man with its black arts, a mere shadow and reminiscence of humanity, a man laid out alive and standing, and already, as one may say, buried under arms with funeral accompaniments, though it may be

"Not a drum was heard, nor a funeral note,
As his corpse to the ramparts we hurried;
Not a soldier discharged his farewell shot
O'er the grave where our hero we buried."

The mass of men serve the State thus, not as men mainly, but as machines, with their bodies. They are the standing army, and the militia, jailers, constables, *posse comitatus,* etc. In most cases there is no free exercise whatever of the judgment or of the moral sense; but they put themselves on a level with wood and earth and stones; and wooden men can perhaps be manufactured that will serve the purpose as well. Such command no more respect than men of straw, or a lump of dirt. They have the same sort of worth only as horses and dogs. Yet such as these even are commonly esteemed good citizens. Others, as most legislators, politicians, lawyers, ministers, and office-holders, serve the State chiefly with their heads; and, as they rarely make any moral distinctions, they are as likely to serve the devil, without intending it, as God. A very few as heroes, patriots, martyrs, reformers in the great sense, and *men* serve the State with their consciences also, and so necessarily resist it for the most part; and they are commonly treated by it as enemies...

...I quarrel not with far-off foes, but with those who, near at home, co-operate with, and do the bidding of those far away, and without whom the latter would be harmless...There are thousands who are *in opinion* opposed to slavery and to the war, who yet in effect do nothing to put an end to them; who, esteeming themselves children of Washington and Franklin, sit down with their hands in their pockets, and say that they know not what to do, and do nothing...They hesitate, and they regret, and sometimes they petition; but they do nothing in earnest and with effect. They will wait, well disposed, for others to remedy the evil, that they may no longer have it to regret. At most, they give only a cheap vote, and a feeble countenance and Godspeed, to the right, as it goes by them...

If the injustice is part of the necessary friction of the machine of government, let it go, let it go; perchance it will wear smooth,—certainly the machine will wear out. If the injustice has a spring, or a pulley, or a rope, or a crank, exclusively for itself, then perhaps you may consider whether the remedy will not be worse than the evil; but if it is of such a nature that it requires you to be the agent of injustice to another, then, I say, break the law. Let your life be a counter friction to stop the machine. What I have to do is to see, at any rate, that I do not lend myself to the wrong which I condemn.

...Under a government which imprisons any unjustly, the true place for a just man is also a prison...If any think that their influence would be lost there, and their voices no longer afflict the ear of the State, that they would not be as an enemy within its walls, they do not know by how much truth is stronger than error, nor how much more eloquently and effectively he can combat injustice who has experienced a little in his own person. Cast your whole vote, not a strip of paper merely, but your whole influence...

(Excerpts from **"On the Duty of Civil Disobedience"**.*)*

Leo Tolstoy

According to the Biblical narrative Adam sinned against God, and then said that his wife told him to eat the apple, while his wife said she was tempted by the devil. God exonerated neither Adam nor Eve, but told them that because Adam listened to the voice of his wife he would be punished, and that his wife would be punished for listening to the serpent. And neither was excused, but both were punished. Will not God say the same to you also when you kill a man and say that your captain ordered you to do it?

The deceit is apparent already, because in the regulation obliging a soldier to obey all his commander's orders, these words are added, *"Except such as tend toward the injury of the Tsar."*

If a soldier before obeying the orders of his commander must first decide whether it is not against the Tsar, how then can he fail to consider before obeying his commander's order whether it is not against his supreme King, God? And no action is more opposed to the will of God than that of killing men. And therefore you *cannot* obey men if they order you to kill. If you obey, and kill, you do so only for the sake of your own advantage—to escape punishment. So that in killing by order of your commander you are a murderer as much as the thief who kills a rich man to rob him. He is tempted by money, and you by the desire not to be punished, or to receive a reward. Man is always responsible before God for his actions. And no power, whatever the authorities desire, can turn a live man into a dead thing which one can move about as one likes. Christ taught men that they are all sons of God, and therefore a Christian cannot surrender his conscience into the power of another man, no matter by what title he may be called: King, Tsar, Emperor. As to those men who have assumed power over you, demanding of you the murder of your brothers, this only shows that they are deceivers, and that therefore one should not obey them. Shameful is the position of the prostitute who is always ready to give her body to be defiled by any one her master indicates; but yet more shameful is the position of a soldier always ready for the greatest of crimes—the murder of any man whom his commander indicates.

And therefore if you do indeed desire to act according to God's will you have only to do one thing—to throw off the shameful and ungodly calling of a soldier, and be ready to bear any sufferings which may be inflicted upon you for so doing.

So that the true "Notes" for a Christian Soldier are not those in which it is said that "God is the Soldier's General" and other blasphemies, and that the soldier must obey his commanders in everything, and be ready to kill foreigners and even his own unarmed brothers—but those which remind one of the words of the Gospel that one *should obey God rather than men* and fear not those who can kill the body but cannot kill the soul.

In this alone consists the true, unfraudulent "Notes for Soldiers."

(From "Notes for Soldiers", pp. 34-35 of **On Civil Disobedience and Non-Violence,** *1967.)*

The following was written in 1899 to Ernst Schramm, a young Hessian who was about to be drafted. It was peacetime, but conscription was enforced under penalty of death. This is Tolstoy's second letter to Schramm. The Hessian post office forwarded it to the young man in Bavaria, leaving us to infer that he resolved his dilemma by choosing exile from his native land.

In my last letter I answered your questions as well as I could. It is not only Christians but all just people who must refuse to become soldiers—that is, to be ready on another's command (for this is what a soldier's duty actually consists of) to kill all those one is ordered to kill. The question as you state it—which is more useful, to become a good teacher or to suffer for rejecting conscription?—is falsely stated. The question is falsely stated because it is wrong for us to determine our actions according to their results, to view actions merely as useful or destructive. In the choice of our actions we can be led by their advantages or disadvantages only when the actions themselves are not opposed to the demands of morality.

We can stay home, go abroad, or concern ourselves with farming or science according to what we find useful for ourselves or others; for neither in domestic life, foreign travel, farming, nor science is there anything immoral. But under no circumstance can we inflict violence on people, torture or kill them because we think such acts could be of use to us or to others. We cannot and may not do such things, especially because we can never be sure of the results of our actions. Often actions which seem the most advantageous of all turn out in fact to be destructive; and the reverse is also true.

The question should not be stated: which is more useful, to be a good teacher or to go to jail for refusing conscription? But rather: what should a man do who has been called upon for military service—that is, called upon to kill or to prepare himself to kill?

And to this question, for a person who understands the true meaning of military service and who wants to be moral, there is only one clear and incontrovertible answer: such a person must refuse to take part in military service no matter what consequences this refusal may have. It may seem to us that this refusal could be futile or even harmful, and that it would be a far more useful thing, after serving one's time, to become a good village teacher. But in the same way, Christ could have judged it more useful for himself to be a good carpenter and to submit to all the principles of the Pharisees than to die in obscurity as he did, repudiated and forgotten by everyone.

Moral acts are distinguished from all other acts by the fact that they operate independently of any predictable advantage to ourselves or to others. No matter how dangerous the situation may be of a man who finds himself in the power of robbers who demand that he take part in plundering, murder, and rape, a moral person cannot take part. Is not military service the same thing? Is one not required to agree to all the deaths of all those one is commanded to kill?

But how can one refuse to do what everyone does, what everyone finds unavoidable and necessary? Or, must one do what no one does and what everyone considers unnecessary or even stupid and bad? No matter how strange it sounds, this strange argument is the main one offered against those moral acts which in our times face you and every other person called up for military service. But this argument is even more incorrect than the one which would make a moral action dependent upon considerations of advantage.

If I, finding myself in a crowd of running people, run with the crowd without knowing where, it is obvious that I have given myself up to mass hysteria; but if by chance I should push my way to the front or be gifted with sharper sight than the others, or receive information that this crowd was racing to attack human beings and toward its own corruption, would I really not stop and tell the people what might rescue them? Would I go on running and do these things which I knew to be bad and corrupt? This is the situation of every individual called up for military service, if he knows what military service means.

I can well understand that you, a young man full of life, loving and loved by your mother, friends, perhaps a young woman, think with a natural terror about what awaits you if you refuse conscription; and perhaps you will not feel strong enough to bear the consequences of refusal, and knowing your weakness, will submit and become soldier. I understand completely, and I do not for a moment allow myself to blame you, knowing very well that in your place I might perhaps do the same thing. Only do not say that you did it because it was useful or because everyone does it. If you did it, know that you did wrong.

In every person's life there are moments in which he can know himself, tell himself who he is, whether he is a man who values his human dignity above his life or a weak creature who does not know his dignity and is concerned merely with being useful (chiefly to himself). This is the situation of a man who goes out to defend his honor in a duel or a soldier who goes into battle (although here the concepts of life are wrong). It is the situation of a doctor or a priest called to someone sick with plague, of a man in a burning house or a sinking ship who must decide whether to let the weaker go first or shove them aside and save himself. It is the situation of a man in poverty who accepts or rejects a bribe. And in our times, it is the situation of a man called to military service. For a man who knows its significance, the call to the army is perhaps the only opportunity for him to behave as a morally free creature and fulfill the highest requirement of his life—or else merely to keep his advantage in sight like an animal and thus remain slavishly submissive and servile until humanity becomes degraded and stupid.

For these reasons I answered your question whether one has to refuse to do military service with a categorical "yes"—if you understand the meaning of military service (and if you did not understand it then, you do now) and if you want to behave as a moral person living in our times must.

Please excuse me if these words are harsh. The subject is so important that one cannot be careful enough in expressing oneself so as to avoid false interpretation.

("Advice to a Draftee", April 7, 1899.)

Mark Twain

The War Prayer

It was a time of great and exalting excitement. The country was up in arms, the war was on, in every breast burned the holy fire of patriotism; the drums were beating, the bands playing, the toy pistols popping, the bunched firecrackers hissing and spluttering; on every hand and far down the receding and fading spread of roofs and balconies a fluttering wilderness of flags flashed in the sun; daily the young volunteers marched down the wide avenue gay and fine in their new uniforms, the proud fathers and mothers and sisters and sweethearts cheering them with voices choked with happy emotion as they swung by; nightly the packed mass meetings listened, panting, to patriot oratory which stirred the deepest deeps of their hearts, and which they interrupted at briefest intervals with cyclones of applause, the tears running down their cheeks the while; in the churches the pastors preached devotion to flag and country, and invoked the God of Battles, beseeching His aid in our good cause in outpouring of fervid eloquence which moved every listener. It was indeed a glad and gracious time, and the half dozen rash spirits that ventured to disapprove of the war and cast a doubt upon its righteousness straightway got such a stern and angry warning that for their personal safety's sake they quickly shrank out of sight and offended no more in that way.

Sunday morning came—next day the battalions would leave for the front; the church was filled; the volunteers were there, their young faces alight with martial dreams—visions of the stern advance, the gathering momentum, the rushing charge, the flashing sabers, the flight of the foe, the tumult, the enveloping smoke, the fierce pursuit, the surrender!—then home from the war, bronzed heroes, welcomed, adored, submerged in golden seas of glory! With the volunteers sat their dear ones, proud, happy, and envied by the neighbors and friends who had no sons and brothers to send forth to the field of honor, there to win for the flag, or, failing, die the noblest of noble deaths. The service proceeded; a war chapter from the Old Testament was read; the first prayer was said; it was followed by an organ burst that shook the building, and with one impulse the house rose, with glowing eyes and beating hearts, and poured out that tremendous invocation—

"God the all-terrible! Thou who ordainest,
Thunder thy clarion and lightning thy sword!"

Then came the "long" prayer. None could remember the like of it for passionate pleading and moving and beautiful language. The burden of its supplication was, that an ever-merciful and benignant Father of us all would watch over our noble young soldiers, and aid, comfort, and encourage them in their patriotic work; bless them, shield them in the day of battle and the hour of peril, bear them in His mighty hand, make them strong and confident, invincible in the bloody onset; help them to crush the foe, grant to them and to their flag and country imperishable honor and glory—

An aged stranger entered and moved with slow and noiseless step up the main aisle, his eyes fixed upon the minister, his long body clothed in a robe that reached to his feet, his head bare, his white hair descending in a frothy cataract to his shoulders, his seamy face unnaturally pale, pale even to ghastliness. With all eyes following him and wondering, he made his silent way; without pausing, he ascended to the preacher's side and stood there, waiting. With shut lids the preacher, unconscious of his presence, continued his moving prayer, and at last finished it with the words, uttered in fervent appeal, "Bless our arms, grant us the victory, O Lord our God, Father and Protector of our land and flag!"

The stranger touched his arm, motioned him to step aside—which the startled minister did—and took his place. During some moments he surveyed the spellbound audience with solemn eyes, in which burned an uncanny light; then in a deep voice he said:

"I come from the Throne—bearing a message from Almighty God!" The words smote the house with a shock; if the stranger perceived it he gave no attention. "He has heard the prayer of His servant your shepherd, and will grant it if such shall be your desire after I, His messenger, shall have explained to you its import—that is to say, its full import. For it is like unto many of the prayers of men, in that it asks for more than he who utters it is aware of—except he pause and think.

"God's servant and yours has prayed his prayer. Has he paused and taken thought? Is it one prayer? No, it is two—one uttered, the other not. Both have reached the ear of Him Who heareth all supplications, the spoken and the unspoken. Ponder this—keep it in mind. If you would beseech a blessing upon yourself, beware! lest without intent you invoke a curse upon a neighbor at the same time. If you pray for the blessing of rain upon your crop which needs it, by that act you are possibly praying for a curse upon some neighbor's crop which may not need rain and can be injured by it.

"You have heard your servant's prayer—the uttered part of it. I am commissioned of God to put into words the other part of it—that part which the pastor—and also you in your hearts—fervently prayed silently. And ignorantly and unthinkingly? God grant that it was so! You heard these words: 'Grant us the victory, O Lord our God!' That is sufficient. The *whole* of the uttered prayer is compact into those pregnant words. Elaborations were not necessary. When you have prayed for victory you have prayed for many unmentioned results which follow victory—*must* follow it, cannot help but follow it. Upon the listening spirit of God the Father fell also the unspoken part of the prayer. He commandeth me to put it into words. Listen!

"O Lord our Father, our young patriots, idols of our hearts, go forth to battle—be Thou near them! With them—in spirit—we also go forth from the sweet peace of our beloved firesides to smite the foe. O Lord our God, help us to tear their soldiers to bloody shreds with our shells; help us to cover their smiling fields with the pale forms of their patriot dead; help us to drown the thunder of the guns with the shrieks of their wounded, writhing in pain; help us to lay waste their humble homes with a hurricane of fire; help us to wring the hearts of their unoffending widows with unavailing grief; help us to turn them out roofless with their little children to wander unfriended the wastes of their desolated land in rags and hunger and thirst, sports of the sun flames of summer and the icy winds of winter, broken in spirit, worn with travail, imploring Thee for the refuge of the grave and denied it—for our sakes who adore Thee, Lord, blast their hopes, blight their lives, protract their bitter pilgrimage, make heavy their steps, water their way with their tears, stain the white snow with the blood of their wounded feet! We ask it, in the spirit of love, of Him Who is the Source of Love, and Who is the ever-faithful refuge and friend of all that are sore beset and seek His aid with humble and contrite hearts. Amen."

(After a pause.) "Ye have prayed it; if ye still desire it, speak! The messenger of the Most High waits."

It was believed afterward that the man was a lunatic, because there was no sense in what he said.

Acknowledgments

Author	Page	Source
Edna St. Vincent Millay	189	"Conscientious Objector" From COLLECTED POEMS, Harper & Row Copyright 1934, 1962 by Edna St. Vincent Millay and Norma Millay Ellis
Albert Camus	190	Excerpted from "Neither Victims nor Executioners", an essay first appearing in the French Resistance newspaper *Combat* August 1946. Translated by Dwight MacDonald and reprinted in *Politics* July-August 1947.
Dorothy Day	193	Excerpted from *Catholic Worker* editorial "On the Use of Force" September 1938. Used with permission of *Catholic Worker*.
Mahatma Gandhi	195	Excerpted from NON-VIOLENCE IN PEACE & WAR by M. K. Gandhi and SELECTIONS FROM GANDHI by Nirmal Kumar Bose. Used with permission of Navajivan Trust, Ahmedabad, India
Martin Luther King, Jr.	196	Abridged from pp. 61, 62, 63, 65, 181-182, 191 (deletions to be indicated by ellipsis) of WHERE DO WE GO FROM HERE: Chaos or Community?, by Martin Luther King, Jr. Copyright 1967 by Martin Luther King, Jr.
		Abridged from pp. 71, 72, 74, 75 (deletions to be indicated by ellipsis of THE TRUMPET OF CONSCIENCE, by Martin Luther King, Jr. Copyright 1967 by Martin Luther King, Jr. Reprinted by permission of Harper & Row, Publishers, Inc.
Peter Maurin	199	"War and Peace" from RADICAL CHRISTIAN THOUGHT — EASY ESSAYS by Peter Maurin. Used with permission of *Catholic Worker*.
Thomas Merton	201	Excerpted from "Preface to Vietnamese Translation of No Man Is an Island", and "The Christian in World Crisis", in THE NONVIOLENT ALTERNATIVE by Thomas Merton. Copyright 1971, 1980 by the Turstees of the Merton Legacy Trust. Reprinted by permission of Farrar, Straus and Giroux, Inc.
A. J. Muste	204	From OF HOLY DISOBEDIENCE by A. J. Muste, Pamphlet 64, Pendle Hill Publications, Wallingford, PA 19086. Used with permission.

Henry David Thoreau	208	Excerpted from WALDEN/ON THE DUTY OF CIVIL DISOBEDIENCE by Henry David Thoreau, Collier Books/Macmillan, 1962. Used with permission.
Leo Tolstoy	210	"Advice To a Draftee", April 7, 1899 used with permission of Houghton Library, Harvard Translated by Rodney Dennis
		Excerpts from "Notes for Soldiers" in TOLSTOY ON CIVIL DISOBEDIENCE AND NON-VIOLENCE. Used with permission of Bergman Publishers.
Mark Twain	214	"The War Prayer" from EUROPE AND ELSEWHERE by Mark Twain. Copyright 1923, 1951 by the Mark Twain Company. Reprinted by permission of Harper & Row, Publishers, Inc.

Photo Acknowledgements

Page   Photo description — Photographer/Source

8   Diana Davies, Swarthmore Peace Collection

10 **Vietnam June 1966**
    US Army Photograph, CC34850   AVSG-S-4115-16

14 **CPS Workers in Coshocton, Ohio, May 1942**
    Richard Wurts, AFSC Archives —
    Swarthmore Peace Collection

21 **Jeanette Rankin**
    Schlesinger Library, Radcliffe College

24 **Minister's Demonstration, October 16, 1946**
    Fred Harris Photographs, Swarthmore Peace Collection

25 **CPS Construction Project**
    NISBCO Archives

26 **CPS Workers in Hospital**
    NISBCO Archives

29 Shawn Perry, NISBCO

30 **Mushroom cloud from Nagasaki bombing,**
    National Archives, 208-AA-249-E-1

33 **Pope John Paul II**
    Saw Lwin, United Nations Photo

35 **Billy Graham**
    Sojourners Magazine

38 **Rabbi Isidor Hoffman**
    Rabbi Hoffman

40   William Sauro, New York Times
46   Shawn Perry, NISBCO
50   Mark Miller, Catholic University Cardinal Yearbook
60   **Demonstration January 4, 1973**
     Theodore Hetzel, Swarthmore College Peace Collection
92   Ed Spivey, Sojourners Magazine
129 National Archives, 208-YE-17
164 **Hiroshima after August 1945 atomic bombing**
     National Archives, 243-H-6
176 Ed Spivey, Sojourners Magazine
188 **Mahatma Gandhi**
     Swarthmore College Peace Collection
192 **Dorothy Day**
     The Milwaukee Journal
195 **Martin Luther King, Jr. August 1965**
     John Spragens, Montreat, NC
200 **Thomas Merton**
     John Howard Griffin
205 **A. J. Muste**
     WIN Magazine Archives, Swarthmore College
         Peace Collection

Publication of
The Tenth edition of
WORDS OF CONSCIENCE
was made possible in part
by a grant from
Anna H. and Elizabeth M.
Chace Fund Committee

NOTES

NOTES

NOTES